Becoming an URBAN PLANNER

Other Titles in the Series

Becoming an URBAN PLANNER

A Guide to Careers in Planning and Urban Design

Michael Bayer, AICP

Nancy Frank, Ph.D., AICP

Jason Valerius, AICP

American Planning Association

WILEY

John Wiley & Sons, Inc.

Library of Congress Cataloging-in-Publication Data:

Bayer, Michael.
  Becoming an urban planner : a guide to careers in planning and urban design / by Michael Bayer, Nancy Frank and Jason Valerius.
      p. cm.
  Includes bibliographical references and index.
  ISBN 978-0-470-27863-5 (pbk.)
  1. City planning--Vocational guidance. I. Frank, Nancy (Nancy K.), 1954- II. Valerius, Jason. III. Title.
  NA9013.B39 2010
  307.1'216023--dc22
                          2009018435

Bayer: To Michelle, Adam, and Clark
Valerius: To Amy and Rhys
Frank: To Bill

CONTENTS

ABOUT THE AUTHORS

MICHAEL BAYER, AICP, is a senior planner with Environmental Resources Management in Annapolis, Maryland, where he develops comprehensive plans for local governments. He has a master's degree in urban planning from the University of Wisconsin–Milwaukee. As a planner and journalist, he has researched and written extensively about land use, transportation, urban redevelopment, and environmental policy.

NANCY FRANK, AICP and Associate Professor, is chair of the urban planning program at the University of Wisconsin–Milwaukee, where she teaches planning theory and environmental planning. She holds a Ph.D. from the Rockefeller College of Public Affairs & Policy at the State University of New York at Albany. In addition to her teaching and research, Dr. Frank is the founder of a charter high school in Milwaukee, the School for Urban Planning and Architecture.

JASON VALERIUS, AICP, is a senior planner with MSA Professional Services, Inc. in Madison, Wisconsin, where he leads a team of planners and urban designers engaged in a wide range of planning for local government and private development clients. He has master's degrees in architecture and urban planning from the University of Wisconsin–Milwaukee and has made planning and design for sustainable communities a focus of his practice.

PREFACE

WHAT DO I WANT TO DO IN MY CAREER? This question is universal and is one urban planners ask themselves even years after they've entered the profession. For most people, there is no simple answer, because the choices we have are limited only by our imaginations, our experiences, our knowledge, and the opportunities that surround us and that we are able to create for ourselves and for others.

Deciding to enter the planning profession is a key point in a person's life. While many resources exist to guide a person through the process of choosing a school or introducing particular fields of planning, to date there has been no one guide that provided this information with real-life examples to demonstrate planning as it is lived. *Becoming an Urban Planner* seeks to serve an important function—to provide a portrait of urban planning through the eyes of its practitioners.

Although planners touch everybody's lives in many ways, from the moment we open the door to the time we park our car or bicycle at the end of the work day, very few people outside of the profession understand what planning is and what planners do.

Segments of the public have become more informed about planning as smart growth and New Urbanism have become prominent public issues and we as a nation grapple with growth, sprawl, traffic congestion, infrastructure, land use, and revitalization at scales from the street to the mega-region.

The challenges provided by these issues have inspired countless people to become urban planners. What many have quickly found is that these problems are complex and must be addressed across disciplines, both within planning and by collaborating with allied professions.

At its core, urban planning is about problem solving: identifying problems, analyzing these problems to create a basis for decision making, working with communities and stakeholders to develop alternatives, and, ultimately, to implement solutions that address the problems and result in tangible benefits. This problem solving happens in many contexts: in governments and the private sector, in small towns and large cities, on site-specific issues with a few key players, and on global problems that involve thousands of people. The input on these issues spans the gamut as well: from small public meetings and focus groups to large interactive gatherings featuring web-based involvement tools where people provide input using the latest advances in technology.

Even planners who commit early to a particular specialization within planning and become expert in specific planning tools and contexts cannot anticipate how their careers will evolve and what issues they will confront in the future.

Becoming an Urban Planner addresses this complexity through the eyes of more than 80 planners working across the United States and Canada in a variety of situations. Through this book, we try to put a face to this complexity, inspire potential planners to explore planning as a career, and provide all of the information you need to make a decision to pursue planning and chart a course for your career.

We have paired information on the field of planning with the real-life experiences of planners. We outline the skills the profession requires and how to hone them, both in school and as professionals. We also outline potential career paths and describe what people in these positions do. We identify lessons learned, what to aspire to and what to avoid. We have interviewed people who are broad generalists and others who have devoted their careers to a particular aspect of planning. For each, we have asked planners to describe how they have arrived at where they are.

By the end of the book, we hope that you, as a potential urban planner, have a clear understanding of what urban planning is and what planners do so that you are able to make an informed decision on your own career path, with thoughts in mind about how successful planners have charted their own paths to success.

ACKNOWLEDGMENTS

PLANNING IS A COLLABORATIVE PROCESS, and so it is fitting that this book is the product of a collaborative effort. To view the profession through the eyes of practitioners, we relied on the willingness of dozens of planners from across the United States to share their thoughts, feelings, motivations, stories, successes, failures, challenges, and lessons learned with a wide audience. Their collective experience is shared here, and we owe them an immense debt of gratitude.

Every planner who participated in this book provided an insight into planning that informed us as authors about the profession and its future. Because of the limits of the format, in many cases, we could only communicate an outline of what many planners shared with us in depth. One of the great joys of planning is the unlimited potential of experiences it provides us through the variety and breadth of projects on which we work. These projects, more than any textbook or technical knowledge we acquire, really define us as planners. We appreciate the willingness of so many of our colleagues to serve as these lenses so that planners-to-be can understand how a career in planning can play out in real life.

Many people willingly dug into their archives of art to share them with us, in particular Dan Burden, Barry Miller, Dana Bourland, Rick Bernhardt, Ronald Bailey, and Paul Olsen.

We also recognize David Holden, AICP, of PB PlaceMaking; Sue Schwartz, FAICP, of the City of Greensboro; and Dr. Ruth Yabes of Arizona State University, for reviewing drafts of the manuscript.

Finally, but not last in our minds, is John Czarnecki of John Wiley and Sons, our editor and colleague, who reached out to us and enabled us to work on this fascinating project. Without his help, guidance, and doggedness, we would not have completed it.

MICHAEL BAYER, AICP

NANCY FRANK, Ph.D., AICP

JASON VALERIUS, AICP

Personal Acknowledgments

I am indebted to my wife, Michelle Landrum, and children, Adam and Clark, who sacrificed their evenings and weekends to allow me to work on this project, while I attempted to balance it, myself, with the life of the planner and all of the demands and experiences of my day (and night) job. The act of balancing career and personal life within urban planning is an art not always well executed, but in the end, is tremendously rewarding.

I also owe thanks to Uri Avin, FAICP, who helped me bridge the public and private sectors and introduced me to his vast network of planners across the country, many of whom are represented in this book. I must acknowledge Craig Watson, RLA, with whom I've had many conversations about mentorship and team building and the role that planners can and should play in the professional development of others.

MICHAEL BAYER, AICP

To my wife, Amy Payne, I owe heartfelt thanks for the patience with the late nights and weekends diverted toward this effort.

JASON VALERIUS, AICP

Thanks to my students for their patience with me in the final stretch in completing this book. Tomorrow is another day, and tomorrow my students are at the top of my "to do" list. Thanks, too, to my colleagues for their constant support along the way. As always, I am grateful for my husband's patience, encouragement, and support. I owe tremendous gratitude to the many planners who have shared their wisdom with me over the years. But finally, and especially, my great thanks to my former students Michael Bayer and Jason Valerius, who are valued colleagues and who made this project sing.

NANCY FRANK, AICP

① Becoming an Urban Planner: What Planners Do

URBAN PLANNING IS A PROFESSION that offers a wide range of opportunities for people with many different talents and aspirations.

Yet, unlike the occupations of doctor, architect, lawyer, or engineer, the work of the urban planner is not well known to people outside the profession.

The name of the profession, "urban planning," is straightforward and descriptive. Urban planners plan for the future of urban areas. But this literal description of the work of an urban planner only scratches the surface of the role of urban planners. Planners work to ensure that cities have what they need to grow and prosper, including:

■ Places where people can live

Planners estimate the number of households that will need to be housed in the coming years and recommend where within the community land should be set aside for homes to be built. In the process, planners work with communities to determine the proportion of homes that will be single-family houses, duplexes, or multi-family housing and the proportion that will be targeted for home ownership versus rental. Planners also work on policies affecting the price of housing in a community, to ensure that low-income and moderate-income residents (like store clerks, restaurant staff, nursing assistants, and teachers) have comfortable and affordable housing available to them.

■ Places where employers can build shops, offices, and factories

In addition to working to identify the best places within a community for locating factories, shopping areas, and offices, planners also work to attract jobs to communities. Economic development planners study the local economy to identify needs and create programs to fill those needs. For example, planners work with employers and local educational institutions to make sure that the students receive training in the skills required by local industries or by the industries that the community would like to locate there.

■ Transportation facilities (roads, rail, airports, and seaports)

Planners study transportation systems to determine when additional transportation facilities are needed, where they should be built, and the mix of transportation options that should be available. Planners collect and analyze information to find out whether the growth and prosperity of a region is hampered because the transportation network does not provide sufficient access to some locations in the community or because congestion is creating excessive delays in getting from one place to another. Planners know that industry needs an efficient transportation system for moving raw materials in and manufactured products out. While the number of cars per person has steadily increased since the nineteenth century, planners work to create a balanced transportation system in which residents can choose to live in areas that are designed to make biking, walking, and transit (buses, light rail, and commuter rail) more successful.

■ Clean water for drinking and washing and systems for managing wastes

Planners work with civil engineers to ensure that basic urban infrastructure—sewer and water— will be available as a community grows. How a community grows can have a dramatic effect on the cost of providing sewer and water services. For example, laying out a neighborhood with large lots served by sewer and water requires more spending on pipes and requires more maintenance by the city in the future. Planners work with communities to understand the effects of land use decisions on the cost of providing sewer and water services and to modify land use policies as needed. Planners also work with hydrogeologists and civil engineers to develop plans for the sustainable use of sources of drinking water, to ensure that the supply of water will remain sufficient in the future.

■ Places where people can recreate

Planning for parks, open space, and community facilities like ice rinks, athletic fields, and community centers is important to any community. Planners study the age distribution of the population as it is today and as it will be in the future. A city with a growing number of school-age children requires a different mix of recreation facilities than a city with an aging population entering retirement. Planners seek a fair distribution of parks and open space across the community.

■ Places where people *want* to be

Planners know that it is not enough simply to meet basic needs for housing, shopping, working, and recreation. People choose where to live, work, and play based on many factors, and the physical design of urban places is one of those factors. Urban design considerations—how tall should our buildings be, how far should they be set back from the street, where parking for cars and bikes should be located—are an important aspect of the urban planning puzzle. Decisions and rules regarding the physical design of the community determine the appearance and character of the place and can either attract or repel people and investment in the community.

■ Community development

Some planners focus on community organizing and community development, seeking to increase social justice, reduce poverty, and "build vital and thriving under-resourced communities" (National Congress for Community Economic Development, 2009). Most planners working on community development work in areas with high levels of poverty and low levels of education, employment, and income, whether in central city neighborhoods, suburbs, or rural areas. They provide assistance to small businesses, bring resources to the community for improving the quality of affordable housing, and develop programs for increasing the skills and job readiness of residents.

■ Supplies of energy

Planners have always worked with energy utilities to predict future energy demands and to locate sites for new energy facilities, such as power plants, natural gas pipelines, or petroleum storage areas. Today, increasingly, planners are at the forefront in identifying ways in which communities can reduce their energy needs and plan for the future of renewable energy resources.

Employment in Planning

Planning is a relatively small but growing field. In 2006, the Department of Labor reported 34,000 jobs held by urban and regional planners (Bureau of Labor Statistics, 2009). This compares to 132,000 architects, for example.

U.S. News and World Report rated Urban and Regional Planner as one of the "Best Careers" in 2009 (U.S. News, 2009). The Bureau of Labor Statistics projects a 15 percent increase in the number of planning jobs between 2006 and 2016—faster than average for all occupations (Bureau of Labor Statistics, 2009).

Two-thirds of planners work for the government. Usually, planners work for city or county governments, but they may also work for a metropolitan planning board or regional planning agency. Some planners who are publicly employed work for state or federal agencies, such as the National Park Service, the Federal Emergency Management Administration, the Department of Transportation, Environmental Protection Agency, or Housing and Urban Development.

The fastest growing segment of the planning job market is in the private sector (Bureau of Labor Statistics, 2009). Twenty-five percent of the planners surveyed by the American Planning Association said that they worked for private consulting firms, and 2 percent worked for private developers. Planning consultants work in the private sector, but frequently their clients are local governments. That is, although the planner works for a private firm, the firm is hired by a city to do planning on the city's behalf. Even when planners work for private developers or when their consulting client is in the private sector, planners' code of ethics calls upon them to take the public interest seriously in all of their work (American Institute of Certified Planners, no date).

Many planners work for government agencies. Planners who work for cities, villages, and towns work with elected officials (the mayor and city council members) and the planning commission, helping them to understand the community's planning needs and opportunities and to make good decisions about the community's future. CITY OF PIEDMONT.

Planners work in all kinds of cities—from large cities with millions of residents to small rural hamlets with fewer than a hundred homes. In addition, whether a planner works for an individual city, for a regional planning agency or for a private client, planners are always thinking about the connections between the place where they focus their work and other places beyond those borders. Roads and train tracks extend in every direction from the city where a planner works. People live in one city, but they may work in another and shop is dozens of other cities. People buy goods and services that come from around the globe. Political boundaries, such as city limits, define a city planner's main focus, but the skillful planner is always looking at how the place where the planner is currently focused is connected to other places near and far.

SIMCITY™

Since 1989, scores of children and adults have been introduced to the field of urban planning through the computer game SimCity. Players take on the role of urban planner (though officially designated "mayor" in the game), deciding how much land to devote to housing, industry, and commercial buildings (offices and stores), building roads and rails and heliports, and setting aside land for parks, zoos, and police stations. As the game unfolds, players see how their decisions affect the number of people who want to move to the city, the taxes generated from houses, offices, and factories, the level of traffic congestion, and the amount of pollution. When taxes get too high or traffic congestion becomes too intense, people move away, looking for less expensive places to live or places with a higher quality of life. The game also teaches that planners need to expect the unexpected, as a host of natural and human-caused disasters can suddenly descend upon the city. SimCity has done more than dozens of books like this to interest people in the work of planners.

This book picks up where a game like SimCity leaves off, showing you not only what planners do, but also how to prepare for a career in planning and the opportunities within the field.

A Young Profession: Planning Emerges in the Late Nineteenth Century

Planning is not only a small profession; it is also a relatively new profession. It emerged out of the urban crises at the end of the nineteenth century. Rapid population growth combined with a laissez-faire economic philosophy created multiple challenges for cities: water supplies fouled by human and animal waste, air choked by smoke from coal-burning industries and wood burning in homes, and a chaotic streetscape with telegraph, telephone, and electrical wires strung erratically above an underground tangle of pipes and tunnels. Jon Peterson (2003) describes the elements that led to the establishment of city planning as a separate profession in 1909. First, the public health movement in the late nineteenth century recognized the relationship between land use and disease. Until the germ theory became well accepted in the late 1890s, medical science did not always understand why people who lived in certain parts of the city were more likely to become ill. One theory was that wet ground, vapors from swamps, and bad smells carried disease. As a result, public health professionals and civil engineers advocated for well-planned sewer and water systems, drainage of wet areas in cities, and the creation of city parks where people could enjoy fresh air away from the smoke and dust of the city streets.

Sewage Treatment Plant. Planners worked side by side with public health professionals and engineers in the late nineteenth and early twentieth centuries to promote sewage treatment. Initially, sewage systems were designed to merely move filth-laden water out of homes and off of streets. During the early twentieth century, new methods of treating sewage evolved, so that it became less dangerous to people and less harmful to the environment. This plant, first built in 1925, was one of the first in the United States to use microorganisms to break down the contaminants in sewage. Planners create sanitary sewer service area plans to make sure that the city does not develop too fast, outpacing the sewage treatment plant's available capacity. FROM THE AMERICAN GEOGRAPHICAL SOCIETY LIBRARY, UNIVERSITY OF WISCONSIN–MILWAUKEE LIBRARIES.

AN AGE OF IDEALISM IN DESIGN

Concerns about the urban environment also led to utopian efforts to build model towns. Some plans were designed by self-trained visionaries, like Ebenezer Howard, who designed a utopian plan for "garden cities of tomorrow." Other plans were commissioned by landowners seeking to create an idyllic place for the "wealthier classes," such as Riverside, Illinois. And others were the result of the visions of industrialists like George Pullman, who commissioned a town plan with housing and shops for the workers in the company's railroad car factory.

A key event in the development of the planning profession was the work of architects, landscape architects, and engineers in the design of the grounds for the 1893 Chicago World's Fair. Later dubbed the "White City," the fair introduced the idea of master planning and caught the public's imagination. Following the fair, the architects and landscape architects who had designed the White City were commissioned to create plans for cities across the country.

The World's Columbian Exposition (1893), also known as the Chicago World's Fair, brought the first Ferris wheel and the birth of city planning in the United States. Key figures in the development of planning as a profession led the planning for the exposition, including Chicago architect Daniel Burnham and the "Father of Landscape Architecture," Frederick Law Olmsted. Decades would pass before these three professions—planning, architecture, and landscape architecture—became distinct fields and much overlap continues today. CHICAGO HISTORY MUSEUM, ICHI-02524, 1893.

DEVIL IN THE WHITE CITY

Erik Larson's book, *The Devil in the White City: Murder, Magic and Madness at the Fair That Changed America,* is an entertaining look at the creation of the "White City" and some of the notorious activities that accompanied the fair. The *New York Times* lauded Larson's fusion of history and entertainment, noting that "truth is stranger than fiction." The book is a good read that teaches much about the early pioneers in urban planning—and the times in which they worked.

Planning in Boston, Chicago, Cleveland, and Washington, DC, all showed the imprint of the Chicago World's Fair. In 1909, the first National Conference on City Planning was held in Washington, DC.

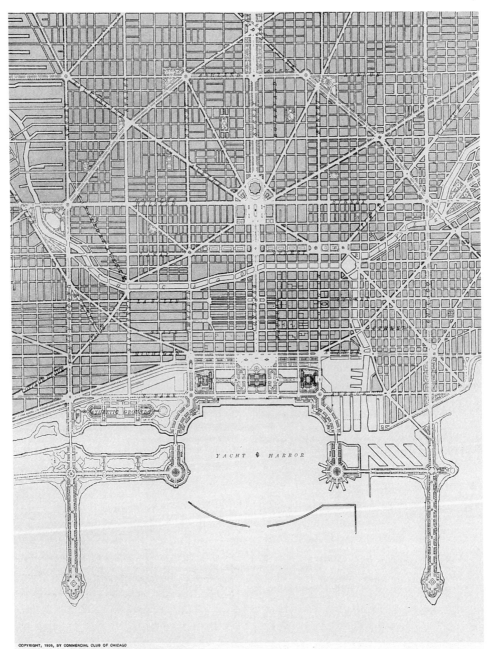

COPYRIGHT, 1909, BY COMMERCIAL CLUB OF CHICAGO

CX. CHICAGO. PLAN OF THE COMPLETE SYSTEM OF STREET CIRCULATION; RAILWAY STATIONS; PARKS, BOULEVARD
CIRCUITS AND RADIAL ARTERIES; PUBLIC RECREATION PIERS, YACHT HARBOR, AND PLEASURE-BOAT PIERS; TREATMENT
OF GRANT PARK; THE MAIN AXIS AND THE CIVIC CENTER, PRESENTING THE CITY AS A COMPLETE ORGANISM IN WHICH
ALL ITS FUNCTIONS ARE RELATED ONE TO ANOTHER IN SUCH A MANNER THAT IT WILL BECOME A UNIT.

Plan for Chicago (1909). CHICAGO HISTORY MUSEUM, ICHI-39070, 1909.

THE ADVENT OF ZONING

At this stage in its development, planning had reached a new level. It was not about merely designing a single park or a housing district. It was about taking the scope of an entire city and understanding the relationship among the elements of a city—moving people from place to place, providing a lively and inviting atmosphere, keeping people safe and healthy, and creating a canvas on which commerce could prosper.

This expansion of the scope of planning posed challenges, however. When planning was undertaken for a single site—whether for a new housing district like Riverside, a new town like Pullman, the civic center in Cleveland, or the Chicago World's Fair grounds—the designers had only to worry about persuading the client to agree to the ideas set forth in the plan. Typically, the land was entirely under the control of the client. If the client liked the plan, it simply had to be built. Moving to the scale of an entire city, encompassing an area of 40, 50, or 60 square miles was another matter entirely. Multiple landowners could not be corralled into agreeing to a single plan. If the plans were to become more than grand ideas on paper, some means of implementing them—within the context of democratic government—had to be found.

U.S. Constitution. Planners are required to limit their activities to doing things that are consistent with the U.S. Constitution and the powers that each state government allows municipalities to exercise. Enabling statutes are the state laws that allow local governments to regulate land use. Those regulations must also conform to the requirements of the U.S. Constitution. When zoning-enabling statutes were first created, some property owners believed that the state and local government had infringed upon the owner's right to property, in violation of the U.S. Constitution. The U.S. Supreme Court, the final authority on what is constitutional, frequently rules on the constitutionality of planning laws and actions. U.S. ARCHIVES.

While those trained in the design professions continued to put together grand ideas about how places should look, others tackled the problem of channeling urban growth and development through the hundreds of private decisions made by landowners about their real estate. The regulation of land use was not new, and municipal officials were inventing new kinds of regulations as the challenges of urban life continued to mount. Restrictions were placed on locations where certain activities could be carried out. For example, slaughterhouses were relegated to one part of the city. Restrictions were placed on the heights of buildings even as engineers invented new ways of making buildings taller. Outside of the downtown area, the restrictions on the height of buildings were even stricter. These restrictions led cities to identify specific zones within the city where some activities were allowed and others restricted.

In 1916, New York City was the first city to adopt a comprehensive zoning code that covered all property within the city. In 1924, the federal government completed a draft of a model zoning-enabling statute, encouraging state legislatures to empower municipalities to exercise zoning powers. In 1926, the U.S. Supreme Court upheld the zoning code of the city of Euclid, Ohio, as a proper exercise of local government power.

The advent of the era of land use regulation also meant that a new category of government bureaucrats would be needed to administer these new codes. In 1914, Newark, New Jersey, became the first city in the United States to hire a planner on its staff rather than relying on consultants.

After the 1920s, planning continued to develop along two separate tracks. One track focused on the design of urban spaces. These planners, who often had some training in architecture or landscape architecture, envisioned how a space would be used and how it would look, and they communicated those ideas through drawings and maps. The second track in planning focused more on the skeleton of the city, mapping out the major areas for shopping, housing, and factories, and putting into place the local ordinances that would govern how property owners might use their land and the size and scale of buildings that might be erected on a site.

POLICY PLANNING EMERGES SIMULTANEOUSLY

A third track within planning—policy planning—also has its roots in the late nineteenth century. In 1907, the Russell Sage Foundation completed detailed studies on the employment and living conditions of workers in Pittsburgh. The authors recommended a new kind of policy response, beyond the tenement regulations that had been in place for at least 20 years prior to the study. The authors focused on public policies aimed at the working conditions within factories, including the long hours and lack of financial security of workers. They recommended legislation to end the 12-hour workday. This recommendation reflected a growing understanding that many urban issues are interrelated.

Policy planning became an increasingly prominent component of the profession throughout the twentieth century, especially at the federal level of government. Planners helped develop policies to meet the needs for jobs and housing during the Great Depression of the 1930s, and then to deal with commodity scarcities during World War II. In the postwar era planners helped create policies to meet the surge of demand for housing and transportation, especially the interstate freeway system. In the 1960s planners helped combat poverty as part of the Great Society movement spearheaded by President Lyndon B. Johnson.

PLANNING AND SOCIAL INJUSTICE

The ferment of the 1960s also alerted planners to issues of social justice and participatory democracy. Planners entered an era of self-reflection and saw many things about the profession that they did not like. Planners had ignored the needs of poor and minority communities. Spurred by visions of urban renewal and gleaming freeways cutting across city neighborhoods, planners had been blind to the unjust negative effects that such policies had had on poor neighborhoods.

Planners redefined their role. Prior to the 1960s, most planners would have identified themselves as experts whose opinions on matters relating to the development of cities should be accepted by the public and community leaders as they would accept the opinions of an attorney or doctor in their respective fields of expertise. After the 1960s, a growing number of planners accepted the idea that planners need to consult with the people who live and work in communities and to apply their expertise to assist the community in achieving its goals. At the same time, planners recognized that the values and interests of the most vocal participants in the planning process may not be shared by other segments of the community.

Public participation is now a staple of almost every planning process. Planners reach out to all segments of the community to hear their views on how the city meets their current needs and what their vision for the future looks like. In the 1960s, this approach focused largely on including racial and ethnic minorities that had been left out. Today, planners also seek to ensure that the voices of the physically disabled, children, the elderly, and single parents are included in the planning process.
COURTESY OF DAN BURDEN, GLADDING JACKSON.

PLANNING IN THE LATE TWENTIETH CENTURY

The 1970s awakening of environmentalism resulted in a wave of federal regulations and initiatives to curb pollution, and planners engaged in work to protect watersheds, reduce air pollution, and protect the habitat of endangered species. The interest in environmental protection was a major influence on the development of the Smart Growth movement in the late 1980s and 1990s.

Factory closings during the 1970s and 1980s drew many planners into local economic development efforts. As this process continued and accelerated in the 1990s and 2000s, planners helped pursue similar efforts at a regional scale. Policy planners continue to work in all of these areas. An increasing number of policy planners work on issues related to energy and climate change.

Today, the three major approaches to planning (design, land use planning, and policy planning) are coming together in a more integrated way. While individual planners may have specialized skills in one or two of these areas, planning is carried out in teams that include all of these skills, and few plans are created that do not touch upon all three areas in some way.

Abandoned factories became a common sight in cities across the United States beginning in the 1970s. Initially, employers moved their factories to new locations with better access to truck transport on the edges of cities. Later, many industrial operations moved to locations in the south. More recently, employers have moved operations to foreign countries to lower their costs of producing goods. Often, when factories moved out, they left behind deteriorating buildings and underground contamination that hampered reuse of the sites. FROM THE AMERICAN GEOGRAPHICAL SOCIETY LIBRARY, UNIVERSITY OF WISCONSIN–MILWAUKEE LIBRARIES.

In Milwaukee, Wisconsin, an old rail yard has been redeveloped for new industrial facilities and park space, honoring the area's heritage by preserving two smokestacks, providing visual interest and symbolizing the prior use of the site. NANCY FRANK, 2009.

Plans envision the future. The comprehensive plan for Kona, Hawaii, envisioned the future through both words and pictures. Over 1000 participants attended public workshops where they shared their ideas for how the community should grow. Planners took that information, along with technical information about trends and needs, to create a plan for moving toward the future that participants said they preferred. ACP VISIONING+PLANNING

Urban Planning Is about the Future

One of the distinguishing characteristics of urban planners, no matter what their approach to planning, is their focus on the future. The future is always shrouded in a fog of uncertainty. No one can predict what the future will bring. But planners are in the business of attempting to anticipate the future and recommend strategies to help cities thrive as the future unfolds.

Planners work with elected officials, businesses, and residents to create a vision of the future. Then, by studying current conditions and trends, the planner develops suggestions for actions that will allow the city to achieve its vision. Planners collect information about population, the economy, and the environment. This information allows planners to understand whether the city is growing in population or shrinking and whether employers are moving into the city and creating new jobs or moving away because of suburbanization or globalization. Planners look at whether the supply of houses is likely to be sufficient to meet the needs of residents over the next 20 years, whether the existing transportation system allows people to get to jobs, shopping, school, and recreational activities without safety problems, unacceptable delays, and increasing pollution. Where problems are identified, planners then strategize ways the city government can work with residents, businesses, and other units of government to solve those problems and achieve their vision for the future.

LOW-INCOME SENIOR HOMEOWNERS:
TOTAL HOUSEHOLDS & COST BURDEN (1990 VS. 2000)

Measure	1990	2000	% Change
Total households	19,153	15,042	−21%
Cost burden > 30% of household income	4,135	6,043	45%
Cost burden > 50% of household income	1,897	3,367	78%

Source: City of Seattle Comprehensive Plan, 2005.

Urban Planning Is about Place

Google the word *planning* and one comes to realize how planning relates to every part of life. One finds retirement planning, wedding planning, and health system planning—and many others. All planning shares an orientation toward the future. "Urban planning" is different from the others because of its focus on "place." This focus on place is even deeper than the profession's focus on urban places. Urban planning focuses on shaping the nature of places, including the built environment (houses, stores, offices, and factories) and the natural environment (fields, forests, waters, and wetlands). Planners shape the built and natural environment in many ways.

Why did you become a planner?

> As a kid, I was always fascinated by buildings, places, maps, and the world around me in general. This led me to pursue a career as an architect. However, after studying architecture in college for two years, I found that my interests were less in designing individual buildings and more in the morphology of places and the dynamics of regional transportation networks, as well as how these relate to one another. This realization led me to change majors from architecture to urban affairs and geography.

Upon graduation into a tough job market and still not exactly sure what I wanted to do with my life, I took a job at a consulting firm in the Washington, DC, area as a cartographer, primarily drafting and editing FEMA flood maps.

While it wasn't what I wanted to do, and the pay was quite low, I knew that it would help me get some practical experience and serve as a stepping-stone towards something more suitable. Several months into the job, I was given the opportunity to transfer into the company's planning group, doing more challenging professional work, where my career as a planner began in earnest.

Stuart Sirota, AICP, TND Planning Group

Land use planners shape how a community uses the land and spreads out across the land as more and more people move to the city. Transportation planners shape the built environment by increasing the ease with which people can travel to some places rather than others. When transportation planners design streets for cars moving at 45 miles per hour, pedestrians are unlikely to walk

Shopping areas along roads that are designed entirely for moving traffic quickly are no place for pedestrians. Few people will hazard crossing the street on foot. As a result, areas like these—so common in suburbs built in the second half of the twentieth century—increase the amount that people drive, pollution, carbon emissions, and energy consumption. Many suburban communities are rethinking how to plan for shopping areas, and planners are helping them to find ways of making their shopping areas more pedestrian-friendly. NANCY FRANK, 2009.

between places along the street, and developers design their sites to accommodate people arriving by car. Economic development planners may focus their efforts on attracting new businesses to office parks built on former farm fields or, instead, they may focus on cleaning up former industrial sites and attracting new businesses to locate on these recycled lands. In each case, the focus is on developing plans, policies, and programs for a specific place.

You are invited to help

Build a Better Neighborhood

Please come and learn how you and your neighbors can

Take Back the Streets

Neighborhood Meeting!

Traffic Calming Charrette

With Walkable Communities Expert, Dan Burden

Friday, April 16 – 6:30 PM to 9:00 PM

Saturday, April 17 – 9:00 AM to 12 Noon

Sunday, April 18 – 1:00 PM to 3:00 PM

Meet at Burtness Auditorium

Cottage Hospital Pueblo and Bath Streets

Questions? 897-2509
¿Preguntas? 564-5385

info@OakParkTrafficManagement.org
Neighborhood Traffic Management Program

▲ Traffic calming refers to a set of techniques communities can use to slow down traffic to allow pedestrians to travel more safely and more efficiently in areas where high speeds and high traffic volumes have made walking difficult. COURTESY OF DAN BURDEN, GLATTING JACKSON.

▶ In newly developing areas, planners and urban designers design narrower streets, on-street parking, and other visual cues to reduce traffic speeds and give pedestrians and bicyclists a safer and more comfortable environment. COURTESY OF DANA BOURLAND

Urban Planning Is about Helping Other People Make Decisions

All communities are concerned about the future and faced with decisions that will shape that future. Whether deciding where to allow growth or restrict development, deciding how to attract businesses and grow jobs, or deciding what type of transportation improvement is most worthy of scarce public dollars, community leaders need help finding and choosing among alternatives. Urban planners study the options and make recommendations for the preferred solution to a problem, but the decisions are usually made by elected officials.

Why did you become a planner?

❯ I was always interested in public policy. I majored in economics and political science at Claremont McKenna College (it was Claremont Men's College at the time), but I wasn't sure which aspect of public policy interested me the most.

During my sophomore year in college, I spent a semester in Copenhagen, then backpacked through Europe. That exposed me to European cities and how different they were from Southern California where I grew up. That's when I first became interested in cities and how societies choose to physically organize themselves.

Another influence was when I took the train across the country while in college. On the train, I saw the backside of cities, often traveling through their depressed communities. The poverty in some areas was shocking to me, and I became increasingly interested in economic development. I still hadn't heard of city planning. I was just interested in the public policy issues such as housing, poverty, and community development.

My senior year, I went to the college career office to learn about graduate schools. I thought about getting a master's in public policy or international development. I noticed a flyer about a program at Berkeley that focused on housing, environmental, and urban economic development policies—all issues that interested me. When I read further, I discovered it was a program in city and regional planning. This was the first time that I learned that city planning was a specific discipline.

William Anderson, FAICP, City of San Diego, California

The Planning Process

Whatever the issue at hand, planners engage in a number of activities to help find and select from a range of possible solutions. First, they collect and analyze information about the problem, to understand the causes and consequences, as well as solutions that have been tried before. Next, they clarify the outcomes that a policy solution must achieve to be considered a success. Third, they identify a number of alternatives for solving the problem. These alternatives may be based on efforts that have been tried in other places or planners may come up with entirely new approaches for solving the problem. Finally, they try to predict the outcomes that are likely to occur under each alternative, and they present these results to decision makers, usually appointed or elected public officials.

Residents participating in a planning workshop. CRAIG OWENSBY/METRO NASHVILLE PLANNING DEPARTMENT.

Stakeholder: Anyone who feels they have a stake in the decision because they will be affected by it or because they care about the outcome.

An essential component of this planning process—finding, evaluating, and selecting alternatives—is public involvement. Elected officials are acting on behalf of the entire community. They want to make smart choices, and they also want to choose with the confidence that those decisions are supported by voters and stakeholders throughout the community. Planners are responsible for bringing the public into the process by facilitating public meetings at crucial stages in the planning effort, especially at the beginning before a plan exists, in the middle when a draft plan or preliminary set of options is available for review, and at the end just before a decision is made.

STUDY APPROACH

The study proceeded in three stages: existing conditions compilation, land use and transportation evaluation, and preferred alternative selection. A final set of framework plans and streetscape guidance were developed to support the preferred alternative. Three reports were produced from this analysis: *Existing Conditions and Plans*, *Transportation and Land Use Evaluation*, and *Framework Plans and Street Typology*.

In the course of the study, seven combined transportation and land use scenarios were developed, analyzed, and evaluated. These scenarios evaluated both existing and future conditions in the study area. Included were two alternative scenarios, Alternatives 1 and 2, each with a short-term time horizon (2015) and a long-term time horizon (2030). Evaluation of the scenarios measured: how well the scenarios work from an urban design perspective; how well the scenarios result in connectivity; and how well the scenarios promote integration of the entire study area.

Source: Richard Bernhardt, FAICP, Springfield Connectivity Study, August 2008, ES-1.

Getting People Involved in the Process

GIANNI LONGO

Principal, ACP Visioning + Planning

New York, NY

How did you become interested in planning and, ultimately, visioning as a public involvement tool?

❭ I have always been a city person. All my life, someone has lived above me or below me. So I began to deal with city issues from the standpoint of public awareness and public involvement. I wanted to take the European experience and apply it to my American experience, professionally.

Through the National Endowment for the Arts, I published a series of books about learning from cities.

The city of Chattanooga, Tennessee, saw this work and asked me to do an assessment of their community. I developed a plan for the city that wasn't conventional. It was really about how to organize neighborhoods, animate neighborhoods, and create opportunities for social interaction, with a focus on the creation of public places.

How have you applied this experience to your subsequent work?

❭ What became very clear to me from the Chattanooga project was that dialogue has to be more than one way. Instead of deciding what should be, planners need to ask the community: What do you want to do? This is a shift in the public involvement process.

In the past, planners would develop a plan, then have a public hearing to inform the public about it.

Then, almost by necessity, planners would ignore the public's comments, and in the end, the public might sue the city because it had no ownership in the plan.

Certain principles are fundamental to the process of public participation. One is inclusiveness. Instead of a top-down process, it should be from the center out. We try to begin with a small group of individuals or planners or a couple of city council members to begin the process and then move out to larger and larger groups. It's like throwing a pebble into a pond.

Another principle is transparency. A public hearing is a very intimidating type of setting where people who stand up and give speeches can only grandstand. We, as the public, never learn anything from this type of communication. Instead, planners need to make a firm link between the public involvement process and implementation. If the public is aware of what is going on, they are more likely to be supportive of it.

The techniques depend on what you're trying to accomplish. There is an array of techniques that we use. We do a lot of brainstorming, where we develop goals by collecting a large number of ideas from a group. We use technology, like visualization and electronic keypads to collect data. We use modeling. And we stay visible. There is never a time when the consultant disappears in the process.

Public involvement is not easy. It can be a challenge to get people to take time out of their lives to participate in a planning process. Historically, the people who were most affected by planning decisions were left out of the process. Today, planners often exert special effort to be sure to include those who will be affected most but who may be hard to reach—people working multiple jobs, people with limited English reading skills, and those with limited transportation options. Public meetings and surveys are staples of the process, but getting people to those meetings and getting them to respond to a survey requires creativity and persistence. Planners use a variety of communication strategies to alert people to their opportunity to get involved, including websites, emails, posters, direct mail, and notices in the papers, community and church newsletters, and announcements at community meetings.

Once people are engaged in the process, getting feedback on what they think the community should do also requires creativity. Like elected officials, the general public will have their opinions about what to do, but they will also look to the planner for information about the options. The planner's role is to inform people based on the best available information. To do this, the planner facilitates a public discussion of the options that allows all voices to be heard. Then, the planner writes up an accurate summary of that discussion to inform decision makers.

Urban design projects often utilize a special type of public process known as a charrette. The charrette approach originates from architecture and urban design, but has become a staple of public participation in land use planning as well. In its traditional form, a team of designers will set up a temporary work space in the study area, such as an available downtown storefront.

SUSTAINABILITY VISIONING SESSION

The City of Middleton is working with MSA Professional Services, Inc., Seventh Generation Energy Systems, and GDS Associates, Inc. to prepare a Sustainable City Plan for Middleton. What do you want the future of Middleton to look like? Please come to the Sustainable City Plan visioning session to provide input and learn more about the plan. The plan will focus on the following key areas:

Wednesday, July 8, 7:00pm
Middleton Senior Center
7448 Hubbard Avenue

- *Energy*
- *Land Use*
- *Transportation*
- *Water Resources*
- *Solid Waste Generation and Management*
- *Economy/Food/Fair Trade*
- *Public Outreach and Education*

Questions? Contact Abby Attoun at 827-1043 or aattoun@ci.middleton.wi.us

Visioning session invitation poster. COURTESY OF ABBY ATTOUN, CITY OF MIDDLETON, WISCONSIN

ORIGINS OF THE WORD CHARRETTE

The French word "charrette" means "cart" and is often used to describe the final, intense work effort expended by art and architecture students to meet a project deadline. This use of the term is said to originate from the École des Beaux Arts in Paris during the nineteenth century, where proctors circulated a cart, or "charrette," to collect final drawings while students frantically put finishing touches on their work.

Source: NCI Charrette System, http://www.charretteinstitute.org/charrette.html

that the historic character should be preserved regardless of the decision. Several respondents mentioned the hotels and motels along Tulane as prime candidates for redevelopment.

GALVEZ

- All respondents (5) stated a mixture of both rehab (where possible) and new development (if buildings not structurally sound or unmarketable) was desired.

8. Are there any specific buildings (historic, neighborhood landmarks, etc) in your neighborhood that you feel strongly about? 10 years from now, what places do you still want to be in the neighborhood?

TULANE

- 85% stated the Dixie Brewery was an important asset that should be saved, while 43% (3/7) mentioned the Falstaff building. Others mentioned Anita's Grill and any historic brick buildings should be rehabilitated.

GALVEZ

- The 3 respondents all stated that the old historic homes should be saved if possible, and new residential developments should not "cheapen" the value and historical character of the neighborhood.

9. Are there any specific buildings or lots that you would like to see removed and/or redeveloped into something else?

- Respondents stated buildings that were not structurally sound should be removed, especially the abandoned hotels. Existing homes that are repairable on Galvez should be redeveloped with/ historical character.

10. What type of experience would you like to have while walking or driving along the corridors? Do you want to see/feel a difference between Tulane and Galvez?

TULANE

- Respondents had varied responses, including a historic character focus, "downtown USA" with/ walkability & retail, and more traffic oriented, mixed uses.

GALVEZ

- Responses varied; most wanted a general neighborhood feel with/less traffic and walkable neutral ground.

11. What image do you want visitors to have of each of the corridors? 10 years from now, if you were to describe Tulane and Galvez to an outsider, what would you like to tell them?

- Most respondents wished for a safe, walkable, vibrant neighborhood reflective of traditional & eclectic New Orleans character.

COMMON THEMES

- The impact of the LSU expansion was mentioned 6 times by respondents as an influential factor impacting green space, residential relocations, housing needs, and commercial needs.
- The need for planned green-space and park lands was a recurring theme mentioned 9 times by respondents. Safety, location, and accessibility were cited as potential concerns.
- The need for public transportation improvements, namely electric rail car and bus stop improvements was mentioned 4 times.
- Respondents repeated the need for homeownership and professional job creation to solidify and stabilize this area as economically prosperous and independent.

PUBLIC PARTICIPATION APPENDIX D

After conducting interviews or other public participation activities, planners summarize the information and include the summaries in appendices attached to the planning document. Planners need to be able to write clearly and accurately about what people said. COPYRIGHT 2007. TULANE/GRAVIER REGULATING PLAN AND FORM-BASED CODE, PREPARED FOR THE PHOENIX OF NEW ORLEANS BY MATT AHO, ALISON KOPYT, BRAD LENZ, AND MEAGAN LIMBERG.

Planners encourage participants at a planning charrette to pick up markers and write their ideas on maps of the community. CRAIG OWENSBY/METRO NASHVILLE PLANNING DEPARTMENT

Over a 2–3 day period, the team will hold a series of meetings with stakeholders to ask questions and offer ideas and designs. In the time between meetings they will study the project area and work on design ideas, allowing the public to stop by at any time to view and discuss the work in progress. The charrette concludes with a public meeting at which final ideas and drawings are presented and discussed, allowing the designers to make a final recommendation based on the feedback and support of people affected by the changes that may occur.

A variation of this approach provides maps, aerial photos, and other representations of the community and invites participants to mark up the maps, identifying areas with issues that need to be addressed or features that could be added to improve the area. A planning charrette may take a few hours or a couple of days.

Buyer Beware: Things You Might *Not* Like about a Career in Planning

Most professions have a downside—circumstances that come with the job and are a common source of frustration or complaint. So too does planning.

Many jobs in planning require attendance at public meetings of one kind or another, and most such meetings are scheduled after 5:00 in the evening. It may be possible to find a role in a larger organization, public or private, that does not have this requirement, but the typical planner will attend 1–2 night meetings per week, getting home well past the dinner hour. This fact of the planner's life can interfere with after-work recreation activities and complicate family scheduling.

NIGHT MEETINGS: BALANCING WORK AND FAMILY

Working at home—with the dual full-time responsibilities of caring for a child and home, and completing my professional responsibilities—is quite a challenge.

Every day is a new balancing act between meeting deadlines, caring for my son, and completing daily household tasks. There are always conflicts and the right choice is never clear-cut.

Kathie Ebaugh, AICP, Bell David Planning Group

Another issue that some planners find frustrating is the role of politics in planning. Professional planners are trained to identify problems, develop solutions to those problems, and facilitate decisions by public officials to choose a solution. This final step in the process is where things get complicated. Public officials bring to their roles a vast array of differing values and interests that may or may not align with the planner's recommendations. Decisions and actions may be delayed by prolonged debate, sometimes over seemingly insignificant issues.

POLITICS AND PLANNING

Often, in planning, we called ourselves the "Department of Damage Control" and were disappointed that our plans were always being ruined by community realities. But, in retrospect, I think that this is the point of planning: working from an ideal to a best scenario based on reality, and doing that well takes far more skill than just dreaming up the textbook "perfect" solution.

Joan Kennedy, City of Hampton, Virginia

A planner's work may take decades to be realized, but elected and appointed officials come and go at a much more rapid pace, resulting in shifting priorities. Some planners take this in stride and enjoy the challenge, while others are simply frustrated by the process.

A third source of dissatisfaction is the lack of immediate reward after a plan is completed. An architect can point to a completed building a year or two after finishing the design, but planners frequently work on a much longer time horizon. Decisions about how and where a city should grow and change are realized only gradually as private developments are proposed, approved, and constructed over many years.

These concerns should be considered by the aspiring planner, but they should not scare anyone away from the profession. For most planners these issues are outweighed or entirely negated by the attractions of the work. Planners have the opportunity to influence decisions that shape cities for decades and develop programs that can have dramatic effects on quality of life. The work varies from project to project, bringing new challenges and opportunities for personal and professional growth. And, like other professions dependent on frequent communication and interaction, planning offers a steady supply of new friends and professional acquaintances.

WAITING FOR SOMETHING GOOD TO HAPPEN

While it can be frustrating at times, when you look back at what we are trying to do, it is critical that we figure out how to grow smarter in Maryland, the U.S., and for the planet. You get to do many different things, work with interesting people, and all for a good cause.

Richard Eberhardt Hall, AICP, Maryland Secretary of Planning

What Kind of Salary Can a Planner Expect to Make?

The Bureau of Labor Statistics provides information about the salaries of 35,000 jobs categorized as planning jobs. The agency's May 2007 survey found that the median salary for urban and regional planners was $57,907 (Bureau of Labor Statistics OES). Fifty percent of planners earned between $46,000 and $73,000. Twenty-five percent earned more than $73,000. Just 10 percent of planners earned less than $37,000; this group is probably made up primarily of planners early in their careers and planners working for nonprofit organizations.

PERCENTILE WAGE ESTIMATES FOR URBAN AND REGIONAL PLANNERS

Percentile	10%	25%	50% (Median)	75%	90%
Hourly Wage	$17.76	$22.00	$22.00	$35.15	$42.59
Annual Wage	$36,950	$45,750	$57,970	$73,110	$88,590

How to read this table: Ten percent of urban and regional planners surveyed earned less than $36,950. Half of the planners surveyed earned less than $57,970. Ninety percent of planners surveyed earned less than $88,590 annually.

Source: Bureau of Labor Statistics, Occupational Employment and Wages, May 2007.

Planners working in local and state government are at the lower end of the salary range as well. The best salaries are found in the private sector, where planners often work in architectural and engineering firms. The average salary for planners in private firms ($67,000) is about 15 percent higher than the average salary for planners working in local and state government ($58,400) (Bureau of Labor Statistics OES).

Skills for Becoming an Urban Planner

Planners are asked to find so-lutions to all sorts of problems. In preparing to become an urban planner, students need to develop the skills required to solve complex problems and capitalize on opportuni-ties. Planners need strong research skills, including the ability to find information, analyze it, and make accurate conclusions based on the information. Planners need to be able to communicate well, both orally and in writing, to different audiences. Planners need some skill in analyz-ing numbers—population numbers, numbers of housing units, numbers of jobs, miles of bike trail, dollars collected in property taxes. Planners in some specialties—transporta-tion, economic development, policy analysis, for example—need more skill in working with numbers than in other specialty areas.

▲ Planner Dana Bourland addresses a group of developers at a conference hosted by the Financial Times. Public speaking in front of many different kinds of audiences is one of the planner's most-used skills. COURTESY OF DANA BOURLAND.

▶ Two examples of the ways that planners need to be able to work with numbers. The table titled "Percentile Wage Estimates for Urban and Regional Planners" shows household composition, showing change over time and how households are expected to continue to change through the year 2020. The numbers in the table are percentages. For example, in 2000, the last time that the U.S. Census collected this information, the proportion of all households in Seattle that was composed of one person living alone was 40.8 percent. This proportion has been climbing slowly over time, and is expected to continue to climb into the future. The graph shows a steady decline in the number of Seattle households with children. Planners forecast that this decline will continue through 2020. Planners use graphs to communicate numerical information in a way that communicates with readers more quickly than a large table of numbers. With a graph, a reader can more quickly see any trend in the numbers. CITY OF SEATTLE.

Seattle's Comprehensive Plan | *Toward a Sustainable Seattle*   H-A17   A

Housing Figure A-12
Percent of Seattle Households by Type, 1960-2020

Household Type		1960*	1970*	1980	1990	2000	2010	2020
Family								
	Married couple without child	29.4	30.7	25.5	22.4	19.7	20.6	21.3
	Married couple with child	32.5	23.8	14.8	13.4	13.0	13.3	12.4
	Parent with child & without spouse	3.8	5.3	6.9	6.7	6.3	5.4	4.9
	Other family without child	5.3	4.8	4.8	5.2	4.8	5.6	5.8
Non-family		28.9	35.3					
	One person living alone			38.2	39.8	40.8	41.0	41.9
	Two or more persons without child			9.4	12.1	15.0	14.1	13.5
	Two or more persons with child			0.5	0.4	0.3	0.1	0.1
Total		100.0	100.0	100.0	100.0	100.0	100.0	100.0

*Refers to own child of the head of the household rather than any child in the household.
Sources: 1960 - 2000: U.S. Census Bureau, decennial censuses, 1960 to 2000; 2010 and 2020: forecast by City of Seattle Department of Planning & Development, July 2004, based on data from U.S. Census Bureau, decennial censuses, 1990 and 2000; Washington State Office of Financial Management King County Age Forecasts; and Puget Sound Regional Council 2010 and 2020 population projections for Seattle.

Housing Figure A-13
Seattle Households with Children, 1960-2020 (percent)

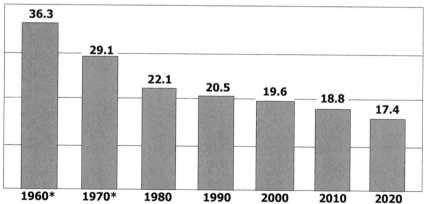

| 1960* | 1970* | 1980 | 1990 | 2000 | 2010 | 2020 |
| 36.3 | 29.1 | 22.1 | 20.5 | 19.6 | 18.8 | 17.4 |

Sources: 1960-2000: U.S. Census Bureau, decennial censuses, 1960 to 200; 2010 and 2020: forecast by City of Seattle Department of Planning and Development, July 2004, based on data from U.S. Census Bureau, decennial censuses, 1990 and 2000; Washington State Office of Financial Management King County Age Forecasts; and Puget Sound Regional Council 2010 and 2020 population projections for Seattle.

Because the problems that planners are typically asked to address have a geographic component, planners need a good understanding of geography and skill in using tools for mapping and analysis of spatial information. Where in the region is job growth the strongest and how does that relate to where unemployed workers reside? What would happen to property values if a new freeway interchange were constructed and how far from the interchange would the impact be felt?

For those planners who choose to focus primarily on the design of urban spaces, training in one of the design professions—usually coursework in architecture, landscape architecture, or urban design—prepare the planner to understand urban spaces and how the streets, buildings, and the spaces in between can be arranged to make an aesthetically attractive, economically vibrant, and environmentally sustainable place.

Creating and interpreting maps is a big part of planners' work. ACP, a planning consulting firm, created this map to frame conversations during a three-part intensive charrette process, named *Blueprint Plus* for the City of Fort Wayne, Indiana. The charrette helped local stakeholders to develop a vision to guide public policy and private investments in downtown, design the public places and the buildings that frame the vision, and identify site-specific catalyst projects. ACP VISIONING+PLANNING.

A lively street in Boston. This historic district has many of the elements that urban designers seek to re-create in newly developing areas. JASON VALERIUS.

The next chapter will provide more detail on the education of urban planners. Chapter 3 will review ways that a beginning planner can gain valuable job experience through internships and similar opportunities. Then, in Chapter 4, practicing planners will share their stories about the choices they made, the work they do, and the advice they offer to those interested in the profession.

❷ Becoming an Urban Planner: Education

GETTING THE RIGHT EDUCATION is one of the first steps in becoming a professional urban planner. Planners need a broad education because of the wide range of issues that planners address in their daily work. In addition, most planners obtain more specialized education focusing on the forces that drive the growth and decline of urban areas and the tools available to control and direct those forces.

Becoming an urban planner requires at least a bachelor's degree, and a master's degree is highly recommended. Because of the wide diversity of jobs that planners occupy, the educational paths that planners take to their careers are equally diverse. This chapter begins with the most common educational paths to a career in planning.

What Research Shows about Planners' Education

The American Planning Association (APA) is the largest organization of city and regional planners in the United States. APA has almost 30,000 professional members, which is close to the total number of planners identified by the Department of Labor in its survey of the profession. APA members are typically employed in public planning agencies or private planning consulting firms. They most commonly work on land development planning, land use code enforcement, transportation planning, and environmental planning. Fewer APA members are involved in economic development planning, planning for housing, and park and recreation planning. At the end of the chapter, alternative paths leading to careers in other subfields related to planning are described.

In 2008 APA conducted a web-based survey of its membership. These results are useful for understanding the typical educational path taken by planners engaged in the areas of planning represented by the APA membership. APA reports the results from 14,397 planners who provided salary data and who indicated that they were employed full-time as planners (American Planning Association).

Ninety-four percent of the planners surveyed had received either a master's degree (62 percent) or a bachelor's degree (32 percent). Of those planners who held a master's degree, two-thirds of them received their master's in urban planning. The remaining third held degrees in public administration, geography, business, and other fields. Of the 32 percent of surveyed planners who had only a bachelor's degree, a third held a bachelor's in planning. Geography was the next most common undergraduate major for planners with bachelor's degrees only.

Clearly, the typical educational path to a career in planning is to obtain a master's degree in planning, with 42 percent of all planners surveyed by APA having a master's in planning. Before getting into the details about selecting a graduate program and understanding what students learn in a master's program in urban planning, a student needs to think about how to best prepare for a planning career and for graduate study *before* getting to graduate school.

Preparing for a Professional Education

The professional degree in planning is the Master of Urban Planning, and similar degree designations. Long before enrolling in a master's program in urban planning, however, a student interested in a planning career can prepare by seeking out opportunities to learn more about planning and to hone skills that will be required in graduate school and in a planning career.

Rick Bernhardt, FAICP, executive director of the Metro Planning Department in Nashville, Tennessee, addresses a group of residents and business owners as a normal part of his daily work. FAICP stands for Fellow of the American Institute of Certified Planners. This designation indicates that Mr. Bernhardt has been elected to this honorary status in recognition of his achievements as a planner. CRAIG OWENSBY/METRO NASHVILLE PLANNING DEPARTMENT.

Barry Miller found his interest in planning at an early age. Here, Miller imagined and drew a skyline as viewed from across a bay. While drawing skills are not essential to being a successful planner, most planners agree that it can be a big advantage because so many aspects of planning involve visual elements. BARRY MILLER.

Perhaps the most important thing to remember about preparing to be a planner is that planners need to think *holistically* about problems and solutions, seeing all sides of an issue and recognizing how things are interconnected in cities and their surrounding area. That means that planners need to be well rounded, with knowledge about a wide range of topics. The second most important thing to understand about preparing for a planning career is that planners spend most of their day *communicating*. Planners need to be proficient writers and speakers. As much as 90 percent of a planner's day will be spent reading, writing, and talking with other people. A survey of practicing planners conducted by Ozawa and Seltzer (1999) found that planners considered communication skills to be among the most important skills for planners.

Planners also need to be able to work with numbers, although advanced math is not generally required for day-to-day activities for most planners.

Probably the best way to prepare to think holistically about urban problems and urban futures is to pursue learning across a wide range of fields. Literature teaches planners about people and their environments—and hones critically important reading skills. Art and art appreciation give future planners an understanding of how visual qualities (light, color, form) create the physical environment in cities.

◀ Like most planners, Dana Bourland (foreground), senior director of Green Communities for Enterprise Community Partners, meets with stakeholders. Dana works with city staff, developers, and residents to develop green and affordable housing options. LLOYD WOLF.

▼ In large cities and small, planning involves people from many different social and cultural backgrounds. Public meetings, in which members of the community share their views, are a staple of planning practice. © GOVERNMENT OF THE DISTRICT OF COLUMBIA, 2006.

Planners need to work with a wide range of people in the community. Gaining an understanding of the diverse cultures and histories of different subgroups in American society is excellent preparation for planners.

History gives planners an understanding of the past, which helps planners to anticipate how actions today may affect the future. Social studies give students an understanding of the governmental, business, and social organizations in which planners work and which are necessary to implement planners' ideas.

Finally, an understanding of science gives planners a clearer understanding of the relationship between cause and effect, an appreciation for basing decisions on high-quality information, and an understanding about the physical and environmental forces affecting cities—from the causes of earthquakes and floods to the resource demands of cities and the impacts of cities on the natural environment.

New residential subdivision with stormwater detention pond. Understanding the science of water quality and water quantity helps planners do a better job of managing the effects of rainwater in cities. Polluted rainfall is the biggest source of water pollution in most places today. Stormwater management has become a critical part of planners' work in laying out new subdivisions and in redeveloping older parts of existing urban areas. NANCY FRANK, 2009.

Fond du Lac and North Avenue Green Infrastructure Initiative

Prepared by Center for Resilient Cities
(formerly the Urban Open Space Foundation)

December 2007

CENTER FOR RESILIENT CITIES

Good Living Well Grounded

For decades, planners and engineers designed and implemented gray infrastructure—steel and concrete pipes and channels that carried wastes and polluted rainwater away. Out of sight; out of mind—or so people once thought! Today, planners understand that nature can provide ecosystem services, cleaning pollutants naturally, *if* cities are designed *with* nature rather than in opposition to nature. Trees and native grasses can help to clean pollutants before they reach urban streams, decrease the intensity of summer heat in cities, and provide habitat to animals, such as birds—and people, too. CENTER FOR RESILIENT CITIES, 2007.

James Segedy shows how stormwater facilities can be integrated into even the densest urban settings. This form of green infrastructure is also known as Low Impact Development. Like green infrastructure, it seeks to both integrate nature into urban environments and mimic the actions of nature to improve water quality and manage water quantity. ILLUSTRATION BY LOHREN DEEG.

Future planners should take classes in:

- Environmental studies to understand the dynamics of the natural environment and the interaction between humans and the natural environment.

- Economics to understand how the market operates, including what makes a successful business and what makes a successful regional economy.

- Art and design—whether graphic design, fashion design, or architectural design—to prepare the future planner to think creatively about visual appearances and skills for communicating those ideas to others.

- Geography to learn about ways of both understanding and depicting the physical and social environment—from the preparation of topographic maps, showing the elevation of hills and valleys and waterways around which cities are built, to the creation of maps using Geographic Information Systems showing such things as income, home ownership or health status in different areas of a city or region.

- Ethnic studies to gain cultural competence beyond one's own cultural upbringing.

- Sociology or social psychology to understand the dynamics of complex social interactions between individuals and among a community.
- Government and political science to understand the role of government in creating the preconditions for a desirable community and the limitations on government authority.

Future planners should also seek out opportunities to become engaged in their local communities. Many high schools and colleges require or give elective credit for "service learning," learning by volunteering in a community organization. Future planners should take advantage of these opportunities or volunteer after school or during the summer. Students can volunteer in homeless shelters, in neighborhood organizations, for local environmental groups, or by assisting the elderly with transportation needs. Each of these experiences gives a planner a window into the diverse needs of residents of his or her own community. These experiences can shape the future planner's understanding of the kinds of community facilities that need to be included in a fully comprehensive plan for a city.

Middle school and high school students may be able to link up with a summer or after school program in urban planning. In many cities, competitions are organized by engineering, architecture, and planning organizations that encourage students to learn about cities, urban infrastructure, and the wide range of issues that planners need to understand. A small number of communities in the United States have developed middle schools or high schools focusing specifically on city planning and the related fields of architecture and civil engineering. A sampling of the kinds of programs that are available is summarized on the following pages.

Taking part in a community clean-up is just one way that a young person can get involved in his or her community and learn about the kinds of issues that planners deal with every day in their work. DUNDALK RENAISSANCE CORP.

High school students from the School for Urban Planning and Architecture in Milwaukee participated in the Construction Challenge, developed by Destination ImagiNation® and the Association of Equipment Manufacturers. Although the Construction Challenge focuses more on engineering than planning, students learn about urban infrastructure and the engineering involved in building cities and individual buildings. In 2009, over 2,500 students nationwide participated in 15 regional rallies. The most successful teams advanced to the national competition in Knoxville, Tennessee. PERMISSION GRANTED BY DESTINATION IMAGINATION®.

LEARNING ABOUT PLANNING IN MIDDLE AND HIGH SCHOOL

Opportunities to learn about the planning of cities are available to students of almost all ages.

NATIONAL PROGRAMS

National Engineers Week Future City Competition

www.futurecity.org

This competition is open to middle school students. "The mission of the National Engineers Week Future City Competition is to provide a fun and exciting educational engineering program for seventh- and eighth-grade students that combines a stimulating engineering challenge with a "hands-on" application to present their vision of a city of the future." Students compete in building the most successful city on SimCity. Students build a scale model of their ideas for the city of the future. Learning focuses mainly on planning for urban infrastructure.

Construction Challenge

www.constructionchallenge.org

This competition is open to both middle school and high schools students. Students compete in teams of 5–7 students, learning about the infrastructure of cities and other design-related issues in engineering. Although the competition is geared more toward teaching about engineering than planning, the future planner will learn lots of valuable skills through this program, and learn a bit about cities at the same time. In 2009, Construction Challenge regional rallies were held in 15 locations in the United States and Canada.

EXAMPLES OF LOCALLY AVAILABLE PROGRAMS

After-School and Summer Precollege Programs

Box City Program, American Institute of Architects (selected state chapters)

AIA state chapters across the country sponsor the Box City program, designed for pre-middle-school-aged children. The AIA-Colorado describes the program as a unique children's event that is open to the public and promotes an understanding of historic preservation and urban design by combining art, architecture, creative thinking, city planning, design, construction, fun and learning into one comprehensive educational experience." Contact the local or state chapter for the American Institute of Architects for more information.

Exploring New York Landscapes, Barnard College

www.barnard.edu/pcp/4weeks.html#landscapes

This course explores the built environment, with local application to the city of New York. Students are taught to think critically about "how the natural environment, immigration, political decisions, urban planning assumptions and corporate profits have shaped the neighborhoods of New York City." Students "take to the streets to understand how cities develop and change."

Summer Workshop, Ball State University, Muncie, Indiana

www.mundeleinmustangs.com/CollegeAndCareerResourceCenter/
CollegeSummerPrograms.htm

Designed for high school juniors, "participants engage in creative problem solving, spatial understanding, field studies, graphics, and model making. The workshop is a primer for the course work in the CAP program that includes architecture, landscape architecture, and urban planning."

Citizen Schools Boston

The program is offered by Citizen Schools Boston to give "minority and low-income students the knowledge that they have a voice in the development of their neighborhoods. . . . The competition [is] arranged for teams of students to meet weekly with officials from the city's most prestigious design and architecture firms as their apprentices." (Woolhouse 2007).

Urban Science Simulation Game, University of Wisconsin–Madison

coweb.wcer.wisc.edu/eg/?cat=14&limit_cat=63
An interactive computer simulation, Urban Science is designed to teach students in middle school and high school about their city and "to see the world through the eyes of a problem-solving urban planner."

PUPS for PUPS, University of Wisconsin–Milwaukee

www.uwm.edu/SARUP/prospective/precollegeprograms.htm
This is a fun name for a seriously fun summer and after-school program. PUPS for PUPS gets Milwaukee's urban youth directly involved in urban planning concepts and neighborhood problem-solving activities. Student participants learn about careers in urban planning.

Urban Civil Engineering Summer Institute, New Jersey

www.nj.gov/highereducation/precollege2004/ProgDescPage75.html
A five-week program that teaches ninth-graders "principles of engineering, mathematics, computer programming, and applications, transportation, urban planning and design, and communications."

Specialized Middle Schools and High Schools with a City Planning Theme

Academy of Urban Planning, Brooklyn, New York

www.aupnyc.org
"The Academy's urban planning, theme-based curriculum draws students out of the classroom and into their communities to develop skills that will move them toward higher education and professional careers. With New York City as a laboratory, students tap into their innate curiosity for the world around them."

School for Urban Planning and Architecture, Milwaukee, Wisconsin

www.supar.org
This charter high school was founded by the faculty and alumni at the University of Wisconsin–Milwaukee. The project-based curriculum teaches students the skills and professions involved in planning, designing, and transforming communities to create a better future.

Discovering the Planner in You: The Eighth Grade

❭ I can trace my career journey back to 8th grade, when I applied for, and was accepted into a phenomenal experimental program called Ecology Box, a program that taught me all about the importance of place.

For half of the school year, students in the "EcoBox" program didn't take any math, science, English, or social studies classes. Instead, we went on educational field trips and participated in hands-on workshops held by a local nature center (The Hitchcock Nature Center in Amherst, Massachusetts).

We spent most of our school time in a gym that had been converted into several different microenvironments, each with its own rules and ambience. In one corner, a parachute hanging from the ceiling served as a tent; inside it was a quiet, meditative space. Another space was designed to look like a typical classroom, with orderly rows of chairs. Another was a creative area with paints, colored pencils, and other art supplies laid out on a tarp. A comfortable sofa and bookcase were the anchors of another space. The gym also had a door that led directly outdoors.

For the conclusion of the program, we were asked to do an independent project, and present it in any of these spaces, using any format we chose. I decided to do research on the quarry behind my house. It still astonishes me that I was allowed to leave school, unaccompanied by an adult, to go to the town library and Town Hall, where I searched property records. I took photos of the quarry and interviewed the owner.

From the interview, I realized that my perception of the quarry was very different from that of the owner. For my friends and me, it was a favorite playspace, and for him, it was a property to protect. I also noted how my classmates behaved in the environments set up in the gym, and how they preferred certain spaces over others.

This experience profoundly changed me. It set me on a journey to discover the ways different community members relate to a place—how they perceive it, how they inhabit it or control it, and even how they incorporate a place into their own identities. I also have a strong belief in equity and diversity, so for many years, I have wanted to learn what made a place welcoming to some, and hostile to others.

Corinna Moebius, Bordercross Consulting Group, Miami, Florida

A few specific skills are going to be important for succeeding in becoming an urban planner. These include communication skills—written, verbal, and graphic communication—and basic mathematics.

Communicating in Words

Becoming comfortable with writing and learning how to write in a wide range of styles should be a focus of the future planner's preparation in grade school, high school, and college. This preparation might include classes in creative writing, persuasive writing, journalism, and formal research writing. One day a planner will need to write a formal report and the next day prepare a marketing flyer to attract new businesses to a revitalized commercial area. Learning to write clearly and succinctly will prove especially valuable, as the planner's audience is usually composed of busy people with limited time to read reports.

Funding the Vision

Vision Partnership Program

Phoenixville Region Adopts Comprehensive Plan

Congratulations are in order for the Phoenixville Region on the successful adoption of their regional comprehensive plan. The plan was officially adopted by the final municipal member on February 6, 2008, following several years of developing and refining the plan. The Phoenixville Region consists of the Borough of Phoenixville and the townships of Charlestown, East Pikeland, East Vincent, Schuylkill, and West Vincent. The region's municipalities have also adopted a cooperative implementation agreement consistent with the provisions of the Municipalities Planning Code. The implementation agreement will allow them to provide for land uses on a regional basis upon bringing their zoning ordinances into consistency with the regional comprehensive plan.

The region worked with a team of consultants with expertise in the areas of land use, transportation, environmental planning, marketing analysis, and economic development to complete the plan, with Kise, Straw and Kolodner of Philadelphia serving as the lead project planner. The plan received funding from the County's Vision Partnership Program and a Land Use Planning and Technical Assistance Program (LUPTAP) grant from the Pennsylvania Department of Community and Economic Development, with the individual municipalities funding the remainder of the effort. The region is to be commended on seeing this complex planning effort through to adoption.

The Borough of Phoenixville, along with the townships of Charlestown, East Pikeland, East Vincent, Schuylkill, and West Vincent officially adopted their regional comprehensive plan.

Active VPP Contracts
Spring 2008

Municipality	Comprehensive Plan	Zoning	Subdivision	Official Map	Revitalization Plan	Special Study
East Bradford	■					
East Brandywine	■					
East Coventry		■				
Franklin		■				
Highland			■			
Honey Brook Twp.		■		■		
Kennett Twp.			●			
London Britain	●					
London Grove		■				
Modena			●			
New London		■				
North Coventry	■					
Pennsbury			●			■
Sadsbury			■			
Tredyffrin	■					
Upper Uwchlan	■					
West Marlborough	■					
West Nantmeal			●			
West Nottingham			●			
Oxford Region	■					

■ Private consultant retained
● Chester County Planning Commission retained

Because of the importance of including the public in developing plans for their communities, planners try to keep the public informed by sending out periodic newsletters about the progress of the plan. Here, a newsletter article describes the completion of the Phoenixville Comprehensive Plan. CHESTER COUNTY PLANNING COMMISSION.

LIVE·EARN·PLAY·LEARN

Creating simple logos is another way that planners use their communication skills. Using tools like PhotoShop and other graphic software, planners create logos, report covers, and newsletter layouts that are eye-catching and engaging. JACK YOUNG – CITY OF BALTIMORE.

Public speaking is another critical skill. While a few planners can find positions in which they are able to avoid public speaking, the overwhelming majority of planners will find themselves addressing an audience of 10 to 30 people at least once a month, and usually more often. Planners regularly make presentations to the planning commission and to the legislative body for their clients or employer (e.g., city council, county board, or the board of a regional authority). Such meetings will be attended by the appointed and elected officials serving on the board or council and by members of the general public and the press. The planner needs to be comfortable in front of the group and communicate clearly and effectively.

At other times, especially when a new plan is being prepared, special public meetings are held to allow the public to provide

Whether presenting at a public workshop or at the monthly planning commission meeting, planners need strong public speaking skills. Practice is the key to becoming comfortable talking in front of people. Courses in public speaking and debate are essential at both the high school and college level. CHESTER COUNTY PLANNING COMMISSION.

comments and suggestions about the plan. The planner typically presents an overview of the plan and then moderates a discussion. Such meetings can attract large audiences, with 50 or 100 or more people attending, sometimes including irate citizens who are unhappy about past planning results or proposed changes in their community. Again, being able to speak to such a large group in a poised and effective manner is an important skill in planning.

How do you deal with confrontation?

❯ I think it's important to argue issues, not personalities. You have to be respectful of the person on the other side . . . . They are your client, essentially. You have to put yourself in a position where you don't dictate to them, you have to act as a facilitator. And then you have to make a decision. In that situation, you need to communicate to the person and help them understand why you're doing what you're doing. And, for you as a planner, you want to leave the conversation knowing that they may not like the law or the policy that you're discussing, but that doesn't mean they don't like you as a person.

Nine of ten people will leave the office and understand what you did and respect why you're doing it. The other one in ten is a mutant case. There is no way of resolving those situations, and you'll just have to live with it.

Brad Steinke, City of Apache Junction, Arizona

Students considering a career in planning should seek out opportunities to practice public speaking. Public speaking courses are offered at both the high school and college level. In addition, many high schools and colleges offer extracurricular programs in public speaking (often called "forensics") and debate. These are excellent opportunities to gain experience in both speaking from a prepared outline and responding extemporaneously ("off-the-cuff" and "on-the-spot") to questions and opposing viewpoints.

Communicating through Pictures

Plans use pictures almost as much as words to communicate problems and possible solutions. Having the ability to work with drawings, photographs, maps, and graphs is useful for every planner. Although many planners do this effectively simply by placing these pictures into a word processing document (such as Microsoft Word), a growing number of planners are using more sophisticated document design and image manipulation software such as Adobe InDesign and Adobe Photoshop to create eye-catching documents or before-and-after illustrations of a proposed project.

Some planners may have the luxury of working with a graphic designer on staff or on contract who takes the planner's text and "makes it pretty." But in many communities, especially smaller communities, the planner will need to be able to do some of this work. So the savvy future planner will want to learn one or more publishing software programs and gain some experience in "pasting up" text and graphics. Volunteering to do the newsletter for your local neighborhood association is an excellent way to gain this experience—and learn something about communities and their needs at the same time.

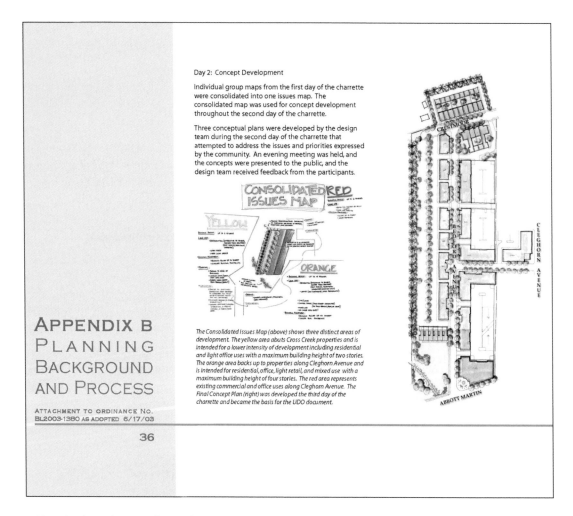

Day 2: Concept Development

Individual group maps from the first day of the charrette were consolidated into one issues map. The consolidated map was used for concept development throughout the second day of the charrette.

Three conceptual plans were developed by the design team during the second day of the charrette that attempted to address the issues and priorities expressed by the community. An evening meeting was held, and the concepts were presented to the public, and the design team received feedback from the participants.

The Consolidated Issues Map (above) shows three distinct areas of development. The yellow area abuts Cross Creek properties and is intended for a lower intensity of development including residential and light office uses with a maximum building height of two stories. The orange area backs up to properties along Cleghorn Avenue and is intended for residential, office, light retail, and mixed use with a maximum building height of four stories. The red area represents existing commercial and office uses along Cleghorn Avenue. The Final Concept Plan (right) was developed the third day of the charrette and became the basis for the UDO document.

APPENDIX B
PLANNING
BACKGROUND
AND PROCESS

ATTACHMENT TO ORDINANCE NO.
BL2003-1380 AS ADOPTED 6/17/03

36

▲ Here, the planner has created a page layout using a desktop publishing program, combining text and graphics to tell the story of the design charrette held in relation to the Bedford Avenue redevelopment plan and the three alternatives developed out of that charrette. CRAIG OWENSBY/METRO NASHVILLE PLANNING DEPARTMENT.

▶ The planner placed graphs, tables, maps, photos, and text together on the page to describe how well the plan for the area is achieving goals related to housing density and clustering of development to save natural areas from encroachment. CHESTER COUNTY PLANNING COMMISSION.

Sample indicators

Indicator
Proposed Housing Units Consistent with Landscapes

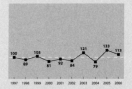

Purpose statement
The major purpose of Landscapes is to change the development pattern away from sprawl. The urban and suburban landscapes and suburban and rural centers can best accommodate growth and the rural landscape is least appropriate for development. Proposed housing development plans indicate the location of future residential development.

Description
Percent of total proposed housing units located within the Landscapes growth areas (urban and suburban landscapes, and the suburban and rural centers).

Livable Landscapes

LEGEND
Livable Landscapes
rural
rural center
suburban center
suburban
urban
Municipalities

Data for 2007 index

	Proposed housing units			
	Base year 1997		Comparison year 2006	
	Housing units	Percent	Housing units	Percent
1. Rural	1,469	37%	1,941	29%
2. Rural center	14	0%	280	4%
3. Suburban	2,089	53%	1,689	26%
4. Suburban center	199	5%	25	0%
5. Urban	203	5%	2,665	40%
Total	3,974	100%	6,600	100%
Total–Landscapes #2-5	2,505	63%	4,659	71%

Indicator calculation

$$\text{2006 Indicator Value} = \frac{\text{Comparison year}}{\text{Base year}} \times 100 = \frac{0.71}{0.63} \times 100 = 93$$

Indicator trend

100 105 89 81 92 84 121 79 133 113

1997 1998 1999 2000 2001 2002 2003 2004 2005 2006

Interpretation
- The percentage of units in Landscapes growth areas (71%) in 2006 was above the base year.
- The current percentage was the third highest value for this measure.
- The percentage of proposed housing units in growth areas declined from the previous year, but that was the best year on record.

Data source
Chester County Planning Commission reviews of development plans.

Indicator
Residential Loans in Urban Areas

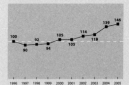

Purpose statement
One of Landscapes goals is to preserve and enhance urban areas in the county. Rehabilitating existing housing, building new housing and preserving historic homes is one way to accomplish that goal. This ratio indicates the proportion of residential loans that support urban revitalization.

Description
Ratio of residential loans in urban landscapes to non-urban areas, relative to the ratio of total housing units in urban areas to non-urban areas.

Urban census tracts

LEGEND
Urban Census Tract
Non-Urban Census Tract

Data for 2007 index

	Residential loans in urban areas			
	Base year 1996		Comparison year 2005	
	Loans	Housing units	Loans	Housing units
County total	9,104	155,613	14,981	186,370
Urban areas	1,625	36,008	3,202	38,434
Non-Urban areas	7,479	119,605	11,779	147,936
Ratio (Urban:Non-Urban)	0.22	0.30	0.27	0.26
Loans Ratio: Housing Units Ratio	0.72		1.05	

Note: Loans include home purchase mortgages and home improvement loans.

Indicator calculation

$$\text{2005 Indicator Value} = \frac{\text{Comparison year}}{\text{Base year}} \times 100 = \frac{1.05}{0.72} \times 100 = 146$$

Indicator trend

100 90 92 94 105 105 114 118 139 146

1996 1997 1998 1999 2000 2001 2002 2003 2004 2005

Interpretation
- The proportion of residential loans in urban areas relative to the number of housing units has increased steadily.
- This indicator has been above the Base Year since 2000.
- This indicates increasing private investment in houses in the urban areas.
- The ratio of 1.05 in 2005 means that there were more loans in the urban areas than non-urban areas relative to the number of housing units.

Data source
Federal Financial Institutions Examination Council (FFIEC), Home Mortgage Disclosure Act (HMDA), Aggregate Table 1; Chester County Planning Commission estimates of housing units

Mapping is another essential function of planning practice. Planners use maps to indicate planned land use, population density, natural resource locations, and lots of other information. Geographic Information Systems (GIS) software allows planners to create maps that show more than just the physical features of a city—like streets and highways and hills and valleys. GIS allows planners to create pictures (maps) of the social and cultural features of the city and to communicate those findings. In one area, in red, is where the average household owns less than one car. In another area, in blue, are areas within a quarter mile of a bus stop. Planners look at the pattern of red areas and blue areas on the map to determine whether some areas of the city have many residents without access to cars but with poor access to buses as well.

▼ This simple illustration was created in GIS. It shows just two layers: an aerial photo and street labels. STEPHEN TREMLETT/MSA PROFESSIONAL SERVICES, INC.

▶ Southeast Orlando, Florida, proposed land use map. Geographic information is stored digitally, allowing planners to pull up maps showing streets and other physical features along with social characteristics of places, such as how the land is being used by people. Then, after analyzing the communities' needs, planners can suggest how land should be regulated, protected, or redeveloped to achieve the communities' future goals. CRAIG OWENSBY/METRO NASHVILLE PLANNING DEPARTMENT.

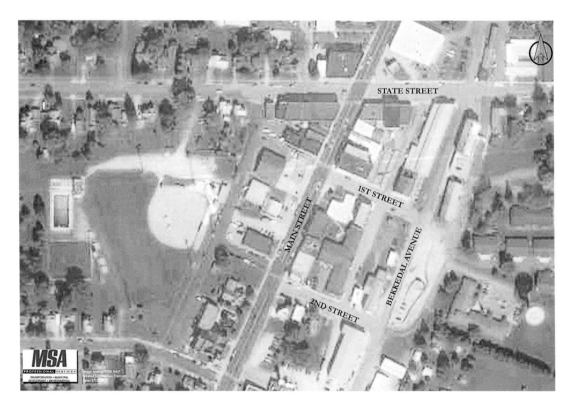

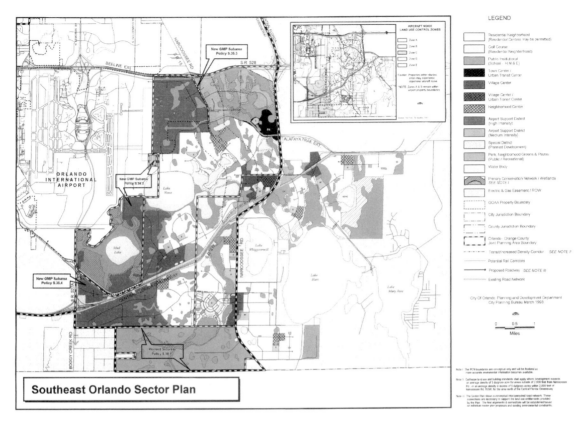

Southeast Orlando Sector Plan

▶ GIS can represent an area in 3D by including data on the topography of an area. Maps like these can help elected officials and the public to understand more clearly how human development is fitting into and affecting the natural landscape. This map includes the following layers: land use, major roads, topography, and proposed development nodes. LOUIS RADA/MSA PROFESSIONAL SERVICES, INC.

Being Comfortable with Numbers

Most planners need only a certain level of "comfort" in dealing with numbers. With a few exceptions, such as transportation planning and regional economic planning, planners will be successful as long as they are not math-phobic and can comfortably cope with some basic math tasks, such as calculating percentages and ratios and solving relatively simple equations. In addition, planners need to be able to represent numbers effectively for public officials and for the general public. The ability to create tables and graphs is an important skill that can be mastered in high school and college.

In high school, future planners should take as much math as their high school offers. In college, a student may want to pursue calculus and trigonometry, though these courses are not required to pursue a graduate degree in planning. Whether required by the undergraduate major or not, a student interested in pursuing a career in planning should strongly consider taking a course in statistics. Typically, rather than taking the statistics courses offered by the mathematics department, a future planner will be well served by a statistics course in any of the social sciences, such as statistics for sociology majors.

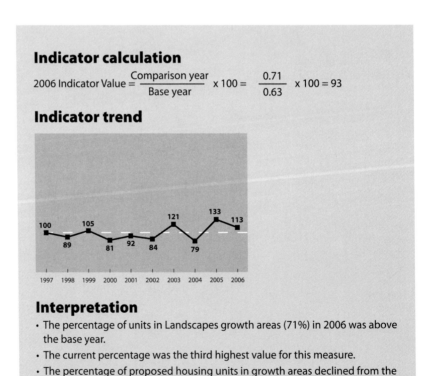

Indicator calculation

$$\text{2006 Indicator Value} = \frac{\text{Comparison year}}{\text{Base year}} \times 100 = \frac{0.71}{0.63} \times 100 = 93$$

Indicator trend

100   105   89   81   92   84   121   133   79   113

1997 1998 1999 2000 2001 2002 2003 2004 2005 2006

Interpretation

- The percentage of units in Landscapes growth areas (71%) in 2006 was above the base year.
- The current percentage was the third highest value for this measure.
- The percentage of proposed housing units in growth areas declined from the previous year, but that was the best year on record.

For most planners, basic math, like that shown here, will be enough to meet planners' daily needs. CHESTER COUNTY PLANNING COMMISSION.

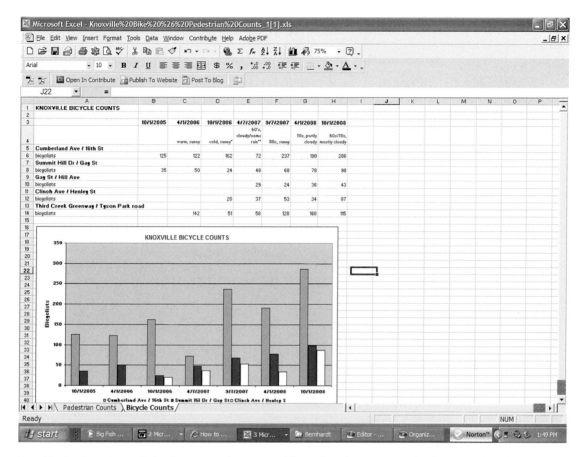

Spreadsheet software is a staple for almost every planner. Spreadsheets allow planners to compile information, do mathematical calculations with the click of a mouse, and convert those calculations into graphs. KNOXVILLE REGIONAL TPO.

During high school future planners should also learn about how to use spreadsheet programs, such as Microsoft Excel. Spreadsheets are used for many purposes. They allow the user to easily organize text and numbers as a table. Spreadsheets also allow the user to carry out simple and complex mathematical calculations—from adding up a column of numbers to finding the average of those numbers, to complex tasks like calculating the amount of money that would be spent on interest payments on a loan for a new high school or for a subsidy to a developer.

In the following table, taken from work of L. Carson Bise II, the planner has compiled figures from the city budget regarding the costs of various public infrastructure and services. Then, the planner presents four alternatives for filling the shortfall in funds available, including two changes to the development impact fee, a local sales tax, and borrowing against anticipated property tax revenue. The planner shows how much each alternative will cost to each dwelling unit in the community—a figure that is more easily interpreted by people than large, raw numbers.

INFRASTRUCTURE FUNDING STRATEGIES

	TYPE OF INFRASTRUCTURE					
	ROADS	SCHOOLS	PARKS	FIRE	EMS	LIBRARY
	GROSS FUNDING NEEDS					
	$253,924,000	$135,090,000	$56,279,330	$7,150,000	$600,000	$21,002,667
	LESS CURRENT FUNDING SOURCES					
Impact Fees	$38,885,529	$0	$13,458,312	$7,500,000	$0	$25,262,221
Unspent STIP Funds	$15,000,000	$0	$0	$0	$0	$0
New STIP funds	$15,000,000	$0	$0	$0	$0	$0
Rural/Critical Lands			$5,000,000			
	EQUALS ESTIMATE OF FUNDING GAP					
NET FUNDING NEEDS	($185,038,471)	($135,090,000)	($37,821,018)	$350,000	($600,000)	$4,259,554
	POTENTIAL FUNDING OPTIONS TO MEET FUNDING NEEDS					
Revision to Existing Impact Fees	$45,000,000 ($1,200 per du)		$10,000,000 ($840 per du)	N/A		
Implementation of New Impact Fee				N/A	$600,000 ($20 per du)	
Local Option Sales Tax	$140,038,471 (15 years)		$27,821,018 (15 years)	N/A		$5,019,158 (15 years)
Bond Issue (backed by Property Tax)		$135,090,000 ($9.94 m/yr)		N/A		

Source: L. Carson Bise II, AICP, President, TischlerBise

A statistics course prepares future planners to be able to describe the communities in which they live and to make educated guesses about the likely effects of pursuing different policies in cities. For example, such courses teach methods of describing groups of numbers (mean, median, mode, quartiles, dispersion from the mean, etc.). This skill is applied by planners in describing the characteristics of a city or subareas within cities and regions.

Planners use information collected by the U.S. Census to describe neighborhoods in terms of the ages of the residents, the income level of the people living in the neighborhood, and the characteristics of the houses they live in. A planner might then compare the costs of housing in the city compared to the incomes earned by people who live there. This allows the planner to determine whether the housing is affordable to those workers so that they do not need to travel long distances between a more affordable neighborhood and their workplace.

Another set of statistical techniques allows planners to determine whether a relationship is observable between two or more sets of numbers; for example, whether home ownership rates in neighborhoods are related to crime rates. If so, then planners might want to consider policies and programs to increase home ownership rates as a strategy for reducing crime in certain areas of the city.

These statistical techniques are not exclusive to the field of city planning. Indeed, all fields of science—from medicine to engineering—draw on the same basic statistical toolkit. At the undergraduate level, it will be most useful to study these techniques in the context of some social phenomenon, whether psychology or social work or economics. Later, in the graduate program in urban planning, the future planner will be required to take a statistics course that teaches the planner how these techniques are applied in city planning.

LENGTH OF RESIDENCY (2000)	Tulane/ Gravier	Orleans Parish	Louisiana	United States
Total occupied housing units	1,566	188,251	1 .656,053	105,480, 101
Moved in 1999 to arch 2000	27.5%	20.6%	18.7%	19.9%
Moved in 1995 to 1998	33.3%	28.5%	26.9%	28.9%
Moved in 1990 to 1994	14.1%	15.9%	15.6%	16.1%
Moved in 1989 or, earlier	25.1%	35.0%	38.8%	35.11%

Source Citation: U.S. Census Bureau. *Census 2000 Sample Characteristics (SF3)*. From a compilation by the GHO Community Data Center. <http://www.gnocdc.org>

AVERAGE RENTAL COSTS (2000)	Tulane/ Gravier	Orleans Parish	Louisiana	United States
Total renter-occupied housing units paying cash rent	1,237	96,257	474,873	33,386,326
Average contract rent	$292	$404	$377	$565
Average gross rent	$406	$518	$490	$657

HOUSEHOLD INCOME TYPE (2000)	Tulane/ Gravier	Orleans Parish	Louisiana	United States
Total households	1,630	188,365	1,657,107	105,539,122
Wage or salary income	54.7%	73.3%	75.4%	77.7%
Self-employment income	6.1%	8.7%	9.8%	11.9%

COPYRIGHT 2007. TULANE/GRAVIER REGULATING PLAN AND FORM-BASED CODE, PREPARED FOR THE PHOENIX OF NEW ORLEANS BY MATT AHO, ALISON KOPYT, BRAD LENZ, AND MEAGAN LIMBERG.

These tables show some of the information that planners use from the U.S. Census. Planners try to portray the characteristics of the neighborhood by describing the residents in terms of age, income, whether they rent or own their own home, and many other variables. Calculating the mean or median and comparing that to a larger area, such as the state or national average is a common technique for understanding where a neighborhood or city stands in comparison to others.

Drawing, Planning, and Urban Design

The planner as designer of the physical environment is a role that planners held during the early history of the planning profession. Some of the earliest and most famous planners in history were trained as architects or landscape architects. Daniel Burnham, who prepared the 1909 plan for Chicago, was an architect. Frederick Law Olmstead, who is known as the Father of Landscape Architecture in the United States, prepared many plans, including a major plan for Washington, DC, known as the McMillan plan.

One of the greatest misperceptions about the field of planning is that modern-day planners spend most of their time *drawing* city plans. While drawing is a skill that is used frequently by some subfields within planning and some related professions that work closely with planners, most planners do not draw. This is quite different from the planning profession in other countries, where planners are routinely trained in drawing—both by hand and by digital means, drafting, and computer-aided design.

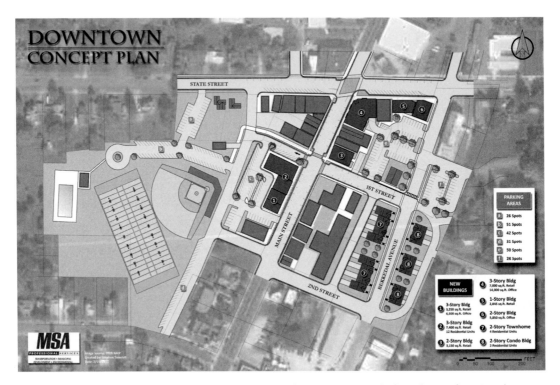

Ideas can be presented in three different views: plan, elevation, and perspective. Here, the future layout of streets and buildings is shown in plan view, sometimes called a bird's-eye view. STEPHEN TREMLETT/MSA PROFESSIONAL SERVICES, INC.

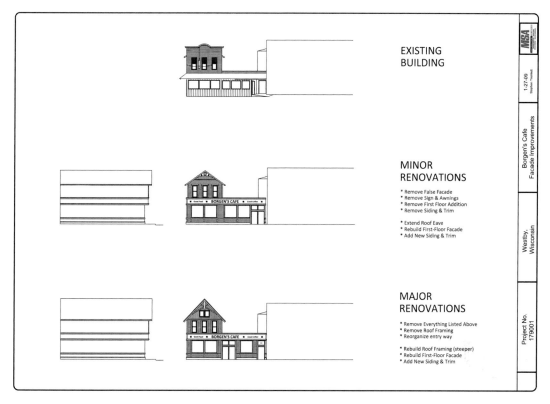

Elevation view. This image shows just the front side of the building, with no attempt to simulate a three-dimensional perspective. In this case, the planner wanted to communicate both the existing conditions and two alternatives for renovating the façade of a building. STEPHEN TREMLETT/MSA PROFESSIONAL SERVICES, INC.

Perspective drawings offer a more realistic 3D image of plans for the future. These can be produced by hand or with the help of computer software. Although scientists believe that humans have an innate ability to see the world in plan view, communicating in pictures helps people to better understand the changes that are proposed and how those conditions compare to current conditions. And many changes cannot be effectively communicated in plan view. For example, in this image, the architectural character of the proposed townhomes and the streetscape established would be difficult to communicate in plan view. STEPHEN TREMLETT/MSA PROFESSIONAL SERVICES, INC.

In the United States the subfield of planning that engages in the physical design of cities and neighborhoods is called Urban Design. Urban designers craft the shapes of streets, blocks, and lots within a development area, as well as the location, height, and character of buildings and public facilities. The urban designer manipulates these variables to give form to the public spaces created by the things we build, knowing that good design attracts people and investment and bad design can lead to failure and neglect, even when all the right pieces are present.

Urban Design and Historic Preservation

You were trained as an architect. How did you make the transition to ecological and historic preservation planning?

❭ When I was designing buildings, I found myself growing more and more dissatisfied with architecture as a profession. I felt the buildings we were designing were self-centered and shallow and were aimed mainly at the architects and not at the users.

When I became exposed to ecological planning, I realized that planning has a broader impact on communities and landscapes than architecture does, and it gave meaning to what I was interested in and what I thought I wanted to do.

The more I studied it, the more I realized that all landscapes have been impacted by human activity and that ecological planning is one way to address the cultural landscape we have created.

Ecological planning provides a way to look at our world, a way to understand it, a way to understand how to improve it over time, and how to accommodate change over time.

Change is going to happen. We have to accommodate it. Preservation planning is a vehicle to improve and change our communities and make them better places to be.

The more that I've studied it, the more I realize that the environment is more important than the design styles of our buildings. It provides a context to our relationships to the broader planet, to our ecosystems, to plant communities and other forms of life. The study of these relationships is fundamental, whereas the study of architectural styles and landscape styles is interesting but, ultimately, superficial.

Planning allows me to look at the broader connections in the world. Historic preservation planning focuses on the human hand in this world.

Peter Benton, AIA, Principal Preservation Planner, Heritage Strategies, LLC

To create a vibrant neighborhood, it is not enough simply to build a mix of residential and commercial uses in the same area. The urban designer's job is to organize these uses and design the environment so that the pedestrian environment is safe and inviting, so that retail uses can realize the greatest possible visibility, so that residential options meet the needs of the intended residents, and so that people value and care for the neighborhood.

Many universities offer graduate degrees in urban design. Urban designers often have multiple degrees, including a degree in planning and another degree in architecture, landscape architecture, or urban design. Students interested in the subfield of urban design should pursue drawing and design classes in high school. Usually, urban designers need to begin their study of architecture or landscape architecture as an undergraduate, and then pursue either the master's in urban design or planning or a dual master's degree.

Both architecture and landscape architecture programs feature training in three keys areas that will help the urban designer: history, design principles, and graphic rendering. Urban design occupies the territory occupied by both landscape architecture and architecture, and so history courses in both fields will likely include the major figures and trends of urban design history. Design principles, such as balance, rhythm and proportion, inform all design fields, and knowledge of those principles can bring focus to raw creative skills. Graphic rendering is essential to the communication of design ideas, and students in these fields will learn a variety of techniques for communicating their design ideas. Historically, an education in architecture or urban design would have included extensive training and practice in hand rendering, from pencil sketching to pen and ink line drawings to watercolor renderings. Indeed, many contemporary designers utilize these methods to illustrate a finished design.

Before. This photo shows a typical suburban street in a commercial area with office buildings. TND PLANNING GROUP.

After. This urban designer's rendering envisions what the street could look like with new policies toward street design and building setbacks, and with new investment from the private sector. This hand drawing relies on the time-tested skills of using pencils, paints, and a steady hand. TND PLANNING GROUP.

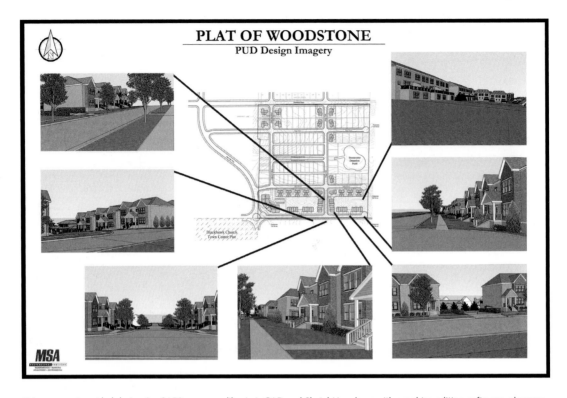

Using computer-aided design (or CAD) programs like AutoCAD and SketchUp, along with graphics-editing software, planners can produce renderings like these. TND PLANNING GROUP.

But the student pursuing design training today will also learn the use of computer programs to create and render designs, such as Adobe PhotoShop, AutoCAD and 3ds Max by AutoDesk, or SketchUp by Google. Some programs allow the user to create animated fly-through views, providing an increasingly realistic impression of the design.

Urban designers may develop advanced skills in all such methods of graphic rendering or may specialize in one or two methods. In comparison, the urban planner who is only modestly skillful in drawing can be an especially valuable member of a planning staff. Planners can use basic sketching or computer design skills to illustrate options for laying out streets or parking areas. Or the planner might draft an idea for a sign that meets the city code. Planners who lack these skills can always work with another professional to produce graphics. But taking the time to learn some basic skills in drawing and computer graphics can give a planner another communication tool—and, as stressed earlier, communication is the planner's most important task.

Some of the skills described in this section can be learned as early as middle school. Others will be learned in high school, while other skills can wait for college or graduate school. Ultimately, the future planner will move on to college in order to prepare for a career in planning, and most will continue to a master's degree. A few will go even farther, obtaining a doctoral degree (Ph.D.) in order to teach and conduct research related to planning.

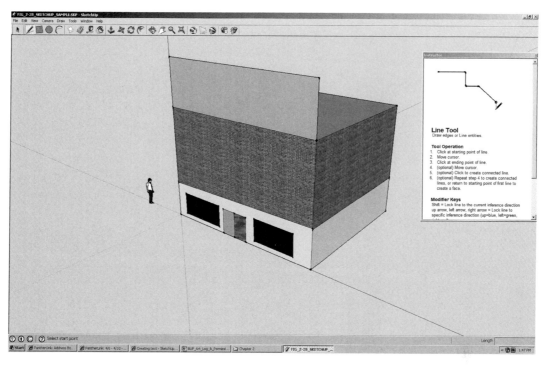

Google's SketchUp software, which provides an easy-to-use interface for 3D design, has become increasingly popular among professional planners. This image shows a sample of what a complete novice can accomplish in about 10 minutes. A pro can produce images like those shown in the previous figure. NANCY FRANK 2009.

Don't say "I can't draw." Even planners who "can't draw" are involved in creating visual images to communicate challenges in an area and how an area is proposed to change in the future. COURTESY OF DAN BURDEN, GLATTING JACKSON.

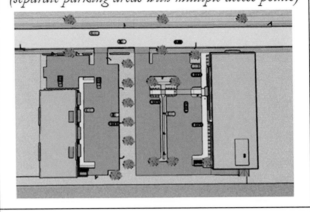

Discouraged Parking Layout
(separate parking areas with multiple access points)

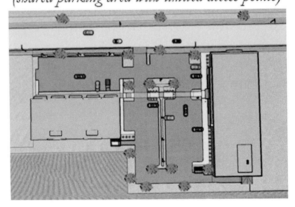

Desired Parking Layout
(shared parking area with limited access points)

This image was created to show a client how two businesses could share a parking lot, reducing the total amount of impervious surface and space devoted to parking. After decades of requiring large parking lots, planners today are working with property owners to try to reduce the amount of urban space dedicated to parking cars. STEPHEN TREMLETT/MSA PROFESSIONAL SERVICES, INC.

Picking a College Major

Few planners have an undergraduate degree in planning, even if they have a master's in urban planning. The survey of APA members showed that only 10 percent possessed an undergraduate degree in planning as their highest degree. Of the more than 120 U.S. and Canadian schools that are members of the Association of Collegiate Schools of Planning, less than a third offer undergraduate degrees in planning (*ACSP Guide*, 13th Ed., 2007). And of those, only 16 undergraduate programs are accredited by the Planning Accreditation Board, the official accrediting agency for educational programs serving the planning profession.

Instead, the planning profession has historically drawn students to its master's programs from a wide range of undergraduate majors. This approach to the education of professional planners is consistent with the idea that planners need to be holistic thinkers drawing on a diverse academic background rather than being narrow technicians with a limited understanding of the context in which they work.

In addition to the small number of programs that offer an undergraduate major in planning, most universities that offer a master's degree in planning offer a smaller number of courses open exclusively to undergraduate students in other majors. Frequently, students may major in any field of their choice and obtain a minor or undergraduate certificate in planning.

The best source of information about planning degree programs at the undergraduate and graduate level is the *Guide to Undergraduate and Graduate Education in Urban and Regional Planning*. The *Guide* is published by the Association of Collegiate Schools of Planning, which is an organization of schools that offer degrees in planning. While the focus of the organization is primarily on U.S.-based schools, many Canadian schools are also members. In addition to providing a profile of each school and programs each offers, the *Guide* also provides introductory information about the field of planning, specializations in planning, and the structure of planning education.

Another source of information about planning degree programs is Planetizen, www.planetizen .com, a website devoted to all things about planning. Beginning in 2007, Planetizen began to collect and publish information about planning education programs. Considerable dissatisfaction exists among planning schools regarding Planetizen's approach to ranking planning schools. Nonetheless, much good information comparing planning degree programs can be found in the Planetizen guide.

COMMON UNDERGRADUATE MAJORS FOR URBAN PLANNING

Geography

Urban and Regional Studies

Economics

Political Science

Sociology

Architecture

Landscape Architecture

Civil Engineering

Environmental Studies or Natural Resource Management

Business, especially Marketing and Real Estate

The *Guide to Undergraduate and Graduate Education in Urban and Regional Planning* is the most complete source of information about opportunities to study urban planning. The Association of Collegiate Schools of Planning makes the Guide available for free online on its website, www.acsp.org, or you can purchase the *Guide*. ASSOCIATION OF COLLEGIATE SCHOOLS OF PLANNING.

Users of the guide should be careful, however, in using the rankings as an authoritative indicator of the quality of planning degree programs.

Most future planners, however, will not major in planning as an undergraduate. Instead, they will pursue every possible undergraduate degree. Future planners can be found throughout the university, from Anthropology to Zoology.

Again, no matter what the major, the future planner will seek out a broad range of electives, making special efforts to hone communication skills, ability to calculate with numbers, and understanding of the diverse cultures and subgroups that make up American cities. If the university offers a minor or certificate in planning, such courses would be a good addition, especially for the student who hopes to work in planning for a few years before pursuing the master's degree.

A FEW GOOD BOOKS AND AT THE MOVIES

In addition to taking classes, a future planner may want to spend some time on the beach with a good book or curled on the couch with a cup of hot cocoa and a good movie.

Nonfiction books that offer a good read include Jane Jacobs's *Life and Death of Great American Cities* and Joel Garreau's *Edge City*. Fiction can also enlighten planning issues. Richard Wright's *Native Son* brings planners into the world of mid-twentieth-century racial oppression. *Invisible Cities* by Italo Calvino takes the reader on a fanciful tour of all the ways a city might look as Calvino's fictional Marco Polo tells tales to Kublai Khan. A rare find is land use attorney Shel Damsky's *Murder and the Comprehensive Plan*, a murder mystery set in the context of a zoning dispute.

Old movies or well-researched period movies set in the nineteenth century, the 1920s, or the 1950s make the history of cities come alive. Futuristic movies, like Fritz Lang's *Metropolis*, *Clockwork Orange*, and *Bladerunner*, stimulate ideas about how cities of the future will evolve and the challenges that planners in the future will face. Other planning favorites include *City of Hope* and *Chinatown*. Every professor will have their favorites. Ask!

The Planners' Network *Student Disorientation Guide* offer dozens of recommendations about good books and movies to bring planning alive.

www.plannersnetwork.org/publications/pdfs/Disorientation_Guide.pdf

And on to Graduate School

As previously noted, almost two-thirds of APA member planners possess a master's degree, usually in planning. The first question any future planner needs to consider in relationship to graduate school is whether to pursue the master's degree at all. What are the advantages of the master's degree and what will be involved in getting it?

One reason students typically cite for seeking a master's degree is to earn a higher salary. APA's salary survey provides good evidence that planners who hold a master's degree earn a higher salary than those without the master's degree. At all income levels, APA member planners who possess a master's degree earn $3000 to $8000 more per year than those who lack this additional education (American Planning Association).

PLANNERS' SALARY BY EDUCATION

	n	25% earn less	50% earn less	75% earn less
Bachelor's	4078	$51,000	$65,000	$85,000
Master's/Planning	5451	$55,000	$70,000	$91,000
Master's/other	2573	$57,000	$72,300	$95,000
PhD/Law	425	$70,000	$85,000	$122,100

Source: Reprinted with permission from the American Planning Association, http://www.planning.org/salary/report/employmentchar. htm, copyright 2008.

A higher income is only one advantage, however. First, the master's degree can substitute for years of experience, giving the master's-prepared planner an advantage in competing for jobs and achieving higher salaries earlier in his or her career. For many supervisory positions, the master's degree is required. In order to be promoted to director or associate director of a planning agency or consulting firm, a master's degree is likely to be required or highly advantageous.

Finally, and most importantly, a master's degree in planning gives the planner a toolbox of knowledge, skills, and experience that prepares the planner for the many challenges in this exciting and diverse field.

PLANNING CERTIFICATION THROUGH AICP

AICP stands for the American Institute of Certified Planners. After receiving their education and completing a minimum number of years of experience, planners can elect to obtain certification through AICP. AICP is managed by the American Planning Association under the executive direction of the AICP Commission.

Planners with a master's degree in planning are required to have worked as a planner for only two years; those with an accredited bachelor's degree in planning need three years of experience. Those with their master's or undergraduate degree in nonaccredited programs or related fields need four years of experience before they qualify to take the exam.

Once planners pass the AICP exam, they must comply with the AICP Code of Ethics and complete at least 30 credits of continuing education every two years. Because only one state licenses planners, AICP certification offers a credential, beyond the master's degree, that indicates a minimum level of competence in planning.

Increasingly, certification is required in order to obtain the associate and senior planner positions, beyond the entry level.

Choosing the Right Graduate Program

For most students, the main factor affecting their choice of schools is location. Often, students' choice of schools is limited to the state in which they reside and can qualify for in-state tuition. The *ACSP Guide*, Planetizen guide, and the list of accredited planning programs on the website of the Planning Accreditation Board shows that most states in the United States have at least one planning program, although not always at a public university. Few states have more than two programs within the state.

After location, students need to consider factors like:

- Is the program is accredited?

- How much financial assistance does the university provide?

- Does the school offer the student's preferred specialization area?

- Does the overall focus of the curriculum and faculty interests, beyond specialization, fit the student's interests? For example, some programs may emphasize physical planning and design while others emphasize policy analysis in planning. Some programs focus on planning for large older cities, while others focus on the problems of growing suburbs or declining rural areas.

- What is the size of the program? How many students enroll as new, first-year students each fall?

- How many faculty teach in the program (including the number who devote themselves full-time to teaching and research in planning)?

- What are the opportunities for studio-based instruction and internships?

- How many credits are required and how long do full-time students take to complete the program?

- How much flexibility does the program allow in tailoring the curriculum to the interests of the student?

What do planning faculty say about selecting a planning program?

❯ My answer to this question really depends upon the background and career goals of the student. However, I think it is important for students to find the right graduate program for them. I ask them about where they want to work (private sector vs. public; what part of the country), what they are interested in (different schools specialize in different areas), and if they are interested more in research or practice. The answers to these questions often determine which programs might be appropriate for that student. One great thing about the Internet is that students can do a considerable amount of research about the various graduate programs that are available to them. I also strongly recommend that they try to visit the schools they are considering (if possible) and talk with a student currently in the program. Another student will typically provide honest answers concerning the positives and negatives associated with the program. The more information you have, the easier it will be to make the right choice.

Dr. Susan L. Bradbury, Iowa State University

What do planning faculty say about selecting a planning program? (Continued)

❯ Ratings have some bearing on doctoral quality, though they are generally years behind the prevailing reality. Ratings have virtually no bearing on the quality of professional master's programs. Key in making these choices regarding master's programs should be any indications that can be secured regarding the commitment of faculty to the needs of professional students. Seek to visit with the chair, perhaps some faculty, and then students before making your decision. Review the curriculum. Is the program fully accredited? Are there emphases that fit your interests? Does the program afford a rich array of opportunities to get first-hand experience through internship and studio work, and through the involvement of at least some adjunct professional faculty in elective offerings? Is the location of the program one that allows you to witness planning's practice in relation to your interests and desired specializations? Are the program's graduates in demand? Have they risen up the ranks as their careers have developed?

Thomas Clark, Ph.D., College of Architecture and Planning, Denver

How did you pick a school for your planning degree?

❯ I only applied to one school. My wife and I had just bought our first home in Silver Spring, Maryland, just a few miles from the University of Maryland in College Park. When I first started researching schools, it became clear that the University of Maryland offered everything I was looking for in a planning program.

The university's Urban Studies and Planning program was considered one of the top programs in the country with an outstanding and oft-published faculty. From a geographic perspective (with its close proximity to the city of Baltimore, the state capital in Annapolis, and the nation's capital in DC), the University of Maryland offered many opportunities for experiential learning. The region has many examples of the successes and failures of planning as well as the growth challenges facing rural, suburban, urban, and inner city communities.

An offer to become a graduate assistant at the National Center for Smart Growth Research and Education also made the University of Maryland an attractive option, with opportunities to study and understand the wide impacts of planning and public policy.

Jason Sartori, Integrated Planning Consultants

❯ I had the desire to pursue an education in environmental science and Alfred University offered such a degree when at that time most institutions were only offering biology degrees with little flexibility in class selection. It was 1975 and many environmental issues, policies, and programs were not formalized in most universities. Alfred University provided me the opportunity to build a multidisciplined program with relatively small class sizes, a lot of field experience, and broad choices when building my program. I enjoyed environmental and land use policy as well as the sciences. Not being able to chose, I ended up with a dual degree.

Alyse Getty, Parsons Infrastructure and Technology, Inc.

❯ I grew up in a typical bedroom suburb on Long Island, New York. By the end of high school, I was aching to get off "The Island," as we called it, and out into the world.

I wanted to experience a new type of environment, so I applied to schools in different regions of the country and in widely varying urban and rural settings. After visiting several campuses, I found myself drawn to Virginia Tech, largely due to its combination of rigorous academics, small-town charm, and breathtaking campus nestled in a valley surrounded by the Blue Ridge Mountains.

Stuart Sirota, AICP, TND Planning Group

❭ I applied to several planning and public policy schools to hedge my bets and because I couldn't decide. One of the schools was Harvard's Kennedy School of Government. They had a city and regional planning program. The planning program focused on urban economic development and housing.

I was accepted by Harvard, as well as several of the other schools. I wanted to experience living in an East Coast city, so even though the UC Berkeley program inspired me to pursue a city planning degree, I picked an eastern school to try something new.

I had such a good experience at the Kennedy School, including course work at the School of Design and at MIT, and a research assistant position at the Harvard-MIT Joint Center for Urban Studies for Bill Apgar, who later became undersecretary at HUD in the Clinton Administration; a summer internship at the National Journal in Washington, DC, with Neal Peirce, the nationally syndicated columnist who writes about local and state government trends around the country, and a post graduate summer internship with the Enterprise Foundation.

William Anderson, FAICP, City of San Diego

❭ While working with the Army Corps of Engineers, several specialists had been retained to conduct an objective review of the Corps as an institution and its practices in the wake of these new challenges. One of those specialists was a professor from Carnegie-Mellon University, and one of the

divisional directors told him about a young trainee that was drawing attention and asking questions that were outside the box.

The two of us had lunch and quickly developed a dialogue and I began working with him part time to facilitate his review. One day he invited me to sit in on one of his classes at the university, which dealt with the Philosophy of Technological Change, which was amazingly resonant with the ongoing experience at the Corps.

CMU had also just launched a new graduate school focused on Urban and Public Affairs, which was formerly a set of electives in the Business School. So graduates effectively attained an MBA degree but with ultimate focus on the public sector.

Disciplines of economics, public policy, advanced statistical methods, and social science were mixed (as was the student base) in an intense 24/7 two-year program of cooperative problem solving. There were numerous large and small-scale group projects that were done for and in partnership with the community.

What I came to like about the school, being a former engineer, was the emphasis on objective, rigorous, quantitative methods, blending research skills with public outreach, and deliberating to arrive at practical but meaningful solutions to transportation, environmental, community development and equity-framed issues. Mine is not a "planning" degree as such but a public policy/public management orientation.

J. Richard Kuzmyak, Transportation Consultant, LLC

❭ I loved the University of Florida and Gainesville. I only applied to master's degrees at UF. It helped that I secured a research assistantship, which paid for my tuition and really gave me a strong introduction to the profession.

How did you pick a school for your planning degree? (Continued)

Planning is, by nature, a profession that involves community involvement. Classes involve fieldwork and public involvement. I find that it helps to have a personal connection to the city and state where you will be in school. I am a third-generation Floridian. If I'm going to be doing community involvement, I want it to be in Florida. Also, you are far more likely to be hired in state, so traveling across the country for school doesn't make a lot of sense.

Alexander Bond, AICP, Center for Urban Transportation Research, University of South Florida

❯ I was 18 and a second-year undergraduate at the University of Illinois. I was a conscientious pre-med student, but the subject never resonated with me. The curriculum was competitive and impersonal, the classes were gigantic and uninteresting, and I found myself sitting in lectures drawing maps and skylines in the margins of my notebooks.

One day I took an alternate route home from class and passed the Department of Urban and Regional Planning. The department occupied a bunch of funky old clapboard houses on a residential street on the edge of campus. Inquisitively, I went inside, picked up a course catalog, and made an appointment to speak with a professor about careers in planning. I still remember that meeting with Lachlan Blair, who was the associate department head at the time. At semester break, I switched my major to urban planning. Looking back, I was very fortunate to be at one of the few schools in the country that happened to have an undergraduate planning program.

During my senior year at U of I, I decided to go straight on to get my master's degree in planning before beginning professional practice. I was still pretty young and felt I needed to expand my skill set before entering the work world. I applied to four graduate programs—three on the East Coast and one at Berkeley. I decided to go to Berkeley because my professors at Illinois raved about the quality of the planning program, the beauty of the place, and the creative energy of the town. At the time, I had never been to California and still considered myself a displaced New Yorker. That was 25 years ago. I live 2 miles from the Berkeley campus today.

Barry Miller, AICP, Planning Consultant

❯ My graduate degree is in geography with a focus in land use planning. I applied to UNC Charlotte because they had an applied geography program, which meant you had real-world work to accompany the classes you were taking. My thoughts were, in the very tough economy of the early 1980s, I was going to have to have practical experience to go along with my degree to get a job. It was a great choice for me. I still could pursue some of my original focus in the environmental arena and develop my interest in planning.

Sue Schwartz, FAICP, City of Greensboro, North Carolina

❯ I wanted to go to southeast for graduate school to be close to both my family and my spouse's family, as we were on the West Coast at the time. I also wanted to go to a growing area where planning was needed, as well as a place where planning was valued. I also wanted to go to a school ranked high in the field, hence UNC-Chapel Hill.

John Hodges-Copple, Triangle J Council of Governments

❯ The academic strength of a planning program is usually the trigger for a decision. For me, there were other equally important factors. For graduate school, I went to an urban university in a large city. Of the two schools in the city with planning programs, one was better regarded academically, the other offered more flexibility in its curriculum and class schedule. I consciously chose the second school.

The more flexible approach to learning allowed me to explore different types of planning in hands-on situations to discover which might suit me best. At various times during a two-year period, I did number crunching for a social research institute, served a legislative aide for a member of the state legislature, and wrote grants for impoverished communities. Those experiences led to a decision to pursue land use policy as a career track.

Marianne Gardner, Fairfax County, Virginia Department of Planning and Zoning

❯ I decided to attend the University of Colorado-Denver for their Urban Planning program, mainly because I was reluctant to leave the state for graduate school. They have the only master's program in Colorado and have a decent reputation.

I spent time in school taking on a dual degree in Urban Design and a certificate in historic preservation, and filled in the blanks with classes I wanted to take in architecture, graphic design, and a study abroad in Rome to focus on architecture and urban design. In retrospect, I shouldn't have limited myself to only Colorado as my choice, but my desire to understand more than planning helped me to get a broad understanding of how it all comes together as a profession.

Jessica Osborne, Colorado Department of Public Health and Environment

ACCREDITATION

The Planning Accreditation Board is composed of planning faculty and practicing planners. The members of the board are appointed by the Association of Collegiate Schools of Planning, the American Planning Association, and the American Institute of Certified Planners. Together, they work to ensure the relevance and quality of planning education for the practice of planning.

Some planning job announcements will specifically require that the master's degree be from an accredited degree program. Generally, however, this is not the case. And many job announcements will advertise for candidates with a master's in planning or a related field. More about those "related fields" below.

Nonetheless, choosing an accredited program provides some minimal assurance that the curriculum is tailored to the job requirements that planners will face after graduation and that the program meets minimal standards of program quality. All accredited master's programs must require a minimum of two years of full-time study for the degree (generally interpreted as at least 48 credits) and must have a primary focus on preparing students to become practitioners in the planning profession.

When a program is accredited, the program undergoes periodic review, usually every six years. During the review, the program needs to produce a report summarizing the program curriculum, student body, faculty resources, research and public service activities of the faculty, and other indicators of program quality. A team of two planning faculty members from other schools and a planning practitioner from outside the local area visit the school for several days, visiting with administrators, faculty, students, and local practitioners.

They subsequently write a confidential report summarizing the strengths of the program and areas in need of improvement. If a program has substantial deficiencies, the program may be put on probation and, ultimately, accreditation may be withdrawn. But whatever the specific outcome of the review, the process always produces ideas for strengthening the quality of instruction and the student experience. The rigorous process of accreditation instills a climate of continuous quality improvement that benefits every program that is involved.

WHAT'S IN A NAME?

When you begin to explore degree programs in planning, you will notice a number of different names: Master of City Planning, Master of Urban and Regional Planning, Master of Urban Planning, Master of Environmental Studies and Planning, Master of Policy and Planning, and others. In general, if the program is accredited by the PAB, the name will tell you little about similarities and differences among the programs. Typically, the names reflect the period in history when the program was founded ("city planning" being preferred among programs that began before 1950 and "urban planning" or "urban and regional planning" being more common among programs that were started after 1950). Similarly, the name of the degree can vary. Some programs offer a Master of Science, others a Master of Urban and Regional Planning or Master of Urban Planning. Again, if the program is accredited, the degree designation can be understood as variation based on institutional policy and history rather than an indicator of program focus or rigor.

Planning programs differ in the number of credits of required coursework. Some programs may have only 15 credits of required courses, with the remainder of the credits (upwards of 33 credits) in electives. Other programs require a greater number of required courses and allow only a minority of credits in electives. In selecting a planning program, students need to inquire about the number of elective courses offered each semester and the reliance of the program on courses outside of the planning program.

THESES, PROJECTS, OR OTHER CAPSTONE REQUIREMENTS

Finally, a prospective student needs to understand whether graduation requires completion of a master's thesis or thesis-like project. Some programs require a thesis, others require an individual project, and others do not require either. In addition, programs differ in the amount of support that they provide to students in working their way through the thesis or project work. In some programs, a large number of students never complete the thesis or project and eventually drop out of the program without completing their degree. In other programs, the completion rate is high, but the quality of theses and projects is highly variable. Whether a program requires a thesis or not should never be a primary criterion for choosing a planning program. Rather, talk to faculty and students to understand the role of the thesis or other capstone experiences in assuring that students graduate with an ability to carry out a substantial, real-world project, whether individually or as the member of a team.

Applying to Graduate School

Typically, the application for admission to a master in urban planning degree program requires submission of an application form, undergraduate transcript(s), letters of recommendation, and a statement of purpose explaining the student's objectives in pursuing the master of urban planning. The ACSP Guide includes information for each program about their admissions requirements.

MASTERS GRADUATION REQUIREMENTS

Hours of Core 33
Hours of Studio or Practice Related Courses 16
Hours of Restricted Electives 11
Hours of Unrestricted Electives 6
Other .... 6 units
Total Required Hours in Planning Program .... 72 units
Thesis or Final Product: .... Thesis, professional project, or Studio III

Joint Master of City and Regional Planning/Master of Science in Engineering

Contact Person: **Cornelius Nuworsoo, Assistant Professor**
Phone: **(805) 756-2573**
E-mail **cnuworso@calpoly.edu**

Year Initiated: 1992 **PAB Accredited**
Degrees Granted through 8/31/07 13
Degrees Granted from 9/1/06 to 8/31/07 1

Masters Specializations

Transportation Planning

MASTERS ADMISSION REQUIREMENTS

University Admission Policy:	Bachelors degree from an accredited institution.
Minimum Undergraduate GPA:	2.5 in last 90 units
Minimum GRE:	Not required, unless borderline GPA
Minimum TOEFL	550-paper, 213-computer
Ranking in Undergraduate Class:	Not Required
Departmental Requirement:	3.0 in last 90 units. Knowledge of basic computer applications; statement of purpose, writing sample, 3 letters of recommendation. CE 221, CE 381 or GEOL 201, CSC 231, Econ 201, Engl 148, Math 143, SCOM 101, Stat 321.

MASTERS GRADUATION REQUIREMENTS

Hours of Core 50
Hours of Studio or Practice Related Courses 15
Hours of Restricted Electives 25
Hours of Unrestricted Electives 0
Other 0
Total Required Hours in Planning Program 90
Thesis or Final Product: .... Thesis, professional project or Studio III

TOTAL MASTERS STUDENT COMPOSITION
2006-2007

US Citizens & Permanent Residents	Male	Female	Total
Hispanics* Of any Race	2	1	3
White	16	11	27
African American	0	0	0
Native American/ Pacific Islander	0	0	0
Asian American	2	1	3
Mixed	1	1	2
Other / Don't know	2	0	2
Non-US Citizens Non- Permanent Residents	1	1	2
Total Students	24	16	40

PLANNING FACULTY

Michael Boswell AICP
Associate Professor. BS (1989) University of Central Florida; MSP (1991) and Ph.D. (2000) Florida State University. **Specializations:** Environmental Planning, Disaster Mitigation Planning, Planning Theory, Sustainable Development.
(805) 756-2496 mboswell@calpoly.edu

W. David Conn
Vice Provost & Professor. BA (1968), MA (1972), and D. Phil. (1973) Worchester College, Oxford University. **Specializations:** Environmental Policy, Planning and Pollution Prevention.
(805) 756-2246 dconn@calpoly.edu

Adrienne Greve
Assistant Professor. BS, (1996) Cornell University; MS, (1999) Colorado State University; Ph.D., (2006) University of Washington. **Specializations:** Urban Ecology, Environmental Impact, Environmental Justice.
(805) 756-1474 agreve@calpoly.edu

Zeljka Pavolich Howard
Lecturer. Diploma of Engineer Architect (1964) University of Belgrade; MS (1972) Florida State University. **Specializations:** Citizen Participation, Community Development, Physical Planning/Urban Design, Neighborhood Planning.
(805) 756-1507 zhoward@calpoly.edu

The ACSP *Guide to Undergraduate and Graduate Programs in Urban and Regional Planning* includes both accredited and unaccredited programs. Here, the first page of information about the programs at the University of Toledo shows that the university offers both an undergraduate major in Geography and Planning, as well as an unaccredited master's degree in Geography and Planning. Under "Program Information," students can find admission requirements and information about tuition and fees. ASSOCIATION OF COLLEGIATE SCHOOLS OF PLANNING.

UNIVERSITY OF TOLEDO

BA/BS   MA/MS

ACSP Member:
FULL

Department of Geography and Planning

2801 W. Bancroft Street, MS 932
Toledo, Ohio 43606-3390
Phone (419) 530-2545
Fax (419) 530-7919

http://www.geography.utoledo.edu/

Dr. Peter S. Lindquist, Department Chair
Phone: (419) 530-4287
E-mail: peter.lindquist@utoledo.edu

PROGRAM INFORMATION

UNDERGRADUATE DEADLINES, TUITION AND FEES
Admission Deadline 2008-09 ....Rolling
Financial Aid Deadline 2008-09 .... N/A
In-State Tuition and Fees as of 2008-09 ....$4,000 per semester
Out-of-State Tuition and Fees as of 2008-09 ....$8,400 per semester
Application Fee $40
Additional Fees: .... Please see University website

GRADUATE DEADLINES, TUITION AND FEES
Admission Deadline 2008-09 for Masters program ....March 30, 2007
Financial Aid Deadline 2008-09 for Masters program............................N/A
In-State Tuition and Fees: ....Approx. $5,800 per semester
Out-of-State Tuition and Fees: ....Approx. $10,400 per semester
Application Fee: $45
Additional Fees: .... Please see University website

Annual Student Enrollment

	Applied 07/08	Accepted 07/08	Enrolled 07/08
Masters	24	12	9

UNDERGRADUATE DEGREE

BA in Geography & Planning

Contact Person: Dr. David J. Nemeth, Undergrad. Advisor
Phone: (419) 530-4049
E-mail: david.nemeth@utoledo.edu

Year initiated:1996

Undergraduate Specializations
GIS, Community Development, Economic Development, Environmental Planning, Historic Preservation, International Development, Land Use/Growth Management, Public Policy, Real Estate Development, Transportation, Urban/Regional Development and Urban Design/Landscape

UNDERGRADUATE ADMISSION REQUIREMENTS
Departmental Requirement: None
Minimum GPA: 2.0
Minimum SAT or ACT Scores: Not Required

UNDERGRADUATE GRADUATION REQUIREMENTS
Hours of Core 12
Hours of Studio Courses...
Hours of Restricted Elective ....
Hours of Unrestricted Elective ....
Total Required Hours In Planning Program 31
Thesis or final product..Not required

FINANCIAL AID INFORMATION
Wide variety available in the Office of Student Financial Aid (Rm. 1200 Rocket Hall)

MASTERS DEGREE

Master of Arts in Geography and Planning

Contact Person: Dr. Patrick Lawrence, Grad. Advisor
Phone: (419) 530-4128

E-mail: patrick.lawrence@utoledo.edu
Year Initiated: 1971

Masters Specializations
GIS, Community Development, Economic Development, Environmental Planning, Historic Preservation, International Development, Land Use/Growth Management, Public Policy, Real Estate Development, Transportation, Urban/Regional Development and Urban Design/Landscape

MASTERS ADMISSION REQUIREMENTS
University Admission Policy: Bachelor's degree from an accredited institution
Minimum Undergraduate GPA: 2.7
Minimum GRE: 500 verbal, 500 quantitative
Minimum TOEFL   550
Ranking in Undergraduate Class: Not Required
Departmental Requirement: No Requiements

MASTERS GRADUATION REQUIREMENTS
Hours of Core 10
Hours of Studio or Practice Related Courses 0
Hours of Restricted Electives 0
Hours of Unrestricted Electives..20
Total Required Hours in Planning Program: 30
Exam, Thesis or Final Product: ....Exam & Thesis

FINANCIAL AID INFORMATION
Internship opportunities, Department awards, University financial aid.

In addition to providing information about admission, tuition, and graduation requirements, the ACSP *Guide* provides information about the composition of the student body and a complete list of the faculty who teach in the program, along with their areas of specialization. This excerpt shows just a single page from the four-page listing for the California Polytechnic State University, San Luis Obispo. ASSOCIATION OF COLLEGIATE SCHOOLS OF PLANNING.

About half of the programs require submission of scores from the General portion of the Graduate Record Exam (GRE). The GRE is a nationally normed exam offered by the Educational Testing Service. It includes sections on verbal reasoning, quantitative reasoning, and analytical writing.

The Graduate Record Exam (GRE) is required for admission by a significant number of planning master's degree programs. The exam is offered in two parts, a general exam and a "subject test." No GRE subject test exists in the field of urban planning, so if the GRE is required at all, in all likelihood, only the general test will be required.

The general test has three parts: quantitative reasoning, verbal reasoning, and analytical writing. The exam is offered throughout the year at testing centers across the United States.

For more information on the GRE exam, visit the website of the Educational Testing Service (www.ets.org) and follow the links to the GRE test taker's site.

Typically, programs require the submission of three letters of recommendation. The most valuable letters speak to the applicant's communication skills, interpersonal skills, and ability to engage in reasoning tasks, like problem-solving and analysis of information. Usually, faculty that the student came to know during undergraduate study will make the best references for graduate school. However, if a prospective graduate student has worked in the field of planning, a letter from someone who can speak to the candidate's planning abilities from direct observation on the job will be given strong weight by most programs.

In most cases, programs prefer to admit students who have an undergraduate grade point average (GPA) of 3.0 or above. If a student's GPA is lower than a 3.0, the program may need additional evidence of the student's ability to perform satisfactorily in the program and may admit the student on probation or some other temporary basis.

Achieving an undergraduate GPA of 3.0 may not ensure a student admission to any program they choose, but should ensure admission at many highly reputable planning programs. The GPA and GRE scores become more critical in decisions programs make about financial aid. Typically, graduate fellowships, scholarships, and assistantships are awarded to students who have the strongest undergraduate records and other indicators of excellent academic performance.

Financing a Planning Education

Fellowships and scholarships are financial assistance that carry no work requirement. The word "fellowship" is usually attached to awards of higher amounts that cover at least the full tuition cost and often include a stipend in addition to tuition. Scholarships are usually smaller amounts, from a few hundred to a few thousand dollars and are not expected to cover more than a small portion of the cost of attending school. Graduate assistantships require work in exchange for financial support. Assistants help professors with their teaching, research, or other projects. In each case, the assistant usually works 10–20 hours per week. Assistantships vary widely in the proportion of tuition they cover and the amount of the stipend that comes with it. In any case, however, any of these awards can greatly reduce the cost of obtaining a planning education. In the case of fellowships and assistantships that carry full tuition remission and a stipend, the school is essentially paying the student to go to school.

Most programs, however, have a limited number of these awards available. Most programs are able to offer substantial support through assistantships to 10 percent or less of their applicants. Consequently, competition is fierce to land one of these awards.

Many students ultimately rely on student loans, summer earnings, and part-time jobs to fund their planning education. Frequently, especially in larger metropolitan areas, after the first year of study—and sometimes earlier—students are able to obtain paid internships in planning agencies and consulting firms that help to defray tuition and living expenses. In addition to paying more than minimum wage, students get valuable practical experience, which complements their classroom experience and is essential in landing that first professional job after graduation.

Planning Curriculum: Knowledge, Skills, and Values

The Planning Accreditation Board specifies the knowledge, skills, and value components that accredited programs must cover in their courses. The knowledge components include such topics as understanding how and why cities form where they do and what causes them to flourish and decline, the history of planning, the process of plan making and policy analysis, and familiarity with specialized subject areas within planning.

The skills component covers topics like the ability to formulate problems and conduct research to develop information addressing the problem; the ability to analyze quantitative information and use computer software to analyze geographic data; the ability to communicate effectively using written, oral, and graphic communication; the ability to work as a team member and team leader; and the ability to apply abstract concepts to real-world planning issues.

Finally, the values component requires that students understand the values of the planning profession. Students are not required to adopt these values as their own, but they should understand why these values are held in high regard within the profession. The value components include appreciation of issues of equity and social justice, the role of government and citizen participation in a democratic society, respect for diversity of views and ideologies, the conservation of natural resources and the preservation of historical and cultural heritage in the built environment, and professional ethics. Programs differ in the emphasis that they give to the various components and how the various components are covered in required versus elective courses. For example, one program may put heavy emphasis on written communication, while another puts more emphasis on graphic communication.

PLANNING ACCREDITATION REQUIRED CURRICULUM COMPONENTS

Knowledge Components

- Structure and Functions of Urban Settlements
- History and Theory of Planning Processes and Practices
- Administrative, Legal, and Political Aspects of Plan Making and Policy Implementation
- Familiarity with at Least One Area of Specialized Knowledge of a Particular Subject or Set of Issues

Skill Components

- Problem Formulation, Research Skills, and Data Gathering
- Quantitative Analysis and Computers
- Written, Oral, and Graphic Communications
- Collaborative Problem Solving, Plan-making, and Program Design

Value Components

- Issues of equity, social justice, economic welfare, and efficiency in the use of resources
- The role of government and citizen participation in a democratic society and the balancing of individual and collective rights and interests
- Respect for diversity of views and ideologies
- The conservation of natural resources and of the significant social and cultural heritages embedded in the built environment
- The ethics of professional practice and behavior, including the relationship to clients and the public, and the role of citizens in democratic participation

Tulane/Gravier Regulating Plan & Form-Based Code

A Guide for the
Redevelopment of
Tulane Avenue
&
Galvez Street

May 2007

THE PHOENIX
OF
NEW ORLEANS

UNIVERSITY of WISCONSIN
UWMILWAUKEE

In many planning programs, students finishing their two-year master's degree complete a major plan for a real client. In this case, students in the Master of Urban Planning Program at the University of Wisconsin–Milwaukee completed a plan for the Tulane/Gravier neighborhood in New Orleans. Working just 18 months after Hurricane Katrina and the levy breaks inundated the neighborhood with flood waters, the neighborhood needed assistance in setting priorities and standards for new development. COPYRIGHT 2007. TULANE/GRAVIER REGULATING PLAN AND FORM-BASED CODE, PREPARED FOR THE PHOENIX OF NEW ORLEANS BY MATT AHO, ALISON KOPYT, BRAD LENZ, AND MEAGAN LIMBERG.

STREETSCAPING STANDARDS

	Sidewalk Width	Crosswalk*	Plantings*	Amenities
Neighborhood	Minimum: 5' 6' sidewalks encouraged where possible	At minimum, crosswalks must be clearly marked with striping in all directions	<u>Planters</u> • Discouraged in right-of-way • Planter boxes must be attached to building <u>Trees</u> • Required every 60 feet, on center Page 39	None required
		Page 39		
Main Street	Minimum: 6' Wider sidewalks encouraged where possible	<u>Major Arterials</u> Crosswalk must be marked by a difference in: • color • texture • materials <u>Minor Arterials</u> Crosswalk must be marked by striping Page 47	<u>Planters</u> • Hanging baskets • Window boxes • Sidewalk planters <u>Trees</u> • Required every 60 feet, on center Page 48	<u>Waste Bins</u> At least 2 per block <u>Bus Shelters</u> Encouraged at major intersections
Urban Transition	Minimum: 8' 10' sidewalks encouraged where possible	All crosswalks must be marked by a difference in: • color • texture • materials Page 58	<u>Planters</u> • Hanging baskets • Window boxes • Sidewalk planters <u>Trees</u> • Required every 60 feet, on center Page 58	<u>Waste Bins</u> At least 2 per block <u>Bus Shelters</u> Encouraged at major intersections
Urban	Minimum: 10' Wider sidewalks encouraged where possible	All crosswalks must be marked by a difference in: • color • texture • materials Page 69	<u>Planters</u> • Hanging baskets • Window boxes • Sidewalk planters <u>Trees</u> • Required every 60 feet, on center Page 69	<u>Waste Bins</u> At least 2 per block <u>Bus Shelters</u> Encouraged at major intersections

CORRIDOR ANALYSIS

26

Proposed development guidelines for the Tulane/Gravier neighborhood. This plan received a Student Project Award from the Wisconsin Chapter of the American Planning Association. COPYRIGHT 2007. TULANE/GRAVIER REGULATING PLAN AND FORM-BASED CODE, PREPARED FOR THE PHOENIX OF NEW ORLEANS BY MATT AHO, ALISON KOPYT, BRAD LENZ, AND MEAGAN LIMBERG.

Specializations

Most planning programs offer one or more specializations, subfields that students may elect to pursue through their elective credits. The most common specialization areas are: land use, environmental planning, economic development planning, transportation planning, housing, social and community development planning, urban design, Geographic Information Systems (GIS), and international development.

Chapter 4 will introduce you to each of these specialty areas in detail, introducing you to planners who work in these subfields of planning. For now, just a few comments about studying for these specializations are important. First, a student who has chosen a particular specialty should be sure to select a program that has sufficient courses available in that area. Second, most programs do not require applicants to identify an area of specialization before enrolling. Finally, some programs may offer specialization options but allow students to pursue a general option, in which a student may take elective courses in multiple specialization areas to increase his or her breadth of understanding.

Specializations may be more or less formal, even within a single program. In some cases, the specialization is a list of courses that are recommended for students seeking a specialty, but no one checks to make sure that the student completes a minimum number of the listed courses. At the opposite extreme, some specializations can be very precisely defined, with their own required courses and with a pre-graduation screening to make sure that the student has completed all of the required elements.

Specializations may also be found in certificate programs, which may be offered by the planning program or by another academic unit on campus. For example, a planner may elect to pursue a certificate in public health policy as part of the master's in planning, even though the public health policy certificate is offered by the School of Public Health.

Again, in choosing a planning program, do your research on the program and understand your own needs and then meet with a program representative to be sure that the program of study that you want to pursue is permissible and feasible. A prospective student needs to understand what courses can be counted toward the planning master's degree and what courses, while related to planning, will need to be taken in addition to the minimum credits for the master's degree. Knowing the answer to this question before enrolling can ensure that a student does not have to add an additional semester or two of coursework because of misunderstandings about the availability of courses and their applicability to the master in planning.

Dual-Degree Options

Many planning programs offer dual degrees with other fields of study, also referred to as "joint degrees" and "coordinated degrees." Such programs allow a student to earn two master's degrees with fewer credits than would be required if the student were to study the same programs independently. Typically, these programs require students to complete the required courses in each program, and the required credits in each program count as elective credits in the other. As a result, the total number of credits for the two degrees can be reduced by 50 percent or more.

Dual-degree programs are often offered between planning and the following fields: architecture, landscape architecture, urban design, engineering, law, and public administration; a smaller number of programs offer dual-degree programs with environmental science and natural resources, business and real estate, and health policy and planning.

Management Skills and a Planning Career

> For many of the years that I have worked as a consultant, I have operated my own planning practice with a staff level reaching as high as 13. This has required that I function as a small business owner.

Consequently, I have to spend time each day on business-related tasks such as personnel management, cash flow analysis, billing, and bill paying.

I have a business manager, but as the owner of the business, it is essential that I stay closely involved in those activities.

Although this work is sometimes a chore, it has helped me develop managerial skills and the ability to appreciate the management and fiscal issues that my clients deal with every day.

Howard Geisler, President, Geisler/Smith Associates

Admission to a dual-degree program can be a bit more complex, because the student needs to meet the prerequisites of two programs. Upon completion of a dual-degree program, however, a student can often find employment equally in either field and can claim a stronger level of expertise than new graduates who hold only the planning degree.

Alternative Paths

Planning is all about exploring alternatives and finding the "best way." For some students who have an interest in planning, pursuing the planning master's degree will not be the "best way" for them. These students should explore alternative paths to a career that allows them to engage the future of communities and the development of the built and natural environment.

PUBLIC ADMINISTRATION

Many students find themselves torn between urban planning and public administration, which focuses on the day-to-day management of cities. The Master of Public Administration program will feature courses on public finance, personnel management, and politics, along with courses on the structure of local government and the interdependencies between local, state, and federal levels of government. Public administration programs also place greater emphasis on administrative regulation as a legal form, while planning programs focus more on the substantive details of the regulations passed by local governments. Some schools offer dual-degree programs in planning and public administration, but many do not.

URBAN STUDIES

Another alternative is a degree in urban studies or urban and regional studies. Urban and regional studies programs can be found at the undergraduate, master's, and doctoral level. These programs focus on cities from a multidisciplinary perspective, and in this way they are similar to planning programs. But they lack—to varying degrees depending on the program—training in the skills and values of the planning profession and the role of planning in cities. Urban and regional studies programs are likely to require fewer credits than a planning degree (30 or 32) but are more likely to require completion of a traditional research thesis. The value of the urban studies degree in landing a traditional planning job varies, depending on the opportunity to complete courses in planning law, land use regulation, and quantitative analysis techniques used by planners.

> *How would you describe the difference between the fields of urban planning, urban studies, geography, and public administration?*

❯ The biggest difference between urban planning and the fields of urban studies and geography is the fact that planning is part of a profession. A profession is an occupation that requires training and specialized knowledge that may include aspects of certification (such as in the case of the American Institute of Certified Planners, AICP), and whose behavior is governed by a code of ethics. Another key difference between these fields is that, although geographers, planners, and urban studies majors all examine aspects of cities and urban environments, planners don't just study cities, they go one step further and ask, what are we going to do about the issues and conditions that exist within our cities?

In other words, geographers and urban studies majors examine cities, but planners examine cities in order to improve conditions and solve problems. Public administration, like planning, is a professional, multidisciplinary field that promotes effective government and strives to address public service issues at all levels or government (local, state, and federal) as well as within nongovernmental organizations (NGOs). Planners are dedicated to protecting public health, safety, and welfare and enriching people's lives as well as the communities in which they live.

Susan Bradbury, Iowa State University

ECONOMICS

Some planners don't call themselves planners. Economic development consultants and specialists are often trained in economics or business. Within economics, they might specialize in labor economics, industrial economics, or regional economic analysis. Within business, they might specialize in marketing or real estate. These practitioners might be employed by larger units of government—large cities or counties, or regional development agencies—or by private consulting firms or land developers. In many cases, individuals with planning degrees work in the same venues doing the same tasks. Generally, however, economic development specialists without a degree in planning may be more engaged in the number-crunching side of the work than on the program development and public meeting side of economic development.

ARCHITECTURE, LANDSCAPE ARCHITECTURE, AND URBAN DESIGN

As previously noted, a number of design professions have historically served as the training ground for planners and continue to engage in planning and planning-related work. Architects, landscape architects, and urban designers may be part of a team of planning professionals, or they may work independently on physical planning tasks. Because of their training in graphic rendering, spatial problem solving, and aesthetics, design professionals are able to more effectively communicate ideas about "place." Unlike planners, however, they may not have the training to understand how to bring that vision to fruition. Urban development is the product of private developers and public regulation. Complex redevelopment projects frequently require a citizen involvement process to win approval and public subsidies or incentives to help developers overcome the challenges of redeveloping an urban site. The design professional is not typically involved in these crucial aspects of urban development unless he or she is also trained in finances and/or planning.

CIVIL ENGINEERING

Civil engineering is another profession that often engages in planning and planning-related activities. This is especially common in relation to the planning of urban infrastructure: transportation, water, wastewater, and stormwater facilities. Like planners and design professionals, civil engineers are taught to engage in problem solving. Engineers' special expertise relates to the technical aspects of the design of urban infrastructure. Engineers can help to understand the critical capacity issues facing cities as they grow, and they can often provide novel and economical solutions to those capacity issues—whether the problem is traffic on the freeway or sewer system overflows.

Engineers are essential members of any urban planning team, but they often lack the training and experience that planners have in understanding the social context of urban infrastructure and the interrelatedness of infrastructure and other urban systems—such as job markets and housing markets. Without that holistic perspective that is the hallmark of planning training, civil engineers sometimes focus too narrowly on the details of moving people and goods as efficiently as possible, missing the bigger picture.

Transportation Planning: Moving People and Goods

What advice would you give an aspiring transportation planner?

❭ Whether you get a master's degree or not, you should strive to get as broad an education and set of experiences to draw from as possible. That can help you to understand how larger systems work.

Become part of national professional organizations. And take advantage of opportunities to work with other disciplines. Civil engineers need to know what planners do and vice versa.

A key question that planners face is whether to stay as a generalist or move into a more specialized role. We need both types: people with advanced degrees that have broad applications across disciplines. But

we also need specialization in transportation fields, on design, engineering, maintenance, and operations. Agencies cannot function without that specialized expertise, whether it's engineering, planning, or financial.

You have to have a willingness to be flexible and to take advantage of experiences as they become available. A lot of people stay in one location after they get their degrees, but if you do that, you may struggle to advance in your career. So I would advise planners to look at opportunities available in your geographic area, but realize that you may need to move to get ahead.

Matthew Moore, Idaho Transportation Department, Boise, Idaho

PLANNING LAW

An alternative path into a planning-related career is through the law. Attorneys may choose to specialize in real estate law or land use law. When a landowner wants to do something with her property, but the neighbors or city government opposes it, they are likely to hire attorneys to present their arguments and to show how the law supports their own side of the argument.

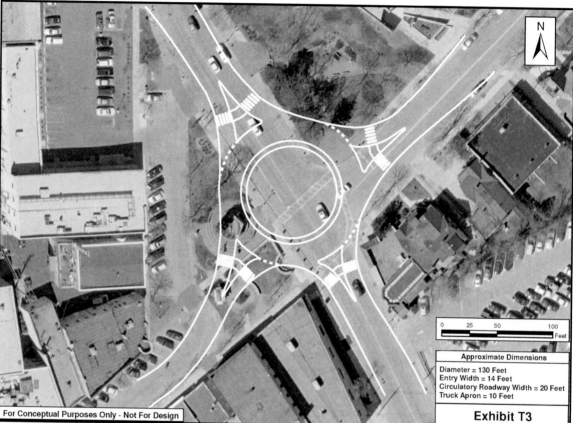

Proposed Roundabout
Wauwatosa Avenue & Harwood Avenue

N

0   25   50   100
Feet

Approximate Dimensions

Diameter = 130 Feet
Entry Width = 14 Feet
Circulatory Roadway Width = 20 Feet
Truck Apron = 10 Feet

For Conceptual Purposes Only - Not For Design

Exhibit T3

This roundabout was designed by a student pursing a joint degree in urban planning and civil engineering. With training in both planning and engineering, the student was able to attend to the technical details of engineering this roundabout at the same time that he considered the effects that this change to the road network might have on nearby businesses, pedestrian and bike movements, and the aesthetics of the area. Transportation engineers get into the details of designing and predicting the performance of transportation facilities, such as adding a new turn signal, widening a roadway, or building a new light rail line. COPYRIGHT 2008. JOHN BRUGGEMAN.

Becoming a Land Use Lawyer

NICOLE LACOSTE
Law Office of Nicole Lacoste
Baltimore, Maryland

How did you end up as a land use lawyer?

❯ After the Peace Corps, I came home to work for the EPA on Superfund projects. I looked young and innocent, traveling around the country to participate in community meetings on behalf of the federal government to address concerns about nearby hazardous waste site remediation. It's where I got my thick skin and learned not to take things personally. Once, at a community meeting, I was asked if I would drink a glass of water from that community's public drinking water source. When I declined, the community member said that since I wouldn't drink the water I was acknowledging that it was contaminated. Another time, I was told by an upset community member that I represented the devil.

I loved the job but burned out on the process. So I went to law school because I was always interested in the policy side of environmental law. If someone asked me what I did with the EPA, I would tell them that I was an environmental protection specialist. I was never a planner. In law school, I excelled in property law and anything to do with land use. I thought, I have a knack for this. One of the professors asked if I thought about getting a master's in planning. I didn't know what he was talking about. I was 27 years old and didn't know what a planning degree was.

I went to talk to one of the professors in the planning program, and he told me about the classes, and about how you could learn how to organize a community meeting. It was exactly the type of work I had been doing in the Peace Corps and at EPA. So I applied and got in and created a joint degree in international and environmental planning, in addition to my law degree.

After I graduated, I moved to Denver and took a job writing zoning codes. After six months, I knew that I was not cut out for sitting isolated in an office for days while drafting tedious zoning code text. I wanted more hands-on interaction with the zoning and land use processes. So I quit and got a job in Baltimore, practicing land use law.

Do you consider yourself to be a planner?

❯ No. Right now, I am 100 percent a lawyer, but there are so many times when I act as a planner to help supplement my skills as a lawyer.

I've been in development meetings where I've made substantive comments about site plans. I can walk into a planning office and talk their language. If you were in a planning office and asked me a question, you'd think I was a planner.

What type of projects do you work on?

❯ Everything from soup to nuts: construction permits, environmental document review, zoning and land use, development approvals and permitting, site plan reviews. I also work on annexations.

Do you keep current on planning issues?

❯ You have to focus on both areas to be able to excel in either area. I'm sure I could get a planning job if I wanted one. I try to be active in the professional organizations of both: APA and ABA.

If I stopped staying current on planning issues, I would waste all that I put into it.

Becoming an attorney requires three years of law school following an undergraduate degree. A few universities offer coordinated degrees in law and urban planning, which allow a student to receive both degrees in less time that the two degrees taken individually.

Conclusion

Whatever an individual's talents, urban planning can offer a rewarding career. Some may find themselves drawn to design, while others take an interest in managing and displaying data that describes an area and its needs. Some may be attracted by the opportunity to work with people and engage with people in solving problems; others may prefer the more solitary work of a numbers-cruncher, analyzing transportation data or economic indicators. The message that every student of planning should take away from this chapter is this: build on your strengths and interests, build up your areas of weakness, and find a learning environment that will help you to discover and grow your passions.

❸ Becoming an Urban Planner: Experience

Question: *What's the best way to get a job in your desired field?*

Answer: *Get experience in your desired field.*

BUT HOW DO YOU GET THAT EXPERIENCE *before* you apply for that first job?

The answer to that question is the subject of this chapter. Students graduating from college are realizing that they need to pursue experience in their field prior to hitting the job market. A January 2009 report by the National Association of Colleges and Employers (NACE) confirmed that over 75 percent of employers prefer to hire new graduates with relevant work experience (Koncz, no date). To an employer, experience means that you can jump into some tasks on the very first day of work and be a productive member of the team while you learn new skills and take on new tasks.

Fortunately, the field of planning offers a wealth of opportunities to get relevant experience before you finish your degree. This chapter describes informational interviews, job shadowing, volunteering, internships, and cooperative education and the ways that a future planner can obtain these experiences.

The order of these activities suggests an increasing level of difficulty, job preparation, and time commitment. A middle-school student can do informational interviews and job shadowing but would have limited volunteer and internship opportunities. High school students and college students are welcomed as volunteers in community organizations related to planning. In addition, high school students and college students may find part-time jobs or internships in planning offices and planning firms doing data collection, research, library assistance, and more general office work.

Informational Interviews

Informational interviews are often the first step in pursuing a job-shadowing or volunteer opportunity. Many job search experts recommend informational interviews with employers in a candidate's desired field. "An informational interview involves talking with people who are currently working in the field to gain a better understanding of an occupation or industry—and to build a network of contacts in that field" (QuintCareers.com, no date). The technique is often associated with the career exploration and job search advice offered by Richard Nelson Bolles in the now-classic book *What Color Is Your Parachute?*

Professionals are often willing to be very generous with their time in talking to someone who shows a genuine interest in learning more about their work. A future planner should prepare for the interview by having a list of questions and show respect for the professional's time by arriving promptly at the appointment time and staying on schedule.

INFORMATIONAL INTERVIEWS

An informational interview for career exploration allows a future planner to ask questions about what it is really like to be a planner.

Suggested questions include:

What are the duties performed during a typical day, week, or month?

Does s/he have a set routine?

How much variety is there on a day-to-day basis?

What are the main or most important personal characteristics for success in the field?

What kind of work/internship experience would employers look for in a job applicant?

How can a person obtain this work experience?

Source: About.com, http://jobsearch.about.com/od/infointerviews/a/infointervquest.htm

In the context of the informational interview or in a follow-up thank you letter, a future planner can ask whether job shadowing the professional would be possible or whether the agency would allow the candidate to volunteer in order to gain a better understanding of the work of the agency and the professionals in it.

Job Shadowing

Job shadowing should be a student's first step on the ladder of increasing experience prior to applying for that first paid job in planning. In fact, prior to applying to an urban planning degree program, students should pursue some sort of job-shadowing opportunity to learn more about what it's really like to be a planner. College students may also want to continue to explore their selected field through shadowing experiences. Ideally, a student should pursue multiple shadowing experiences in different planning settings.

Job shadowing is typically a short-term experience, ranging from an afternoon to a few days or, at most, a couple of weeks. The "future planner" follows a professional throughout the day or week, observing quietly. Between meetings or during other breaks, the future planner might ask questions, and typically the planning professional is eager to explain to the student what the student is observing. For example, a planner may meet with a developer or property owner interested in building something new and needs to discuss the limits imposed by the city's zoning code. After the meeting, the student might be curious to know why the zoning code requires that the building be no more than four stories tall, or what a special use permit is and why it is required for the activity that the landowner wants to undertake on the property.

Because an employer does not need to pay, train, or supervise a student doing a shadowing experience, employers are often willing to open their offices to show an interested young person what the job is really like. In planning, AICP-certified planners are expected, under their code of ethics, to "contribute time and resources to the professional development of students, interns, beginning professionals, and other colleagues." Hosting an occasional student in a job shadow is one way that professionals can meet this goal.

But where to begin? The first step is to identify a planning agency or firm to visit as part of the shadowing experience. One easy place to begin is in the planning department in a student's hometown. Local officials often welcome the opportunity to show a student what they do and how their work affects local residents. In addition to the city or town where a student lives, a student can explore job shadowing with the county planning department, the regional planning commission, or a district office of a state department of transportation, natural resources, or environmental protection.

Another resource for students seeking job-shadowing experience is the state chapter of the American Planning Association. Members of an APA chapter are often eager to tell people about their work and to interest people in the profession as a career. Some chapter web pages also have listings of their members that allow a student to scan for different types of planning agencies.

Other planning-related organizations can also be useful resources. The Congress for New Urbanism attracts planners interested in urban design issues. State and local chapters of the CNU are located in many areas of the country (www.cnu.org/chapters). The Urban and Regional Information Science Association offers programs and networking opportunities with planners involved in the application of Geographic Information Systems, a mapping and analysis tool used by planners.

ORGANIZATIONS FOR STUDENT PLANNERS

American Planning Association, www.planning.org

Chapters in almost every state and in some metropolitan areas. The APA web page provides links to all of its chapters and sections at: www.planning.org/chapters.

Planning Student Organizations, www.planning.org/students/pso.htm

APA encourages all planning education programs to form student organizations that are affiliated with the APA. Typically, the state or local chapter of APA will provide some limited financial support for the organization to support extracurricular educational programs.

Planners Network, www.plannersnetwork.org

Planners Network describes its mission as promoting fundamental change in our political and economic systems. It publishes *Progressive Planner* magazine four times a year, as well as the *Student Disorientation Guide,* "with articles that challenge current planning and educational paradigms."

Congress for the New Urbanism, http://www.cnu.org/

Promotes the principles of New Urbanist–style development as an alternative to sprawl. Members include planners, developers, architects, engineers, public officials, and others interested in promoting more compact and lively neighborhoods and commercial districts.

Urban and Regional Information Systems Association, www.urisa.org

Members are professionals who work with spatial information like Geographic Information Systems. A large proportion of members work in the public sector as GIS professionals.

To make the most of a job-shadowing experience, a student should plan to reflect on the experience. Maintaining a journal about job-shadowing experiences allows a student to formulate questions that might be further explored in subsequent pre-professional experiences.

Volunteer Experience

Chapter 2 described the benefits of volunteer work as a way of learning about different social and cultural groups as part of a student's preparation for being a culturally competent planner. Volunteer experience is also important as a way of developing a resume that will help land that first professional position. Moreover, many scholarship applications require candidates to describe their volunteer experiences, so volunteering can help to pay for education.

Verifying actual conditions in the community, such as the width of a bike lane, is time-consuming but often essential to the creation of a realistic plan. This is a task that an intern or volunteer may be asked to complete. COURTESY OF DAN BURDEN, GLATTING JACKSON.

Volunteering may involve working alongside professionals but engaging in tasks that do not require specialized education. In planning agencies and organizations, a number of tasks engage volunteers in planning-related work. Some examples include:

- Photographing the front of every building along a commercial street or in a particular neighborhood to document the physical condition of buildings as part of the planning process or as part of the redevelopment process in marketing the area to potential developers;

- Collecting basic planning information, such as counting the number of cars using a specific parking lot at different times of day or recording how people are using a local park;

- Contacting residents and businesses to encourage them to participate in upcoming planning meetings in order to help shape the future of their community;

- Producing newsletters or web pages about recent or upcoming activities in the planning department or in neighborhood associations.

WHERE CAN YOU VOLUNTEER IN PLANNING

- Local planning departments
- Regional or state planning agencies or specialized departments related to planning, such as transportation (state department of transportation, regional planning commissions, regional transportation authorities); environmental protection, agriculture, or economic development
- Economic development corporations and community development corporations
- Housing authorities and redevelopment authorities
- Sewer and water agencies
- Neighborhood associations
- Business Improvement Districts
- Business associations for particular geographic areas
- Historic preservation commissions
- Environmental organizations, especially those interested in water pollution and watershed protection, air quality, habitat conservation, and climate change
- Land use organizations, such as 1000 Friends of Oregon

Typically, once a volunteer has proven reliable (shows up when expected) and industrious, a volunteer may be given increasingly complex tasks, leading eventually to an internship.

Internships

No future planner should leave school to embark on her first professional job without having an internship experience. Internship experiences can reduce the amount of time required to land that first job and allow the candidate to obtain a job that involves greater responsibility and a faster ramp to promotions and pay raises.

While anyone can engage in informational interviews, do volunteer work in planning, or job shadowing, an internship generally requires that a person be enrolled as a student. Internships can be paid or unpaid. In addition, students may be able to receive academic credit for the experience, if offered at their university, or may simply do the internship to gain practical experience.

Interning is understood by employers as part of the student's training to become a professional. Because of the training provided by the employer in exchange for the work, internships are often exempt from fringe benefit and salary requirements that apply to other employees. Both parties—the student and the employer—are getting something valuable from the relationship. The student obtains training and the employer gets work at a reduced cost from what would be required to hire a nonstudent.

No planning student should leave college or graduate school without doing an internship. Internships are the steppingstone to a successful professional career.

A planning intern becomes an integral part of the planning team.
CHESTER COUNTY PLANNING COMMISSION.

Why Internships?

❯ My first planning job as a planning intern my junior year was a very good learning experience. I did a comp plan for a very small town of 130 people, Minnesott Beach, North Carolina.

Richard Eberhardt Hall, AICP, Maryland Secretary of Planning

❯ During my University of Denver education, I was lucky to be placed in internships in the Denver City Planning Office and, during my last semester, at a county planning office south of Denver. At the very time that I was graduating, an opening for zoning inspector came open where I was interning, and I applied for and achieved the position. I then worked as a zoning inspector and also a development reviewer during my three years at this county planning office.

Wayne Schuster, AICP, CM, Director, Office of Planning and Environmental Services, Maryland Aviation Administration

Planning directors often will not hire permanent employees unless they have some prior experience. Through an internship, a student sees how the skills and knowledge taught in graduate school are applied, but—more importantly—learns another set of skills and knowledge that cannot be taught at the university. For example, how should a planner talk to an irate property owner who has just learned that a zoning regulation prohibits him from adding a new family room to his home? How do you behave in a city council meeting, especially when a sensitive, politically charged issue is being decided? Where do you go in the city bureaucracy to find out why a new stoplight approved for a busy intersection was never installed? How do you negotiate with a developer to make a proposed project more accessible by foot or by bike, even if the zoning code does not specifically require the changes you seek?

Interns have the opportunity to observe more seasoned planners in action and ask questions later about why the planner approached an issue or an individual in a certain way. This opportunity to learn vicariously and to practice skills in a real-world setting makes an enormous difference, increasing the confidence of the beginning planner and his or her future employer.

Cooperative Education

Cooperative education is a structured educational strategy integrating classroom studies with learning through productive work experiences in a field related to a student's academic or career goals (National Commission, no date). "Co-ops" are similar to the awarding of academic credits for internship work, but more formalized and, in the planning field, much less common. The only planning program in the United States that requires a cooperative education experience is the University of Cincinnati's Bachelor of Urban Planning Program. Students in this program alternate between work and school on a year-round schedule and graduate with at least 18 months of work experience (University of Cincinnati, no date).

Peace Corps and AmeriCorps VISTA

Volunteering through the Peace Corps or AmeriCorps VISTA is an excellent way to get valuable experience, learn invaluable skills, and get a leg up on the competition in the planning job market. The accompanying figure summarizes opportunities for planners in each of these programs. Volunteers in both programs receive a small living allowance to cover basic needs like food, housing, clothing, and transportation. AmeriCorps members who complete their service also receive a small education award. A network of universities provides fellowships and other programs benefiting returning Peace Corps volunteers going on to graduate school. Because of the education benefits associated with volunteering in the Peace Corps or AmeriCorps, many people take this opportunity after graduating with a bachelor's degree but before going on for a master's degree. Some students, however, complete the graduate degree before entering the Peace Corps or AmeriCorps so that they have a larger set of tools with which to assist local communities that they serve.

PEACE CORPS AND AMERICORPS VISTA OPPORTUNITIES FOR PLANNERS

Peace Corps, www.peacecorps.gov

The Peace Corps places volunteers in hundreds of countries in Central and South America, Eastern Europe, Africa, and Asia. Those interested in gaining experience in urban planning may be involved in assisting local people with small business development, community development, and the environment. Volunteers conduct community outreach and needs assessments. "Projects include assessing the impact of planned activities or economic and environmental development on communities, planning infrastructure for primary and secondary cities, planning and controlling budgets, and coordinating activities between governmental organizations and communities" (Peace Corps, "Urban and Regional Development," no date). Peace Corps volunteers also work with communities to protect the environment, "working on projects such as establishing forest conservation plans and developing alternatives to wood as a fuel source" (Peace Corps, "Environment," no date).

AmeriCorps VISTA, www.americorps.gov

AmeriCorps VISTA is often referred to as the "domestic Peace Corps." AmeriCorps VISTA volunteers work anywhere in the United States where people living in poverty need assistance building local capacity to solve their problems. Volunteers interested in urban planning may work in urban or rural locations. Assignments could include working on housing development with Habitat for Humanity, working with watershed groups to clean up polluted waterways, assisting a local organization to set up a micro-enterprise loan program, or organizing at the community level for better access to healthy food.

Peace Corps Leads to Planning Career

How did you become interested in planning?

❯ It was purely by accident. I joined the Peace Corps in Africa and ended up doing a planner's job, working as a community organizer doing interviews and mapping projects. Sometimes I would be involved in the design of a village project; sometimes the most important issues would be related to public health such as pre- and neo-natal health care and AIDS prevention. I would always ask villagers: What can we do to improve conditions in this area? And the answer from mothers and grandmothers would often be: our lives would be better if we didn't have to carry our trash outside the village to the designated dumping area. So I would work with the mayor of the closest prefect to find trashcans and push carts, and we'd arrange to have a guy go around and pick up the trash.

Nicole Lacoste, Law Office of Nicole Lacoste

Networking to Break the Ice

Several of the strategies described in this chapter require the aspiring planner to call a stranger and ask for a meeting. That can be scary to a lot of high school and college students, especially if the call is truly "cold," meaning that you have no connection with the person you are calling.

"Networking" is about expanding your circle of friends and acquaintances by meeting people, learning what and who they know, and finding opportunities to meet the people they know. Young people often begin simply by talking to family members—your mother may have a college friend who is a professional planner. When you call you can introduce yourself as "Laurie's son" and immediately have a common point of connection.

Finding ways to meet people and identify shared interests is a valuable skill that will benefit any person in any field of work. As mentioned previously, one of the best ways of networking in planning is to get involved in organizations that are created to serve the needs of planners.

Volunteering to be a student representative or to do service for the organization—helping to produce newsletters or web content, for example—can introduce you to professionals who can help you "get your foot in the door" for that first information interview—or even for an internship opportunity. There is no better way to build successful relationships with professionals than to be helpful, responsive, and cheerful in assisting organizational board members and other volunteers to achieve their goals. In the process, you will also build communication skills and a commitment to public service that is central to the ethics of the planning profession.

The littlest planners. No one is too young to get involved in planning. These youngsters are expressing their preferences at a public meeting. Increasingly, planners are reaching out to their communities' youngest residents to understand how they experience the neighborhood. Attending planning workshops is a terrific way to learn about planning and to network with professional planners. COURTESY OF DAN BURDEN, GLATTING JACKSON.

CAREER LADDERS: MOVING AHEAD FROM THAT FIRST JOB

After landing that first precious job, what's next? Chapter 4 provides a lot of the answer to that question. One more comment about "getting experience" is needed. Moving from that entry-level position through a successful career with increasing responsibility and salary should be done purposively but with an eye out for opportunities and those once-in-a-lifetime chances. Many of the planners who contributed to this book comment about the role of luck and serendipity in shaping their careers. Reading their stories, one immediately sees that few of their careers moved in a completely straight line. Some started in planning and then branched out into law, public health, Geographic Information Systems, or community organizing. Others started in any number of areas outside of planning and found themselves drawn in by a job opportunity, an influential mentor, or a fascination and desire to learn something new or make a difference for communities in need.

In the next chapter, planners from all levels of practice and many different specialization areas talk about their work and some of the choices that they made along the way.

④ Planners' Many Paths

PLANNING IS A DIVERSE FIELD. Planners fill many roles and work in a range of organizations. Some planners work for local government, others for private firms. Some planners focus on a limited set of problems, such as transportation or economic development, while others are generalists who work on many different issues during the course of a week.

This chapter provides a forum for planners to explain how they came into the profession and to describe their experiences as planners. They talk candidly about their educational and career choices, as well as the challenges and rewards of working in the field.

Many Paths into a Planning Career

Planners take many paths into the profession. As with other occupations, some planners learn about planning from a parent or sister or uncle who is in the field. Many, like Alexander Bond, seem to fall into the profession. Some planners are attracted to the visual side of the practice. Others are especially attracted by the analytic side of the work. Some, like Megan Cummings and Shannon Yadsko, find urban planning to offer a terrific blend of both their creative and visual talents that, at the same time, makes use of their logical and analytic abilities.

Almost all planners are drawn to the profession's focus on making the world a better place. Shannon Yadsko described her favorite thing about her job this way:

The most satisfying part of my job is feeling like I'm making the world a better place by creating communities, and feeling like I am contributing to the quality of life of others.

Planners find great personal satisfaction in their work and the relationships they form with people in the communities where they work.

Entering the Field

MEGAN CUMMINGS, AICP

Transportation Planner and Director of Business Development, Gorove/Slade Associates

Washington, DC

Why did you become a planner?

❯ I had an interest in architecture and economics while in college, and planning was a great mix of the two disciplines. I had an interest in my environment and surroundings, specifically with regard to transportation, and I realized along the way that I could make that my profession.

How did you decide to become a planner?

❯ Like so many others, I stumbled into it. My best friend in high school always knew she wanted to be a planner, but I wanted to be an architect because there was no way I thought that I would have the patience to work in the public sector, which, at that point, was all that I thought that planning was.

After being out of college about three years, I decided that I wanted to get a master's degree in a related field. I did the research and looked into landscape architecture and real estate development. Someone suggested I look into planning. Once I realized that planning was not just a public sector career, I was sold. My entire how-I-came-to-be-where-I-am story is about one door after another opening up in ways that still amaze me to this day.

All policies need to be communicated to citizens in some way, but sometimes we are too reliant on signs. Transportation planners may be asked to identify alternatives to more signs, such as pavement markings or pavement configurations that make illegal parking impossible. MEGAN J. CUMMINGS, AICP.

How did you choose a school for your master's degree?

❯ I did a lot of research. I knew I was interested in transportation and preferred policy to design, so I looked into programs with transportation specialties geared toward policy and analysis. Despite that, my application process was a bit haphazard. I applied to five very different schools (four on the West Coast and one local to DC, where I grew up), and three of them did not accept me, so the choice was almost made for me.

I ultimately chose the University of Southern California. The number one reason was that I wanted to return to the East Coast after school, and the school had a great reputation.

Actually, now that I think about it, the number one reason was because I got a great scholarship. That put the price of a private school education within the range of out-of-state tuition, which as a DC resident I would have paid no matter where I at-

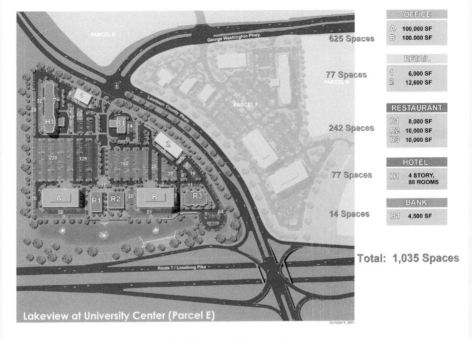

OFFICE	
A	100,000 SF
B	100,000 SF

RETAIL	
1	6,000 SF
2	12,600 SF

RESTAURANT	
R1	8,000 SF
R2	10,000 SF
R3	10,000 SF

HOTEL	
H1	4 STORY, 88 ROOMS

BANK	
B1	4,500 SF

625 Spaces

77 Spaces

242 Spaces

77 Spaces

14 Spaces

Total: 1,035 Spaces

Lakeview at University Center (Parcel E)

AM Peak – 11:00 AM

Planning for new development must feature accommodation for the methods of transportation people will use to get there. In most parts of the country cars and trucks are the primary means of transportation, so adequate parking is essential. Although many communities require a minimum number of parking spaces per building area or capacity, some communities are beginning to set maximums instead to prevent an excess of paved parking lots and to encourage shared parking. The transportation planner uses images like this to illustrate the expected supply and demand for parking. GOROVE/SLADE ASSOCIATES, INC.

tended. And finally, I chose USC because of the well-known Trojan network of alumni and friends that I knew would be a valuable asset in the future. I had learned by then that who you know is just as important as what you know, and that has paid off tremendously.

How did you decide where you wanted to work and how you were going to pursue your job?

❯ Again, I did my research. My specialty is parking, so, one year, I asked every exhibitor at a California American Planning Association conference whom they hire for parking services. I literally went

down each row and asked every person in a booth. They all gave me the same answer, so I knew where I wanted to be. I knew the firm I wanted to join, but I thought it would be years after school before I could get the job I wanted within that firm.

Then, by one of those serendipitous events, I was inspired to pursue a job by a person I met at a cocktail party. He told me a story about going after a job in Paris at a young age, a job that everyone said was impossible for him to get. The next day I perfected my resume and emailed a professor who gave me an introduction to the firm. Within two weeks, I had a job offer for after graduation, with three months to spare.

And after a long search, I was able to find the man from the cocktail party to thank him. He told me to "pay it forward," so I have been trying to inspire other people ever since. Where would I be had I not met him?

Given your experience, how would you counsel someone who is interested in planning as a career or is entering the job market for the first time?

❯ Here are my quick tips:

■ Take as broad a course load as possible, and that goes for graduate school as well as undergraduate. If you do not have any formal planning education, I would strongly urge you to attend planning school.

■ Take advantage of all the school has to offer, especially field trips or study abroad programs. Learning how other people live is vital, not only professionally but personally.

■ Talk to as many professionals in as many different sectors of planning as you can.

■ Always keep an open mind. This goes for the people you meet, your career, your education, and your goals. Sometimes the best direction is unplanned.

■ Do your research—about schools, jobs, your location—then be honest with yourself about what you want to do.

■ Be knowledgeable about current events. Read Planetizen, Cyburbia, the APA website, and local development blogs to really get a feel for the controversial issues as well as successes going on in the community where you want to work.

Using Your Analytic and Creative Talents

SHANNON YADSKO, AICP

Planner, PB PlaceMaking

Washington, D.C.

Why did you become a planner?

❯ I was very math- and science-oriented growing up and entered college in a civil engineering program. However, after a year, I felt like I wasn't being creative enough, so I switched to the architecture school, where eventually I felt like I wasn't being analytical enough. But there I learned of urban planning and found it to be the perfect balance of analysis and creativity. After taking an Intro to Planning course, I knew I had found what I was meant to do.

How did you choose a school for your planning degree?

❯ For my undergraduate degree in planning, it was just luck that I was at a school that had a planning program. For my graduate degree, I was deciding between staying at the University of Virginia (UVa) or attending a large-city school such as Columbia University or New York University. I decided to stay at UVa because I already knew and respected the faculty, and I could complete the two-year program in one year because of my previous work.

How would you counsel someone who is interested in planning as a career and is entering the job market for the first time?

❭ I recommend internships and finding a mentor—two things that established the connections that are indispensable in this field.

What type of work are you doing now?

❭ I work on a lot of background research and initial conditions assessments for projects. I use a variety of research sources to identify the needs and opportunities in an area, then I analyze the existing conditions to find the topics that should be considered for in-depth focus. I work on a variety of projects, including transit station area planning, long-term comprehensive planning, downtown revitalization planning, and GIS.

I read a lot, spend a lot of time analyzing, then putting my knowledge together in a way that's easy to use. My job focuses on what a community should strive to be in 20 years, then working backwards to make sure that the community has the resources available to meet those goals.

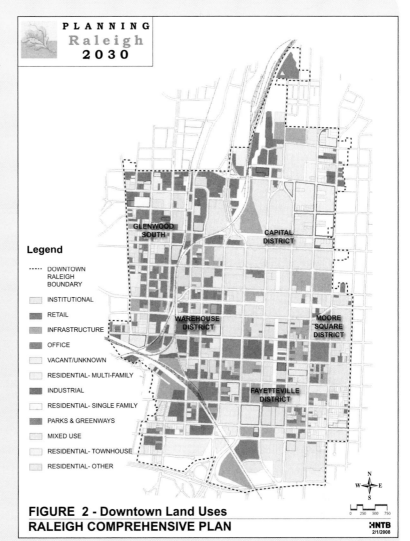

FIGURE 2 - Downtown Land Uses
RALEIGH COMPREHENSIVE PLAN

Comprehensive plans establish a vision for the future of the community and typically address a wide range of topics, such as transportation, housing, economic development, public facilities, and land use. A map describing future land uses, such as this one for downtown Raleigh, North Carolina, is common to all comprehensive plans. Municipal staff and officials use this map to guide their review of development proposals and is part of an effort to revitalize downtown Raleigh. SHANNON YADSKO/HNTB CORPORATION.

Applying a Talent for Mapping

ALEXANDER BOND, AICP

Associate in Research, University of South Florida Center for Urban Transportation Research

Tampa, Florida

Why did you become a planner?

❯ My undergraduate degree was in geography. To be honest, I fell into geography because I wasn't accepted to pharmacy school. But after three years of working with Geographic Information Systems (GIS) in undergrad, I saw that there was the possibility of actually finding a job with my liberal arts degree if I moved into a field that applied GIS to the real world.

The Urban and Regional Planning program at the University of Florida (UF) has a strong GIS component, so it kind of followed to enroll in that master's program. There are far more jobs called "urban planner" than there are jobs titled "geographer."

The policy and administrative track that I've taken in my career began with experiences I had in student government. While I was a student senator, I helped to expand the off-campus bus system. My master's thesis was actually an outgrowth of my work in that area.

Out of school, why did you pursue an internship at the Urban Land Institute?

❯ Long ago I realized that my job needed to have more meaning than making a profit (usually for someone else!). I also knew that I tended to have a holistic view of things, so working for a local

government seemed too small. So for my first job I looked at nonprofit organizations based out of Washington, DC. ULI was a great choice because it exposed me to virtually every side of planning. In the space of one year I worked on downtown redevelopment in Rochester and light rail in Dallas, and co-wrote a book on affordable housing.

I applied to the published internship program on the ULI website. The faculty member I worked for at UF knew some people from her volunteer professional positions, so she was a valuable reference.

How did you make the transition back to Florida?

❯ Before moving back here, my last job was essentially as a lobbyist for Metropolitan Planning Organizations (MPO). MPOs are agencies required to exist by the federal government to plan for transportation improvements on a regional basis. I ran the transportation program at the national level, so I was pretty well known, if only because I sent out a weekly newsletter to all MPOs. When family reasons brought me home to Tampa Bay, I was informed of this position at the local university. This position is largely funded by grants from the Florida MPO Advisory Council, which is the state-level counterpart of my prior job.

What are you doing now?

❯ I perform research work for a variety of grant sponsors. My current sponsors are the Florida MPO Advisory Council, the Florida Department of Community Affairs, and the Federal Highway Administration (FHWA). Projects are usually one to two years in length and address a predefined research problem. Some projects, such as the one from FHWA, simply say to produce a research report due in March 2010. Others, such as the MPOAC, are broken into smaller tasks, such as producing a summary of the state legislative session.

My job has a very flat administrative structure. Most planning agencies are like this. There is one person who is my supervisor, but there isn't much micro-management of my daily or even weekly tasks. Planning agencies seem to place a lot of professional trust in the people working there. I consider this a big advantage of this field.

Do you have advice for people considering planning as a career?

❯ From the earliest stages of your career, build in time to participate in professional associations. It allows you to connect with colleagues, keep up on the latest developments in the field, and shape state and national policy. I have tried to spend 5 hours a month (3% of the month) serving professional groups. If your employer objects to committing this much time, you are working for a short-sighted organization. There are a variety of groups to choose from; just pick one and get involved. I am involved with the American Planning Association and the Transportation Research Board.

I'd also like to warn people against becoming planners who focus solely on technical analysis tools like demand modeling and GIS. These are great tools and wonderful skills to have, but this field is progressing quickly and being overrun by allied fields. Software is constantly evolving to become more user-friendly, which lowers the barrier to entry, and consequently diminishes job prospects

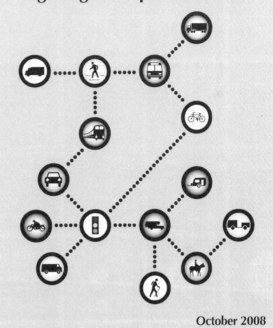

The 2008 Review of Florida's MPO Long Range Transportation Plans

October 2008

Transportation planners predict future demand for all types of travel, and they work to identify the facilities and infrastructure that will be required to meet that demand. As a researcher, Alexander Bond studies transportation planning methods and practices. This study evaluated long-term transportation plans across the state to compare their policies and assess their effectiveness as communication tools. ALEXANDER BOND

over the long term. Engineering grad schools across the country are churning out software specialists, and when it comes to advanced computer software operations, a planner cannot hope to compete with an engineer. Planners earn their keep by injecting the human side into government decisions.

Why did you become a planner?

❯ I was born to be an urban planner. If there was such a thing as being genetically predisposed, then I got the gene. Growing up in Brooklyn, I was obsessed with cities—drawing them, visiting them, studying them, and mapping them.

In elementary school, I spent hours drawing elaborate cityscapes on my Etch-a-Sketch, memorizing the shapes and populations of each state and country, and reading the world atlas the way other kids read comic books.

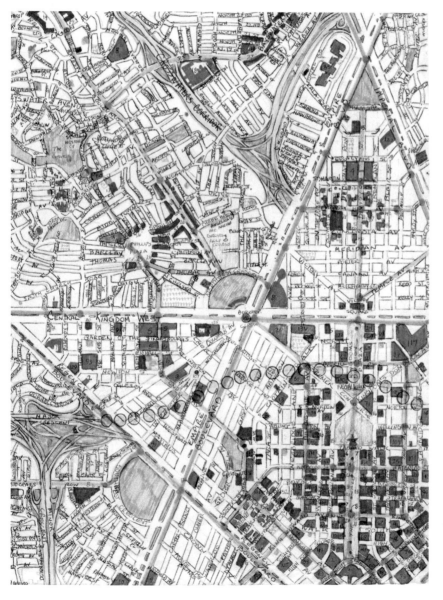

Many planners have fond memories of childhood games creating imaginary cities, but few were as focused as Barry Miller in their youth. Decades before he helped lead the comprehensive planning process for Washington, DC, Barry created this detailed map of a place he called Ocean City. BARRY MILLER.

When I was 11, I organized an anti-pollution club comprised of 20 neighborhood preteens. We wrote a book called *Pollution: It Stinks* and organized neighborhood recycling drives. By my teenage years, I had begun creating elaborate maps of fictitious cities, complete with thousands of named streets, mass transit diagrams, and even imaginary travel brochures and census reports. Some of the maps were over 100 square feet, with intricate detail on each panel.

When I was in junior high school, we moved from New York to a rural part of Connecticut. At that point, I designed an entire country (located in the Pacific Ocean midway between Hawaii and California), complete with wire-bound road atlases for more than a dozen imaginary cities. The atlases included diagrams of shopping malls (listing all the stores), detailed skyline drawings, and narrative reports on key issues. I still have these atlases and keep thinking I should scan them for my website.

Fortunately, my teenage obsession with city planning was put to good use. When I was 15 or 16, I started earning extra income helping my father's business associates by preparing sales opportunity maps for major U.S. cities. I planned their travel routes to sales appointments, and created adhesive dot maps showing sales trends in major U.S. metro areas. I was also able to take independent study classes in high school and earn English and Social Studies credits for my imaginary city designs.

Strangely enough, I entered college at 17 as a biology major, with the intent of becoming an optometrist. I think I was trying to fulfill my parents' wishes ("my-son-the-doctor"), and honestly did not realize that my hobby/obsession might be a legitimate career. It was only a matter of time before I would find my true calling.

Barry Miller, AICP, Planning Consultant, Berkeley, California

❭ Like a lot of people, I fell into it. I took some geography classes and was equally interested in urban and environmental geography. Going to college in Pittsburgh was an incredible urban experience. I became intrigued by city and neighborhood issues so much I double-majored in geography and in urban studies.

When I applied to graduate school I still had my sights set on environmental geography, specializing in energy conservation and natural resource management, but two things happened. Federal policy drastically changed in 1981 and most of those jobs dried up. The second event was when my advisor in grad school convinced me to take his land use planning class my first semester. As part of the class, we conducted background data collection and analysis for a neighborhood plan next to campus. I was hooked.

Sue Schwartz, FAICP, City of Greensboro, North Carolina

❭ A college professor encouraged me to pursue a career in urban planning to merge my interests in public policy, community development, and local government management. After college, I went to work as a community planner working in community development, economic development, and neighborhood development projects. Then after receiving a master's degree in planning, I transitioned into a senior level city planning position.

Kathie Ebaugh, AICP, Bell David Planning Group

❭ I was interested in problem solving and had good analytic skills, so I went into civil engineering as an undergrad. Partway through my undergraduate years, I became more interested in the application of engineering in society, so I double-majored in public policy.

My first job was in transportation planning, but I grew more interested in the connections between issues, so I broadened my focus from transportation to include land use and environmental planning.

John Hodges-Copple, Triangle J Council of Governments

Why did you become a planner? (Continued)

❯ The usual answer is "to make the world a better place" and that would be my answer too (not too creative, I admit, but sincere), except I would substitute "community" for world.

I grew up in Alexandria, Virginia, and loved everything political. The democratic process (the one with the little "d") is an open, organized way to foster debate and bring about change that can benefit many. I am fascinated by the physical realm too and how people use space.

What better way to get to be in both worlds than through planning? I got an undergraduate degree in political science, became curious about why some communities felt vibrant and alive, and went to graduate school in planning to find out.

Marianne Gardner, Fairfax County, Virginia

❯ In my undergrad years, I was bouncing from major to major without any firm direction. Then one day a geography professor asked me if I'd ever considered urban planning as a profession. I said "urban what?" He explained and offered to create a new curriculum

Sometimes a planner needs to find creative ways to communicate and provide perspective on complex issues. To illustrate the land consumed by a proposed suburban freeway interchange, the Triangle J Council of Governments (a regional planning organization) superimposed the footprint of the interchange on downtown Raleigh, North Carolina. TRIANGLE J COUNCIL OF GOVERNMENTS.

at University of Wisconsin–Whitewater that allowed me to be the first student to graduate with an emphasis degree in urban and regional planning.

If not for this professor, I would probably be walking the beach and making $12 an hour as a marine biologist. Wait . . . where did I go wrong?

Brad Steinke, City of Apache Junction, Arizona

❭ I became fascinated with architecture in grammar school and got a degree in architecture from the University of Michigan. I went into the Navy after school, and as I reached the end of my tour, it was obvious that I was way behind all of my classmates.

I spent part of my tour in Vietnam as construction advisor to the Vietnamese and later selected and designed five naval bases for U.S. forces. I decided to apply for a graduate degree in city planning and was accepted at the University of North Carolina. In those days, it was a quite natural transition from architecture to city planning.

Lane Kendig, Kendig/Keast Collaborative

❭ While I was in graduate school at the University of Michigan, I had the opportunity to work on a resettlement and relocation project for a proposed dam on the Mekong River in Laos and Thailand. Through the project, I had to deal with the eco-

Park planning requires time in the field studying the site. Here Richard Sussman tours the site of the Preah Vihear Temple in Cambodia to find ways to make it more accessible to visitors. COURTESY OF THE NATIONAL PARK SERVICE.

nomic and social ramifications of moving a lot of people, looking at what would happen when the place became inundated and what measures could be taken to address those impacts. Although the project did not proceed, it led to other work in planning and sparked my interest in the field.

Richard Sussman, National Park Service

Who Influenced You?

Planners must interact with many people to conceptualize and execute their work. From colleagues to community members to clients, planners must collaborate to gather information, brainstorm, structure and frame their ideas, and implement their concepts and recommendations.

Along the way, planners learn from each other and apply those lessons to other projects, sharing their wisdom along the way.

Here practitioners tell about who has influenced them and how they have applied these lessons to their work. Some planners were influenced by some of the great past planners. Others were influenced by experiences along the way. Most planners have had a couple of strong mentors who shaped their approach to planning or who gave the planner sound advice that has stuck to this day.

Who influenced each of the planners is less important than the insights that each planner gleaned from their experiences with their personal mentors.

How have others influenced the way you think about planning?

❭ Many people have influenced me:

Jane Jacobs, whose books captured me as a student in England and then was suddenly there in Toronto, where I was.

Sir Peter Hall, who has combined an extraordinarily deep understanding of the way cities work with senior real-time planning responsibilities.

And, not to forget, John Lennon, who reminds us that "life is what happens while you're making other plans."

Joe Berridge, Urban Strategies

❭ In my formative years, my dad sold World Book Encyclopedias, which meant our house was always full of encyclopedias, atlases, and statistical abstracts. I always had multiple sets of encyclopedias at my disposal and I got a new world atlas every year.

He brought me along on business trips occasionally and I'd do dispatching and map work for him and his colleagues. My parents provided me with the scrap paper and markers to draw my cities and bought me a typewriter so my fictitious city travel books could look more professional. I always had a huge supply of recycled encyclopedias that I could cut up with scissors for illustrations. I'm grateful that I came of age before the digital and Internet era—being creative was more fun then!

Barry Miller, AICP, Planning Consultant, Berkeley, California

❭ There have been so many people who have influenced my career, starting with those whom I have never met but whose research or writing turned on a light bulb for me. There were those who I studied from a distance, either peers or elected officials, who served unknowingly as a role model or a "what not to do" example.

Lisa Hollingsworth-Segedy, American Rivers

❭ Dr. Robert Reich, dean emeritus of the School of Landscape Architecture at Louisiana State University, has been an inspiration to me. His incredible commitment to the school, to his students, and to the profession has always encouraged me to do and accomplish more.

I have also been influenced by Andres Duany and Peter Calthorpe. Both have given me new ways of thinking about planning and have inspired me to expand the type of planning that we do.

Elizabeth "Boo" Thomas, ASLA, Center for Planning Excellence

Maps get people interested in the planning process in a way that words alone cannot, and images like this have the potential to generate excitement about the future. This vision was created by Urban Strategies as part of a detailed planning effort to revitalize Toronto, Ontario's downtown waterfront. © URBAN STRATEGIES INC®.

❯ Dr. Owen Furuseth, my advisor from the University of North Carolina at Charlotte. What Owen said that has stuck most with me is that planning must begin at the grassroots level. To paraphrase a political slogan, "It's the people, stupid."

Early in my career, my mentor was Bonnie Estes, now an assistant planning director for the Durham City/County Planning Department. The lesson from Bonnie I still live is that it is okay to have fun and show your enthusiasm. That's not being unprofessional and is actually an asset to your job.

Finally, I have to say something about the many planners I have met across our state and across the country in my experience with APA and the American Institute of Certified Planners (AICP). What has struck me over and over again is the great work good planners are doing, with very little recognition or fanfare and sometimes at their professional peril. It makes me proud to share their company and humble and grateful that I've had an extraordinary opportunity to learn from them.

Sue Schwartz, FAICP, City of Greensboro

❯ Researching the lives of civic leaders in 1940s Philadelphia—and the example of someone like Ed Bacon—inspired me to think about making an impact on a particular place over a long period of time. In 1947, Bacon organized the Better Philadelphia Exhibition to capture the minds of the public and help rebuild the city after the war. It was a broad vision, and it included participatory workshops for schoolchildren and other innovative approaches to public involvement. Bacon also dabbled in all sorts of minutiae related to the aesthetics of development projects. He may have sometimes been wrong, and he could certainly be arrogant. But I was impressed by the milieu of 1940s Philadelphia, of civic leaders aspiring for a better future, and how Bacon and some of the others continued to remain engaged for so long.

Amy Menzer, Dundalk Renaissance Corporation

Among the lessons from Amy Menzer's role models is this observation: sometimes it is necessary to gain control of real estate to gain control of a community's future. Amy is working to improve Dundalk, Maryland, by improving its housing stock. This renovated townhome now features pervious pavement for its driveway to reduce stormwater runoff. DUNDALK RENAISSANCE CORP.

❯ There is no question that Franklin Wood was my major influence. He was a rarity in the profession. He recognized talent and let his staff develop programs. This approach is in contrast with planning directors who rigidly and politically dictate an agency's work, stifle good planning decisions, or make decisions that are intended not to offend elected officials, which often means dropping anything controversial and, therefore, not making meaningful advances in planning.

Lane Kendig, Kendig/Keast Collaborative

How have others influenced the way you think about planning? (Continued)

❭ My first planning director was the first primary influence of my career. He was a civil engineer who recognized that planning is a team effort that blends the skills of many people to respond to a community's needs.

Howard Geisler, Geisler/Smith Associates

❭ If you want one person, that person without question is former Hampton City Manager Bob O'Neill. He was the one who taught me that, although I came to my job with planning skills, I worked for the citizens of Hampton, not for the "planning profession."

Planning training is just where one starts the job; the trick is to use the knowledge, skills, and abilities you have gained to craft something that works with and for the citizens. Put another way, I don't work for a textbook; I work for a community.

I was heavily influenced by the community, too. Seeing neighborhoods through the eyes of people who actually live and raise their families there helped me to move from seeing neighborhoods as physical places toward understanding them as communities.

Joan Kennedy, City of Hampton, Virginia

❭ Don Edwards has played a major role in my career, and I have the deepest respect for him. He is the founder, principal, and CEO of Justice and Sustainability Associates, in Washington, DC. He taught me about the field of public participation. He taught me about effective practices in the field. He taught me about the art of facilitation (he is the best facilitator I have ever known), and he gave me a chance to speak up and share my ideas with our clients. He taught me—and showed me—how to create an environment where everyone feels comfortable sharing their opinion, and where everyone feels valued.

Corinna Moebius, Bordercross Consulting Group

❭ Lane Kendig, for defending the suburbs and, especially, for creating systems to define and measure community character, quantifying monotony, and advancing the profession within its zoning, traffic, software, and environmental realms.

Mary Means, for inventing the Main Street Program and her ability to "suss out" the psychology of communities where she works.

Improving urban neighborhoods is often about training and empowerment to help residents get engaged in the future of the community. Planners need to establish relationships with residents, both to understand their needs and to gain their trust. Here Joan Kennedy celebrates completion of a "Neighborhood College" training course with residents. CITY OF HAMPTON NEIGHBORHOOD OFFICE.

Paul Tischler, for unapologetically insisting that it's just fine to make a lot of money as a consultant while still doing meaningful, responsible, and inventive work.

Elaine Van Carmichael, AICP, Economic Stewardship, Inc.

❭ In my formative years, my primary influences were the head of the University of Oregon Planning Department (Dr. David Povey) and an economics professor at the University of Oregon (Dr. Ed Whitelaw). I came from engineering and found a lot of what I got offered in planning school just a little fluffy. With economics I found a solid analytical framework that has influenced my views and work ever since.

Terry Moore, FAICP, ECONorthwest

❭ The architect/planner Le Corbusier, whom I studied for two years, was formative in alerting me to the dangers of individual design genius writ large into the landscape as a plan. The huge power of the international movement in planning and its huge, mostly negative consequences, have sensitized me to the unintended consequences of well-meaning intervention and to the dangers of imposing one's personal preferences (usually unacknowledged) on the public at large. This is not a recipe for inaction but has instead moved me towards explicitly developing scenarios to explore options rather than jumping in with a solution.

Uri Avin, FAICP, PB PlaceMaking

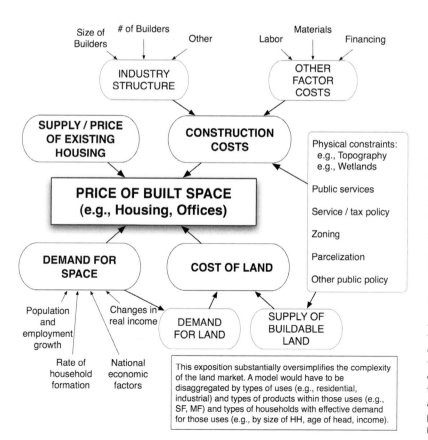

This exposition substantially oversimplifies the complexity of the land market. A model would have to be disaggregated by types of uses (e.g., residential, industrial) and types of products within those uses (e.g., SF, MF) and types of households with effective demand for those uses (e.g., by size of HH, age of head, income).

Planning is a messy process. Well-reasoned planning recommendations based on careful analysis of the problem are sometimes ignored or compromised for purely political reasons. Planners can strengthen their recommendations by citing research findings and providing hard data to illustrate the impacts of each alternative considered. This flowchart tackles the difficult question: "What determines the cost of housing in a community?" Analyses like this can be used to identify and support a strategy to provide affordable housing. ECONORTHWEST.

How have others influenced the way you think about planning? (Continued)

Public involvement is an essential component of the planning process. By bringing residents and stakeholders into the process planners learn about the needs and aspirations of the people who will be affected by the plan. FREGONESE ASSOCIATES, INC.

❯ My mother always has been involved in local politics and public service. Many people do not have public role models in their family or community, so may not be familiar with the options for a government or service career.

David Kuehn, Federal Highway Administration

❯ I have been influenced by various individuals who have been "iconoclasts with a purpose," both inside and outside the transportation planning field. I am completely respectful of persons who will stand up for the objective truth, risk political repercussions to pursue a noble path, and who refuse to accept conventional practice and wisdom simply because it is much easier to play along than to challenge, research, invent, and improve.

J. Richard Kuzmyak, Transportation Consultant LLC

❯ John Fregonese helped me see local planning issues in a longer-term and regional context. He helped me see the value of the relationships you build as you work with stakeholders and clients. John truly listens to people and their ideas before making recommendations. His understanding of the key role of public involvement in planning has also become a foundation for how I approach projects.

Ted Knowlton, AICP, The Planning Center

❯ Betty Deakin and Robert Cervero were my early influences. They both set a standard for rigorous analysis in thinking and talking about the connections between land use and transportation. I got the idealism part right away—it was a rigorous way of thinking about benefits and costs from a planning perspective.

Nat Bottigheimer, Washington Metropolitan Area Transit Authority

❯ Professor Stephen Cohen introduced me to planning and made me realize it was a lot more than urban design. Based on that initial realization, I have been able to combine my interests in economics, political science, history, geography, sociology, engineering, and environmental science.

I have also been influenced by Paul Goldberger, the architecture critic for the *New Yorker*, because he writes about design issues from the perspective of people who live with buildings rather than viewing the buildings as an artistic expression.

Henry Kay, Maryland Transit Administration

❯ Since my focus is alternative transportation, my influences are not planners. Dan Burden, Michael Ronkin, and Mark Fenton have been tremendously inspirational to me. Their work keeps me hoping that we can make a difference in how our communities grow—whether they are shaped for cars or for people.

Kelley Segars, AICP, Knoxville Regional Transportation Planning Organization

Sometimes you just have to get people outside to see their own community up close, even if the temperature is 13 degrees below zero. Here Dan Burden leads a "walkability audit" in Albert Lea, Minnesota. COURTESY OF DAN BURDEN, GLADDING JACKSON.

❯ The people who have had a primary influence on my career are those that, first of all, instilled the importance of values and integrity. While doing environmental education programs, students are an incredible inspiration and I continue to learn in this volunteer role. In the planning arena, there are many that shaped my interests, including leaders such as Arthur H. Carhart and Aldo Leopold, whose early commitment to conservation began a movement about nature and people and that living with the land required an understanding of the interrelationships among species, and the influence of man.

And although the Appalachian Trail did not become the system that Benton MacKaye dreamed, his whole regional planning effort opened the door to concepts beyond the back door. There are so many leading characters that carry weight today.

Alyse Getty, Parsons Infrastructure and Technology, Inc.

❯ Philip Denny Day, my lecturer and undergraduate thesis supervisor at the Department of Regional and Town Planning at the University of Queensland in Australia. Of all the many interesting people I have met in my career, Day has an unparalleled ability to think and express his insights in a compelling and fearless manner.

Whenever I go and sit in the Thomas Jefferson memorial and read his words on the frieze below the dome—"I have sworn upon the altar of god eternal hostility against every form of tyranny over the mind of man"—I think of Philip Denny Day and what he taught me, lessons long since lost on the planning profession.

Geoffrey Booth, Texas A&M University

❯ Barbara Lukermann, a professor at the Humphrey Institute, was my mentor and introduced me to the great and wonderful world of planning. Barbara had a positive and impactful influence on me as a graduate student by helping me think critically about the planning process and opportunities to engage the community. She founded a design team in Minnesota where we spent a weekend in a community addressing a planning issue and delivering ideas at the end of our stay. Experiences like that excited me about ways I could combine my design skills, leadership capacity, negotiation skills, facilitation skills, and an interest in

How have others influenced the way you think about planning? (Continued)

politics, social equity, and environmental justice into one profession.

Dana Bourland, AICP, Enterprise Foundation

❭ It's impossible to identify a single person as an influence.

My father taught me the value of diligence and hard work.

Uri Avin at PB Placemaking and Roger Waldon of Clarion Associates (and formerly Chapel Hill's Planning Director) are two of the most brilliant planners I have worked with. I have learned many lessons about issue analysis, intellectual honesty, and good humor from them.

S. Mark White, AICP, White and Smith Planning and Law Group

❭ Certainly my father has had the most consistent effect on my career. Through weekly calls home, I have shared my successes, discussed my challenges, and received sound advice on my business from him. My father was renowned for his rigor and strategic thinking, and I have tried to combine that

with my mother's ability to communicate well, and her love of theater and people.

Lee Einsweiler, AICP, Code Studio

❭ Stuart Meck has been the most influential person in my career. He is the director of the Center for Government Services at Rutgers University and on a project at APA called Growing Smart.

Stuart had more confidence in my public speaking abilities than I did, and through his prodding and positive feedback, forced me to face my demons by appointing me a spokesperson for the project and sending me to meeting after meeting, conference after conference, to spread the word about our project. After several years of doing 20 to 30 presentations per year to groups as small as five and as large as 2,000, I had completely conquered my fear.

Marya Morris, AICP, Planning Consultant

❭ The New Urbanist writers, most notably Kunstler's "Geography of Nowhere," Peter Calthorpe's "The Next American Metropolis," Peter Katz's "The New Urbanism," Thomas Hylton's "Save Our Land, Save Our Towns," and Jane Holtz Kay's "Asphalt Nation."

Finally, Andres Duany and Elizabeth Plater-Zyberk, two of the leaders of the New Urbanism movement, whom I have had the great fortune to come to know and work with, have had perhaps the greatest influence on me. It has been their wisdom and encouragement that inspired me to take risks and start my own planning firm.

Stuart Sirota, AICP, TND Planning Group

As a group, planners are conflicted about the role of politics. Some detest it, while others, like Dana Bourland, are invigorated by it. Successful planners have strong communication skills and should have the capacity to take leading roles and engage in negotiations with other community leaders while pursuing planning goals. HARRY CONNOLLY.

Where Do You Want to Work?

Planning is a diverse field with many different areas in which a planner might work. In addition to the variety of specializations, planners also can choose to work in a variety of organizations.

Like Megan Cummings, many people initially think that planners only work for the government. In fact, planners work in all three employment sectors: the public sector, the private sector, and the nonprofit sector. In addition, opportunities are available to work in every size organization.

In the private sector, planners most often work for consulting firms. Some planners, like Amy Bonitz, work for development companies. Unlike public planners, planners who work with developers are more likely than any other segment of the profession to see their work quickly turned into changes on the ground.

Size is another consideration. Some private consulting firms have dozens of locations nationally and even internationally. Some local planning offices employ several dozen professional planners and even a larger number of support staff.

Planning comes in small sizes, too. Some planners are sole proprietors of their own businesses and work independently or with a very small staff. Sometimes, these planners work as subcontractors for other planning firms on large projects. In the public sector, too, some planning departments are tiny, with the planner wearing multiple hats and juggling multiple responsibilities. A town as small as a few thousand people may hire a planner to do all of the planning, zoning, and community development work that they need.

Many planners move between the public and private sector, pursuing opportunities for advancement and seeking new challenges. Both have their challenges and rewards.

In this section, planners talk about what it's like to work in different kinds of planning situations. What planners mostly say is that you need to find the niche that feels right. Working with a tight team in a large firm can be just as cozy as working in a small town planning office. Some planners like the fast pace of private practice or the big city planning office. Others find satisfaction in the variety of work tasks they take on in a normal day. Wherever planners find themselves, they almost always find themselves growing—growing more skilled and confident professionally but also growing intellectually. Something new is always happening in planning.

Moving beyond "Public versus Private"

❯ We need to get beyond the old barrier between public and private sector planning. To be an effective planner, you have to work in the public sector and in the private sector. It's one of the terrible splits in planning. I don't know how strong the line is in the U.S., but here in Canada it is quite strong. Planners tend to think that you're either on the red team or the blue team, and I don't think that a separation is a healthy thing.

Planning is essentially about private investment working in concert with the investment of major public agencies on the ground. It's not an art in and of itself. The system is only effective if it's functional.

It's funny. I live in Jane Jacobs' home town, and in one of her later books, *Systems of Survival*, in which she talked about urban systems, she made the point that someone is either a hunter or a governor. That was her way of separating the public and the pri-

Moving beyond "Public versus Private" (Continued)

Successful urban redevelopment efforts require cooperation and collaboration among public and private entities. This image is part of plan to establish a new mixed-use district in London, England. The objective is a sustainable community that capitalizes on recent investments in nearby regional transportation and open space facilities, employs the best environmental practices, and provides jobs for the local community. © URBAN STRATEGIES INC®.

vate. If you're a hunter, you go out and get food and make sure that everyone is well provided for. The governor makes sure all the rules are followed, and followed equitably, and makes sure our other values are respected. In terms of public and private, she would not mix the two. But in all due respect, I think she's dead wrong. And I say that knowing she's not here to wave her craggy little finger at me.

I understand why people are concerned. When you deal with cities, it's a very tricky business. It's how you end up with corruption, projects that sour, and politicians that look like idiots. But all of the big urban regeneration projects have featured a wonderful combination of public values and private implementation. The blend is so mixed, it is difficult to see the distinctions. Separating the two assumes the private sector has no public component and the public sector has not worked with the private, and that's absolutely not the case. If you want to do this type of project and have it implemented, you have to have a mix. And it's like a marriage. The distinctions are blurred over a period of time.

Joe Berridge, Urban Strategies

The Importance of Both Experiences

You have experience in both the public and private sectors. What are your thoughts about working in both capacities? How this has shaped your career?

❭ I can work in both public and private sectors happily. The more important distinctions are the quality of the projects worked on and the quality of the individuals I am working for and with. Both environments can satisfy these criteria. I believe it is essential for planners to spend some time in the public sector. This provides them a good sense of how to implement projects, how government works, and the challenge of ongoing public interaction. Too much time in the public sector, however, can emphasize political, management, and organizational skills at the expense of substantive planning skills, best honed in the private sector typically.

While I have only spent 10 out of 37 years in the public sector, in county government in Maryland, these were the most important and formative experiences of my career. While I have been able to move fairly readily between public and private sectors, these transitions, particularly for senior public officials, are not easy or painless. The private sector discipline of limited time and budget and its focus on production and substantive skills all present potential obstacles to public sector planners.

Uri Avin, FAICP, Practice Leader for Regional Growth Management, PB PlaceMaking

Becoming a Developer

AMY BONITZ

Principal, Bonitz Palmer LLC

Baltimore, Maryland

Why did you become a planner?

❭ I had worked for a nonprofit community design center in Baltimore, Maryland, for three years. My role was to provide donated design services to nonprofit organizations and community groups engaged in community revitalization projects. After working in many communities across Baltimore, I wanted to understand the bigger picture of urban planning and redevelopment, so I applied and was accepted to get a master's in Regional Planning at the University of North Carolina in Chapel Hill.

You moved from the nonprofit side, through planning school, to becoming a developer. Why did you decide to take this route?

❭ I have been working as a real estate developer since 1997. When I graduated from planning school, I could have gone back to the nonprofit, community development world or worked in local government, but I decided that, if I did not work in the private sector, I would probably not expand my real estate development skills, and I wanted to understand how the private sector worked since it is the real driver in our cities.

I chose to work for a very civic-minded developer, so I was able to apply my interest in community development and planning to the kinds of projects we worked on, whether it was a small business incubator or the redevelopment of a mill valley. I found

MASSING PLAN

OFFICE SPACE: 2 MILLION SQ. FT.

RETAIL: 300,000 SQ. FT.

RESIDENTIAL: 2,000 UNITS

HOTEL ROOMS: 500

PARKING SPACES: 10,000+

myself gravitating though to commercial development projects and large, mixed-use projects, which bring new jobs, services, and investment to cities and can trigger broader reinvestment in surrounding neighborhoods.

▲ Development projects such as this one, proposed for a waterfront site in Baltimore, Maryland, offer greater challenges because of their size and prominence, but they also offer greater rewards to the planners and developers that can make it work. This is a digital "massing" plan, illustrating the use, height, and configuration of the buildings. TURNER DEVELOPMENT GROUP.

You worked for a larger firm before establishing your own company. What does your job entail?

❯ I am essentially a project manager. My role is to understand the big picture of what it takes to entitle, market, lease (or sell), finance, design, and build a project and then manage a team and a critical path to achieve a completed, occupied, and profitable project.

I wear a lot of hats. I can be working on putting together a finance package, developing a website, meeting with community members or city agencies, or meeting with architects and contractors all in the same day.

What are some of the experiences that have shaped your ideas of planning and how you approach the projects on which you work?

❯ My experience working in poor urban neighborhoods with the design center taught me that you achieve a better end result if you value everyone's input in the design and planning process. I also think it ignited my drive to understand why the market just abandons some neighborhoods and to learn strategies to bring new investment to inner cities.

Images like this are used by developers for multiple purposes. For large projects, a high-quality graphic can help interested residents and public officials understand the project before it is approved for construction. With approvals secured and construction underway, the developer can use the same image to market the property to potential buyers. TURNER DEVELOPMENT GROUP.

By working for an urban developer I have seen the power of transformative projects where overlooked assets were turned into dynamic new places that catalyzed investment and changed the civic mindset about what is possible.

What is your greatest challenge?

❯ I think the challenge is always how do we find the resources and time to realize the full potential of major redevelopment projects. How do we craft a vision that is not owned just by the private sector but by public and nonprofit partners?

Time is money in real estate so the pressure is always there to move faster, which sometimes backfires if you are trying to build broader ownership and participation in your project. This is particularly true in cities that do not have a strong track record of public/private partnership, where you are on the frontier for new public policies.

What are the most satisfying parts of your job?

❯ Seeing a project take shape as you work with others to craft a program for a building or large-scale project and then start putting the pieces together to make it happen. Real estate is also very concrete—you have a place that is real that you have helped to build, and you can visit it and see people enjoying these places and their companies succeeding and people shopping or living in them.

The least?

❯ I think the length of time it takes to make something happen can wear you out. You have to have a lot of determination and patience for the nitty-gritty details and the ups and downs to see a project through to completion. I also think the public has this sense that all developers are superwealthy and just out to make a buck, and they don't appreciate how challenging urban redevelopment projects can be.

Becoming a Small Town Planner

BEN SMITH

Assistant Town Planner, Windham, Maine

Why did you become a planner?

❯ I grew up in Maine but moved to Massachusetts to work in sales and marketing after college. I became aware of planning as a career while reading about watershed issues and land transfers back in Maine. These issues have very large environmental and social/cultural implications, and through them I found something I could get energized about. Planning was a way to get involved. Since I didn't have a background in biology, forestry, or something similar, I figured planning was a way I could get involved from a policy perspective.

When I became a planner, I made a clean break from my previous work, but the communication, negotiation, and people skills I learned in sales and marketing have served me well as a municipal planner.

How did you end up in Windham?

❯ My first job in planning was an internship at Maine Department of Transportation, where I worked as a facilitator for the Gateway 1 corridor project. This led to a job with HNTB, where I worked as a transportation planner. After a couple years there, I moved to my current position.

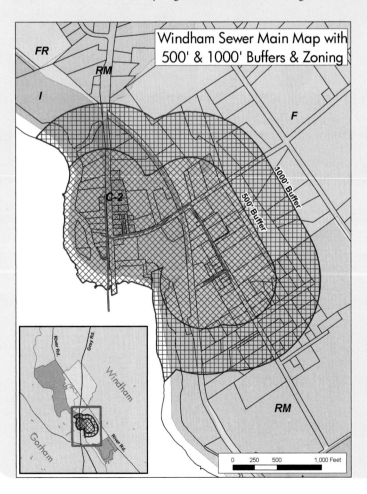

Windham Sewer Main Map with 500' & 1000' Buffers & Zoning

As the "short-term" planner in a small town (Windham, Maine), Ben Smith is responsible for managing administration of the zoning ordinance. Because of the size of the community, he gets more involved in detailed infrastructure analyses than a planner in a larger community with a larger municipal staff likely would. This map reveals which parcels are within 1,000 feet of the downtown sewer main. TOWN OF WINDHAM, PLANNING DEPARTMENT.

Smaller communities such as Windham, Maine, often expand by allowing development to occur at the edge of the jurisdiction along the primary local road. In Windham this pattern is further enhanced by the poor quality of private secondary roads that cannot handle the demands of new development. Planners may be tasked with developing strategies to change this pattern. KEITH LUKE PHOTO, TOWN OF WINDHAM.

How difficult was it to make the transition from the private sector to the public sector?

❯ The most difficult part of making the transition to the public sector is that municipal government is not as nimble as a private consulting firm. The process of starting initiatives, making plans, and anything to do with money seems to take much longer. Also, moving to the public sector involves stepping into an established way of doing things, and inheriting an environment in which it is hard to make changes.

What does an assistant town planner do?

❯ I am responsible for "short-term planning efforts," which includes providing analysis and recommendations on subdivision and site plan applications for the Planning Board and developers.

I have the task of researching and developing ordinance language and zoning changes as develop-

ment proposals are submitted. I am also the planning representative for a town staff committee that is initiating a transportation plan and impact fee strategy for a corridor through the town.

What is your day-to-day routine?

❯ I answer questions from the public and developers over the phone and at the service desk. I review subdivision and site plans, as well as less formal sketch plans for the Planning Board. The Planning Board Chairman and I work closely on meeting agendas. I prepare memos on development application, and for zoning/ordinance changes.

What are some of the particular challenges of working as a planner in a small town?

❯ Infrastructure is a big issue. The only part of town on public sewer is South Windham Village. Ninety-nine percent of the town's population as well as the regional-scale commercial/retail center are all on private septic systems. This really limits density and the types of development that can be located practically anywhere in town.

Private roads are another infrastructure issue. Approximately 35 percent of the town's roadway centerline miles are on private roads that have been built to no standard. This has potential public safety implications for existing development, as well as on the development potential for land accessed by private roads.

What are the most satisfying aspects of your job?

❭ Windham is a town in transition both in how it is developing and how planning is done. For a long time, Windham has been a rural farming community with a seasonal population that swells during the summer. Because land is relatively affordable and the town is within commuting distance of Portland, it is becoming a regional retail center and seasonal cottages are being converted to year-round homes.

Within the Town Office, we are transitioning from a small town, "anything goes," "let's make it easy to help people do what they want, it's their land" mentality to a culture of providing professional services based on sound planning principles.

Within that context, the most satisfying part of my job is being able to introduce planning concepts like "impact fees" and "overlay zones" and creating tools from the ground up, as opposed to strictly administering the systems that the town long has had in place.

What are your goals for the future?

❭ I can see myself being involved with municipal planning for quite some time. The work is interesting, and I still have a lot to learn. That being said, who knows what other opportunities might present themselves in the future at the state level or back in the private sector. All in all, I feel good about the decisions I have made, and I have a positive outlook on building a planning career.

Establishing a One-Person Planning Firm

JASON SARTORI

Principal, Integrated Planning Consultants

Silver Spring, Maryland

Why did you decide to become a planner?

❭ My majors in college were political science and economics, and I've always found myself drawn toward public policy, the social sciences, and issues of economic development.

When I graduated from college, the IT industry was just starting to boom and I found it very attractive. For six years I worked as an IT consultant, managing major technology implementations for companies in financial services.

At some point I became disenchanted with the field and found myself wanting to get back to my original interests by finding a profession through which I could have a more direct and positive influence on people and communities.

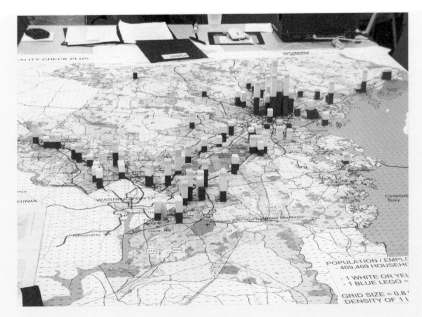

When communities plan for growth simply by looking at a map and considering where they would like to expand, citizen planners frequently identify far more land than is necessary to accommodate projected population growth. The resulting plan enables development over a wider area than necessary, inducing sprawl. Using the "Reality Check" planning tool shown here, participants can explore different growth scenarios in three dimensions, considering development density as well as location. As indicated by the graph, this approach can result in a vision that places more new development within the existing urban boundary. COMPILED BY JASON SARTORI AND THE NATIONAL CENTER FOR SMART GROWTH RESEARCH AND EDUCATION USING DATA FROM REALITY CHECK PLUS EXERCISES, THE METROPOLITAN WASHINGTON COUNCIL OF GOVERNMENTS, AND THE BALTIMORE METROPOLITAN COUNCIL.

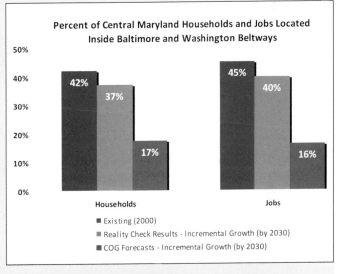

Percent of Central Maryland Households and Jobs Located Inside Baltimore and Washington Beltways

Households: Existing (2000) 42%, Reality Check Results - Incremental Growth (by 2030) 37%, COG Forecasts - Incremental Growth (by 2030) 17%

Jobs: Existing (2000) 45%, Reality Check Results - Incremental Growth (by 2030) 40%, COG Forecasts - Incremental Growth (by 2030) 16%

■ Existing (2000)
■ Reality Check Results - Incremental Growth (by 2030)
■ COG Forecasts - Incremental Growth (by 2030)

At first I thought my interests would lead me to become an architect—as a kid that was one of my original professional dreams—but when I started investigating the School of Architecture at the University of Maryland, I was introduced to the school's planning program and the profession of planning in general.

As an IT project manager, I most enjoyed serving as a conduit between the various players on a project—the software programmers, the client's upper management, the client's customers, and the client's employees. To succeed in that environment, I needed to understand the requirements, interests, perspectives, and priorities that each individual brought to a project, and I needed to understand, communicate, and translate among these multiple "languages."

As a professional planner, I quickly recognized that I could play a similar role in communicating and working with stakeholders. Planners need to understand the concerns and needs of citizens and businesses, the roles and limitations of government, and the abilities of professionals in many fields. Planning offered me a good combination of my interests and experiences.

After graduate school, why did you decide to start your own firm?

❭ In my previous career, I had helped to start a technology consulting firm with seven other people, and that sparked in me a spirit of entrepreneurship. Before graduate school, I briefly worked as an independent project management consultant. That expanded my experience beyond the IT field. I found that working on my own had many challenges but offered great rewards and flexibility.

While in graduate school, I spent a summer working for a local planning agency. I recognized that you cannot simply graduate from a planning program and declare yourself a planning consultant. There is a lot that you need to learn by working in the field, whether in a local or state planning agency or at a large planning firm, skills you never attain from a purely academic experience.

When I graduated, I had an opportunity to lead a major visioning project for the State of Maryland. So I started Integrated Planning Consultants, LLC. As a company, IPC gives me the ability to develop a brand that goes beyond my own individual reputation as an independent contractor. Establishing a limited liability corporation also provided tax and liability incentives.

A few years later, I'm still the only employee of the firm. I value the flexibility this arrangement offers, despite the additional administrative burdens. And while I have called upon subcontractors at times, I hope to grow the company into a full-service firm with more employees (and administrative help!).

What does your job involve?

❭ It depends on what projects are hot at the moment. I could spend a day traveling across the state, interviewing people in Western Maryland for a research project, meeting with project stakeholders in Baltimore, and then going to Annapolis to help a client advocate for changes to state planning policy. Sometimes I sit at my computer all day long preparing materials for a public forum or a project advisory group meeting, researching growth indicators, or writing and editing a research report.

You've talked a lot about what you love about your work. What is the least satisfying aspect of your work as a planner in your own consulting firm?

❭ The least satisfying part of my job must be the administrative aspects of being a company. While it is always satisfying to be able to issue an invoice for a completed project (or even more satisfying to deposit a payment on an invoice), I take little pleasure in maintaining the company ledger or having to serve as my own IT support—sometimes I can spend hours or days trying to resolve an email or Internet connection issue.

What are your biggest challenges?

❭ My challenges relate more to my business and finding the time to work on projects for my clients while pursuing other potential engagements. As planners, we need to better understand the wide and interrelated impacts of planning decisions on communities and society in general.

One thing my experience has taught me is that a comprehensive understanding of these impacts is necessary. You hear a lot of people talk about the need to integrate land use and transportation planning. But I think it's equally important to think about issues related to crime, education, economic development, affordable housing, health and physical fitness, the environment and natural resources, and even global warming. Stakeholders from all these different areas and their related perspectives must be part of the planning and decision-making process. Bringing together all these diverse interests is one of the biggest challenges we face as planners today.

Making Transitions

MARYA MORRIS, AICP

Independent Consultant

Former Senior Associate, Duncan Associates

Former Senior Research Associate, American Planning Association

Chicago, Illinois

Why did you become a planner?

❯ I've had an interest in maps and the notion of place my entire life. In college I majored in economics (after initially trying cartography).

At some point in my first or second year I found the classes offered by the College of Urban and Regional Planning at the University of Wisconsin and realized that there was an actual profession I could pursue that married all my interests. By the end of my junior year in college, I had decided to pursue a career in city planning with a focus on economic development/community development.

How did you choose a school for your planning degree?

❯ I graduated from the UW in August 1985 and there weren't any jobs in Madison. For all my friends (not necessarily in planning), it wasn't a matter of if we were moving away to start a career, it was when.

I moved to Chicago in January 1986 with the plan of entering the University of Illinois at Chicago planning program at some point, but I wanted to work for a while. I had done research on graduate schools of planning prior to moving to Chicago, and found out that UIC's program was known for its emphasis on community development.

Unfortunately, I had no luck finding a job related to urban planning, so I went to work as a secretary at a huge commercial real estate firm. While I learned a lot about office etiquette, interpersonal dynamics, and corporate America in the 14 months I worked there, it was like spending 8 hours a day in an intellectual dead zone. For that reason, I moved up my application for admission to graduate school and started the program in the fall of 1986. The program had a very strong focus on neighborhood and community economic development, which is why I chose to go there.

What are some of the experiences that have shaped your ideas of planning and how you approach the projects on which you work?

❯ I had several experiences as a kid, that in retrospect, were instrumental in shaping my notion of what makes a good neighborhood and a good city and thus why planning is important.

When I was 7 or 8 years old a Victorian-style mansion that had been a stopover point on the Underground Railroad was demolished and replaced by a Radio Shack and a Burger King. I knew there was something inherently wrong with "the system" if that could happen.

Also around that time the high school I later attended was built on unincorporated farmland outside Madison. The school was literally in the middle of nowhere. At the time I regarded the

school district's decision to build it in that location as ill informed at best because most of the students lived in neighborhoods that were too far away to allow for walking or biking to school. I learned many years later that the criteria that school districts rely upon when siting new schools focuses almost exclusively on the size of the parcel, while other considerations, such as student transportation, suburban sprawl, and environmental protection are not taken into account at all. This too was a lesson for me in how decisions get made and the shortsightedness of not taking into account the unintended consequences of decisions such as this.

▼ Despite the continued growth of digital communication options, face-to-face meetings such as this remain an essential component of effective planning. Bringing people around a map and letting them draw in their ideas is an excellent way to engage people and learn from them. KIRK R. BISHOP.

ZONING**PRACTICE** April 2008

AMERICAN PLANNING ASSOCIATION

⊕ ISSUE NUMBER FOUR
PRACTICE SMART SIGN CODES

Digital
Signs:
Context Matters

4

As a consultant specializing in zoning codes, Marya has developed expertise valuable to her clients and to the planning profession. The American Planning Association publishes *Zoning Practice* each month, giving specialists like Marya the opportunity to share that expertise. © AMERICAN PLANNING ASSOCIATION.

As a practicing planner with 20 years' experience at this point, the events that have the greatest impact on me are the many meetings we participate in with concerned citizens, volunteer planning boards, and professional planners who work for local governments. These face-to-face meetings are where planners encounter a diversity of public opinion. Some participants are supportive of what we as professionals gauge as being in the best interest of the public as a whole.

A proposal to include affordable housing as part of a large market rate housing development is one example of how planners must serve a broader public interest that individuals may object to. Others view any attempt on the part of government to plan for the future of the community as too intrusive with respect to private markets and a potential threat to their quality of life. It is enormously challenging to explain and to try to achieve consensus on what constitutes the public interest.

Do you find it difficult to balance the demands of working as a planning consultant and your responsibilities at home?

❯ The personal side is harder than the professional side. It became clear almost immediately after I took the job with the consulting firm how hard it was going to be to work the hours necessary and travel to see clients all while diving in to full-time parenting for the first time in my life. I got married in August and got laid off October 3. I have three stepchildren, and I need so much flexibility with them. I thought I could do it all, and travel the way I did, and work as late as I needed to, and work at home like I need to, but I don't have that kind of energy anymore.

As an independent consultant, what kind of work do you do?

❯ I consult with cities and counties across the country on planning projects and on zoning and land development code revisions.

Describe a typical day in your work as a code consultant.

❯ My typical day involves writing sections of a new ordinance or editing sections of an existing ordinance. I also spend a lot of time conducting research and seeking input from various sources to help establish principles for the regulations before I begin drafting them.

Most land development ordinances can be classified as permissive, moderate, or stringent; the level of permissiveness or stringency that a community decides upon sets the tone for the degree of complexity of the entire code. I also travel to see clients several times each month. These trips might include a full-day work session with planning staff or an advisory group to review a draft ordinance or, when a code is nearing completion, the trip may include presenting the draft ordinance to the city's planning commission or city council.

What is the most satisfying part of your job?

❯ The most satisfying part is that it supports my intellectual curiosity about places, cities, rural areas, suburbs, housing, transportation, the environment, interpersonal dynamics, and politics.

The least?

❯ Writing land development codes can be tedious, especially on the days where the task at hand is formatting a document and not creating new content or implementing new ideas.

Planning Timeframes

Planning, by definition, is a forward-looking profession, focused on plans that guide future decisions. But planners are also engaged in the implementation of plans, especially the enforcement of zoning and land division ordinances. When landowners wish to subdivide their land, build a new building, or begin using property for a new use, someone needs to confirm that the proposed change is consistent with adopted ordinances. Planners often fill this role, too.

Many local planning offices have two divisions: current planning and long-range planning. Current planners focus on developing and enforcing regulations and in creating nonregulatory programs to implement long-range plans. Long-range planners do studies to assess how well the community is doing, identifying problems and opportunities, and creating documents, called plans, to guide future decisions—which will later be made by current planners.

CURRENT PLANNING

After a plan has been approved by the relevant government body, planners next develop an implementation plan, which may include incentives, educational programs, marketing programs, taxes and fees, or regulations. Subsequently, once the new programs, fees, and regulations are approved, planners are often involved in the administration of those programs and policies. The planners who engage in this work are often called "current planners."

When zoning was a matter of measuring whether a setback from the street met the code, zoning administration required little expertise, and no specialized education. On-the-job training was sufficient. As zoning codes have become more complex, however, the task of the current planning section of a planning office has required more expertise and more education. Increasingly, these positions are held by individuals trained in planning.

For example, many communities have revised the zoning ordinance to allow planned unit developments (PUDs). In addition, design guidelines and form-based codes are increasingly common in cities of all sizes. In these variations on traditional zoning, the emphasis of regulation is on building form rather than use and aim to create engaging public spaces.

Administering all of these complex regulations—enforcing the ordinances—is a primary responsibility of planners who work in the current planning section of a planning office. Of course, in small planning departments, this work may be carried out by the same person who does long-range planning, who may also be the same person who directs the planning office. Frequently, communities hire consulting firms to provide code enforcement services in lieu of hiring an additional city employee, especially if the community needs less than full-time service.

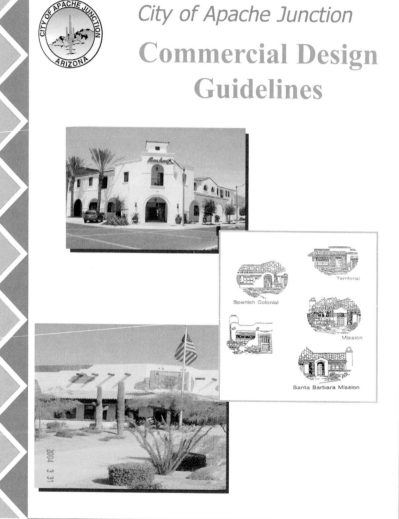

Design guidelines are utilized to provide more specific design guidance than is provided by the zoning ordinance. CITY OF APACHE JUNCTION.

Enforcing Codes and Reviewing Plans

DIRK GERATZ, AICP

Principal Planner, Development Review

City of Alexandria, Virginia

What does your job involve?

❯ As principal planner, I manage the review of development projects. The review consists of working with applicants from the earliest concept of a project to the final review of a building permit.

The process in between involves countless hours of review, negotiation, and analysis. Add to this the public hearings and politics and a project can become a big job. As part of my position, I oversee two junior planners that make up a team. We work together on each of these projects, giving us three sets of eyes for each one. It's a very technical job.

The job involves a lot of coordination. Generally, I am working with three different groups: an applicant, who may be working with a design consultant and attorney, as well as other city departments, and neighborhood groups and the public. Each of these stakeholders may have different wishes and desires, even within city government. Everyone sees a project a little differently. The goal is to get everyone to come to some sort of an agreement, but it can get complicated.

What's a typical day like?

❯ Managing the status of multiple projects is a daily part of my job. We have many deadlines to meet, and I need to ensure that they are met. Deadlines may include the date that comments to the applicant must be sent out, to making sure staff reports are ready to be mailed to the Planning Commission.

Every day includes administrative tasks: checking with my team members, completing time sheets, filling out performance evaluations, and so on. Checking emails and other correspondence takes up a large part of my workday, and I like to stay on top of them.

How did you get involved in development review?

❯ I naturally progressed into this area of planning because of my interest in urban design and my educational background in architecture and urban planning. I believe my strengths are in design (development) review.

What is your biggest challenge?

❯ I would say the most difficult thing is educating others in what "good" planning is and understanding that, for many people, planning is of no importance. As a public planner, especially, you are often taken for granted and not seen as an educated resource that can offer assistance to a builder, developer, neighborhood resident, or business owner.

Over time you learn to make do and try your best to show others that what we do as planners can and does make a difference. With time you can actually point to projects that have been built or programs that have been implemented to show how good planning can be effective in making positive changes to a community.

Is there a particular project on which you thought you had the greatest effect?

❯ While I was a planner in Annapolis, Maryland, I was the staff planner overseeing the renovation of three houses into a new branch bank building. My pride in this project stems from the significant

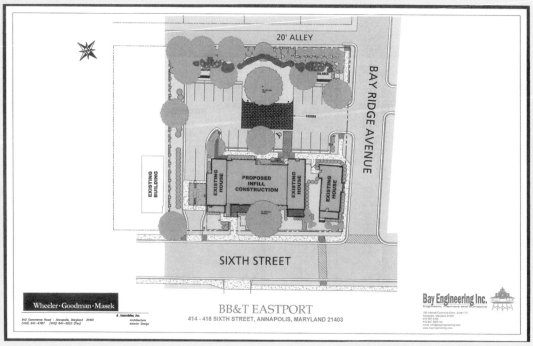

BAY ENGINEERING, INC., ANNAPOLIS, MARYLAND.

BAY ENGINEERING, INC., ANNAPOLIS, MARYLAND.

influence I had in working with the bank and the neighbors to arrive at an outcome that met a number of competing values and desires.

Although it was a small project, it required me to address several important issues in one project: preserving and rehabilitating historic houses, preserving two significant trees, promoting good building design for the new infill structure, reviewing the use of creative bio-retention areas, minimizing the effects of the bank's proposed drive-through, screening the parking and lighting from nearby residential properties, limiting signage, and protecting the character of the neighborhood. These issues are typical of what the development review process addresses, but were all in one project.

What skill sets does someone need in this job?

❯ You have to have some design ability and understand space, scale, and building mass. It helps to have some aesthetic understanding and be familiar with building design. Because you have to work with people, it's good not to be a shy person. I know having this job has really helped me become

◀ Planners involved in development review occasionally have the opportunity to work on unique projects that require innovation and creativity, both by the developer and by the planner. In this project Dirk Geratz helped guide the careful insertion of rain gardens and landscape screening into and between a series of single-family homes, thereby protecting the character of the neighborhood. BAY ENGINEERING, INC., ANNAPOLIS, MARYLAND.

a good speaker. It's a skill you learn as you grow in the career, but I'm not sure you have to have it the day you start.

You need to have the ability to write technical reports, and be able to complete an analysis of a project in terms of codes. And you have to be able to work with other city departments and the public.

There are technical issues that you need to learn about, like air quality and stormwater runoff. In that sense, the knowledge you need is fairly broad, and you will learn a lot about things you may not have to deal with on a daily basis—like traffic counts—but you end up knowing about because it's involved in a project.

What are the most satisfying parts of your job?

❯ The most satisfying part of my job is being able to provide top-notch customer service to the average citizen. I pride myself in being helpful and explaining city procedures to an applicant who has not gone through it before.

The rewarding part comes when the project is successful and the citizen is so thankful that I made it easy to get through what can be a long process.

And the least?

❯ What I find least satisfying is in the lack of leadership and good management within a department or government. In general I am amazed at how poor planners are as managers. It really is two different disciplines.

Addressing the Challenges of Long-Range Planning

KATHIE EBAUGH, AICP

Senior Project Manager, Bell David Planning Group, Venice, Florida

Former Long-Range City Planner, City of Venice, Florida

You have worked in both the public and private sector in long-range planning. What does the job include?

❯ As the project manager for long-range planning, I:

■ Lead a team of planners working on the development of vision-oriented, design-based neighborhood plans, city comprehensive plans, regional visioning processes, architectural guidelines, and other long-range planning instruments.

■ Schedule project tasks to meet target dates and deliverables.

■ Work with communities to lay the foundation for the development and execution of land development regulations that implement the long-range planning policies.

▼ This map illustrates park access within the city, identifying those areas that are within a quarter-mile walk of a park. The neighborhoods with the most parks are located in older, traditionally designed sections of the city. The neighborhoods with the least access to parks and recreation facilities are in newer suburban-style neighborhoods. WADETRIM, INC.

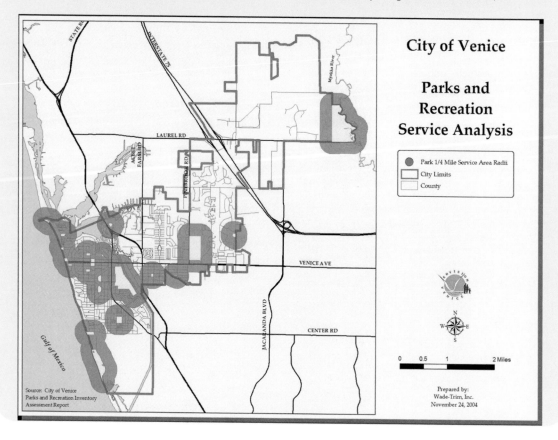

City of Venice

Parks and Recreation Service Analysis

● Park 1/4 Mile Service Area Radii
☐ City Limits
☐ County

0   0.5   1   2 Miles

Prepared by:
Wade-Trim, Inc.
November 24, 2004

Source: City of Venice
Parks and Recreation Inventory
Assessment Report

- Write and design community reports, plans, and other planning materials.
- Facilitate community visioning exercises, workshops, open houses, and public forums.
- Research best planning practices and developing policy strategies that meet the specific needs of the local community.
- Conduct community conditions research by analyzing demographic data, housing and development practices, public service and infrastructure information, transportation systems, environmental conditions, and other community data.
- Determine how to utilize design, maps, photographs, and other graphics to illustrate and support the community's selected policy strategy.
- Present findings at both community meetings and professional conferences.
- Coordinate work efforts with other planners in the region and state.

One of the great things about urban planning is there is no such thing as a "routine" day. Every day has a new focus, new challenge, and new opportunity. This means time management is critical because there is always more than one priority and more than one task that must be completed.

Generally speaking this means that on a daily basis my job requires me to:

- Communicate with other planners involved in the project to coordinate their activities regarding the project.
- Evaluate project status and project needs in order to ensure all tasks are being completed on time and on budget.
- Schedule staff meetings, public events and workshops, plan hearings, and other activities.
- Read and research planning practices in other communities to get new ideas and learn innovative planning techniques.

- Participate in local planning professional events and task forces to stay focused and involved.
- Assess, update, and evaluate job tasks, priorities, and time lines to ensure everything is done appropriately.

What is challenging about long-range planning?

❯ The greatest challenge I have faced is working with communities to establish a future vision for their community that is based on sound planning practices, achieves the local community's needs, and can be bought into by the entire community.

This is a challenge because by there are many diverse interests in a local community—each of whom believe they know what is best for the area's future.

Whether the plan is being developed for a neighborhood, city, or multi-county region, planners are challenged to helping communities make choices about their future that all stakeholders can accept and create a planning vision that all members can support.

This challenge is met by providing communities the tools that help community members and public leaders understand the area's current conditions, guide the stakeholders' choices about future growth and development, and educate communities about how their choices will impact the future.

A particularly difficult component of this challenge is accepting that communities can select the recommendations of the planner, or select an alternative course for their future. Indeed, no matter how well a planner guides the community through the process and decision-making process, the decision, ultimately, belongs to the community.

Even if the community selects an alternative that you, as the professional planner, do not agree with, it is your responsibility to uphold, support, and implement the community's future planning vision.

Improving Quality of Life in the Long Term

MARIANNE GARDNER

Chief, Policy and Plan Development Branch

Fairfax County, Virginia Planning Department

Fairfax, Virginia

What does your job involve?

❯ Internal meetings on projects that range from setting up project-oriented teams (where I might be anywhere on the totem pole) to responding to specific land use proposals, making sure everyone is on schedule with their planning projects, solving problems, asking and answering lots of questions, coaching and mentoring planners, and writing and reviewing staff reports on everything from complex studies to proposed plan amendments on small parcels. On the community side, explaining Comprehensive Plan policies and how they work, and making presentations on specific areas of interest.

In my view, the purpose of land use planning is to promote a better quality of life by creating better places for people to live and work. The Comprehensive Plan provides hundreds of policies and objectives that suggest how this can be achieved. The ability to consider a land use question from several perspectives is an important part of the job because the best outcome represents a balance among the many goals.

Another big part of the job involves trying to anticipate and respond to changing circumstances. Fairfax County, in many ways, represents the American dream with great jobs, neighborhoods, schools, and parks, to name a few attributes.

Proactive planning can help maintain this level of excellence. For example, a recent Comprehensive Plan amendment adopted by the Board of Supervisors encouraging transit-oriented development is reshaping and improving several areas of the county.

What is your greatest challenge?

❯ The greatest challenge is also the area of greatest satisfaction, and that is training and mentoring new planners and then giving them a chance to grow professionally through delegating meaningful work to them.

Why is that so important?

❯ I think there has been a real paradigm shift in how planners approach their jobs. Richard Florida's work on the creative class says that competition for workers in their twenties is becoming intense. In the workplace, we need to speak the same common language, whereas, in the last generation, the culture of organizations was much different.

The planners we are hiring now are more assertive than my generation, and they are also very willing to share what they know. For example, they grew up with technology, and many planners have learned how to present information in beautiful and creative graphic forms. As a result, we are able to publish documents that are not just text, and that makes a gigantic difference with the public in terms of making planning more accessible The relationship of new to more seasoned planners is more of a two-way dialogue: the veterans still have responsibility for training, but those just out of school bring a vibrancy and energy that is an important part of the work culture.

I enjoy working in the public sector. What I love about this job is that we get to work with communities, whether it is the public or elected and appointed officials, to craft planning principles, and then we are given the opportunity to help implement them. Communication and compromise are important parts of the process, so what is learned in this profession has broader application to every aspect of life.

What are the most satisfying parts of your job?

❯ Most is that I continue to learn and be challenged and believe it is possible to make the community a better place.

And the least?

Least is not being able to accomplish everything I would like in a day, a week, or a month. Also the "long" in long-range planning means sometimes there are not immediate results, which can be difficult.

Guide to the
2008
BRAC
Area Plans Review

Fairfax County, VA
The Planning Commission
The Department of Planning & Zoning
January 2008

BRAC stands for Base Closure and Realignment Commission and represents a challenge to communities across the country—economic decline associated with the loss of U.S. military bases. Through proactive planning, communities such as Fairfax County can adapt to these changes. DEPARTMENT OF PLANNING AND ZONING, COUNTY OF FAIRFAX, VIRGINIA.

Creating Comprehensive Plans

BARRY MILLER

Comprehensive Planning Consultant

Berkeley, California

You have extensive experience working on comprehensive plans. What attracts you to this type of work?

❭ My personal bias is that comprehensive planning is the purest form of planning. It combines all the reasons I went into the profession to begin with: it's creative, it's challenging, it's provocative, it's visionary, it's political, and it's big.

I love the big picture aspect of the work, the high level of community engagement, and the fundamental question that a comprehensive plan presents to each resident: What kind of place do you want your city to be in the future? As planners, this question challenges our imaginations and allows us to think and act outside the box.

The multidisciplinary aspect of comprehensive planning is very appealing to me. I enjoy the integration of design, social science, service delivery, engineering, and environmental science. I like the fact that it's citywide, that it's long term, and maybe that it's a little bit abstract and academic. When I'm working on a comprehensive plan, I'm always learning—about a place, about history, about the environment, even about human nature. I also like the high visibility of comprehensive plans—they are often covered by the media and require the active engagement of elected officials.

I like the fact that every plan is different. There are so many aspects of urban planning that feel formulaic (environmental impact reports come to mind). For me, part of the fun of doing a comprehensive plan is finding out what resonates with the residents of a particular city—and then tailoring the plan to be responsive. In the same vein, I like the variety of being a comprehensive planning consultant (as opposed to doing strategic planning for one city only). I enjoy traveling to different regions, and learning about the different dynamics and issues at play.

What does your job involve on a day-to-day basis?

❭ As a sole proprietor, I am typically working on four or five projects at any given time. I multitask between projects as required. Some days I'm lucky enough to focus completely on one project, but usually I'm juggling two or three. At times, I can work quietly in my office for an entire day, but most days I spend at least part of the day in my client's offices. Overall, I spend about 50 percent of my day writing, 25 percent in meetings, and 25 percent doing some form of research. The research is usually web-based, but could involve field surveys, phone calls, library time, and so on.

Occasionally, I'll have a project that is map-intensive, in which case I might be hunched over a drafting table with Prismacolor pencils and base maps, or surfing Google Earth with a pile of parcel maps in my lap. I also do a fair amount of data base management, which can get tedious. One of the downsides of self-employment is that there's no one to whom I can delegate. Occasionally, I will hire interns to assist me, since it's hard for me to spend high-quality work hours on things like survey postcoding, land use inventories, and meeting minutes.

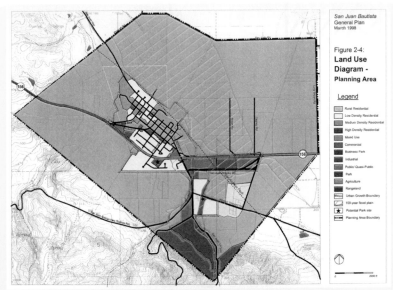

San Juan Bautista
General Plan
March 1998

Figure 2-4:
**Land Use
Diagram -**
Planning Area

Legend

Rural Residential
Low Density Residential
Medium Density Residential
High Density Residential
Mixed Use
Commercial
Business Park
Industrial
Public/ Quasi-Public
Park
Agriculture
Rangeland
Urban Growth Boundary
100-year flood plain
Potential Park site
Planning Area Boundary

BARRY MILLER.

Comprehensive planning comes in all shapes and sizes. As a consultant who travels throughout the country to work on such plans, Barry Miller has helped communities as small as San Juan Batista, California (2000 population 1,700), and as large as Washington, DC (2000 population 572,000). The future land use plan for a large city will utilize more categories than in a small community, but the basic color scheme for general categories of land use is consistent across the profession, including yellows and oranges for residential, reds for commercial, green for parks and agriculture, purple for industrial, and blue for public uses. DC OFFICE OF PLANNING.

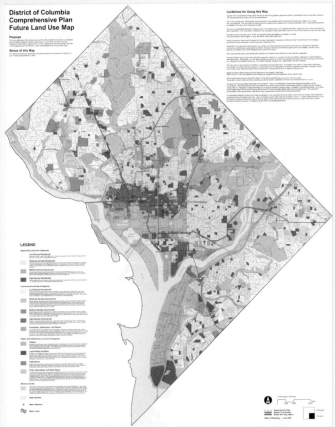

District of Columbia
Comprehensive Plan
Future Land Use Map

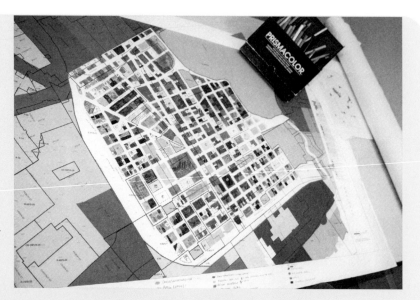

The transition to digital tools for mapping has not yet eliminated the colored pencil. Here Barry Miller has been working with pencil and paper to think through the uses appropriate for downtown Oakland, California. BARRY MILLER.

In my professional practice, I've developed a niche specialty doing comprehensive plans. This largely drives the content of my day-to-day work. I collect data, I analyze it, I map it, I write about it, I draw conclusions, and I make policy and programmatic recommendations. I do a large number of public presentations, and interact with the public at community meetings, public hearings, and in small group discussions. As a project manager, I also spend time managing subconsultants, monitoring project budgets, and working to keep my projects on schedule.

I'm also a small business person, so on a day-to-day basis I have to pay the bills, shop for office supplies, maintain professional contacts, write proposals, prepare invoices, find the best deal on health insurance, and other tasks that most employees take for granted. I'm human resources, accounting, the marketing department, the graphics department, the word processor, the front desk secretary, and the boss all at the same time.

A typical work day for me starts at 9:30 A.M. I send and return emails and phone calls and then turn to "billable" work for the remainder of the day. This might entail writing a plan element, drafting policies, preparing a staff report or memo, creating a PowerPoint presentation, writing talking points, editing a report, and so on. I work until 7 P.M., eating lunch at my desk. I have night meetings one to two nights a week, although there have been times in my career where the frequency has been greater.

What is your greatest challenge?

❯ I've experienced professional challenges and personal challenges. They're very different and it would be hard to say that one is greater than the other.

My greatest professional challenge was managing the Washington, DC, Comprehensive Plan. The plan was to be the mayor's legacy. It had to be written, vetted, and adopted on a compressed schedule that many believed was not doable. I've never worked so hard in my life. On top of the accelerated schedule, the plan had to effectively address profoundly complex urban issues, and pass muster with an incredibly engaged and often suspicious community.

Another challenging project that comes to mind was my very first experience as a planner. I was hired as an intern in a rural East Texas County Planning Department when I was 21, the summer between undergraduate and graduate school. The planning director was fired during my third week on the job and the rest of the professional staff resigned in protest. I effectively became the planning director in one of the fastest growing counties in the country and had no idea what I was supposed to do. I was there for three months. It really made me question my career choice.

On a personal level, the greatest challenge I've had is overcoming some of my basic personality traits. I'm one of those people who wants to be liked by everyone. Yet part of being an effective planner is making tough choices and tradeoffs. It's been hard for me to learn that you can't please everyone all the time. I'm also a perfectionist, and I have a hard time delegating. This is one of the reasons I'm self-employed; I like doing things my own way, to my own standards. I am also very detail-oriented. As I've moved into management, I've found it very challenging to leave the detail to others and focus on the big picture.

What are the most satisfying parts of your job?

❯ The most satisfying part of my job is shaping policy that will influence the future of cities. I feel that it's tremendously important work, and it is very gratifying to see decisions made based on policies I've had a part in. My work provides me with the opportunity to work with many bright, creative individuals in government and private industry. I find the collaboration and creative thinking that goes into a plan can be very stimulating.

In the same vein, I derive a lot of satisfaction helping people participate in and understand the planning process. It is especially gratifying to me when

citizen planners "graduate" from a task force I've staffed, or move on to the planning commission or city council because I've helped get them psyched up about planning. I also really enjoy fieldwork and mapping tasks. To me, the most exciting part of a comprehensive plan is figuring out how and where growth will occur. So any task that involves spatial analysis, creating and testing land use options, and mapping future land uses is very satisfying for me.

What about the least?

❯ The results of my work are often intangible and invisible. Much of my work is "shelf-bound" from the day it is delivered to the client, and I spend a lot of time on interim products that have a shelf life of just a few weeks or months. As a long-range planner, I don't get the satisfaction of seeing "results" the way a current planner or architect does. My plans have 20-year horizons, so it's not like I can point to buildings or highways and say "those are there because the plan I worked on said so." About the only thing I can point to and say "I did that" are some street signs in Houston (I came up with the street names about 20 years ago).

Additionally, my job can also get very intense and exhausting. I typically find myself working nights and weekends, inevitably on tasks that I can't bill my clients for because my budgets are never big enough. I bring work on vacations, and my work-life balance is frequently out of whack. To say I am "time management challenged" would be a comical understatement.

Lastly, I am often stymied by intense bureaucracy. Bureaucracy, and rules that make no intuitive sense, make me crazy. I've also seen some great ideas watered down by vested political interests, and watched the integrity of plans compromised through the political process.

At What Geographic Scale Do You Want to Work?

Planners are not able to control entirely which projects they work on. A planner working for a regional planning agency may be assigned to focus on planning for a small subarea because of a special project focusing on that one place rather than the entire region. A planner in a large city may be assigned to work as a neighborhood planner.

But planners can specialize, to a degree, based on breadth of the geographic areas that they work in. These specializations relate to the kinds of areas that plans are typically prepared for and implemented in.

- Site plans for laying out the buildings, streets, driveways, walkways, and other features of a proposed development site

- District and corridor plans for considering issues of access, identity, and economic development is a specially designated district or street corridor

- Neighborhood plans that consider all of the issues in a neighborhood, including housing character and needs, job access, transportation access, public safety, and many other facets of neighborhood life and character

- Citywide plans, which can be comprehensive in scope, looking at the wide range of issues, similar to a neighborhood plan, or focusing on a single issue, such as a citywide park plan, transit plan, or economic development plan

- State or regional plans, which look at a broad geographic area encompassing multiple communities of both urban and rural character. State and regional plans are likely to focus on a limited number of issues, such as a regional water supply plan or a statewide energy independence plan.

Consulting planners are more likely to work across different scales than public planners. As consulting planners take on new projects, they may find themselves working on a neighborhood plan for a small city one day and on a regional transportation plan the next.

No matter what the size of the area that a planner is working on, many aspects of the job remain the same.

Working with Communities

SUE SCHWARTZ, FAICP

**Neighborhood Planning Manager,
City of Greensboro, North Carolina**

**Department of Housing and Community
Development**

What does your job involve?

❯ I manage the neighborhood planning division
for the City of Greensboro Department of Housing
and Community Development. We are responsible
for the City's Historic Preservation Program and
neighborhood indicators, and we conduct neighborhood and redevelopment planning processes.

How do you spend your time at work?

❯ Meetings! While we all may lament our days being filled with them, in my job they are a critical
part of my day, whether it is checking in with my
staff or working with other city departments on
a project, or meeting with neighborhood leaders.
Our profession is built on collaboration and that is
what those meetings add up to day in and day out.

What are some of the experiences that have shaped your ideas of planning and how you approach the projects on which you work?

❯ I would like to believe my approaches to projects
are always evolving and I am in a constant learning
mode.

Narrowing it down to pivotal experiences I would
say there were three. Early in my career I worked
on greenways. A group of us who did in North
Carolina were in contact with each other pretty
regularly. At some point we decided among the

six or so of us we would put on a two-day state
conference just about greenways. Most of us were
entry-level planners and were too naive to know
we weren't supposed to be able to do that. We had
about 200 people at the first one and put on six
more in subsequent years, the last two being national in scope.

That effort led to the governor of North Carolina
appointing the Greenways Advisory Panel, which I
had the honor of chairing for several years. When I
look back, I can't believe all we achieved with very
little resources. I tend to be a little impatient when
people say they are too busy to put together a lun-
cheon speaker.

In the early 1990s, the mayor of Greensboro wanted
the city to submit an Enterprise Community
Application to the U.S. Department of Housing
and Urban Development (HUD). This was a challenging way of doing business for us, particularly
because of the strong requirements for public input. We hired Mary Means & Associates and Mary
had a much different approach from anything we
had seen before. We went out to some of the worst
economic areas in the city (versus making folks
come downtown to meet). There were focus group
discussions with people we served with programs
but never really talked to directly before like homeless moms and school kids. The way we advertised
our meetings was aggressive, too.

At the last public meeting, a neighborhood resident
from one of our Community Development Block
Grant (CDBG) target areas stood up to speak. I recognized her from several earlier meetings and when
Mary asked people if they had feedback about the
process, she was the first to raise her hand. I will

never forget what she said. "You all show up at our neighborhood, roll out pretty maps, and ask us what we think. This time you asked us 'how are y'all doing?' I appreciate it." Her subtle message to me was very clear. If you want to affect change, you need to know more than just people's opinions on narrow issues. You have to understand what is going on with them, their challenges and triumphs.

We didn't get the grant, but it completely changed how we worked with the community from that point on. Personally, it set me on a never-ending quest to learn facilitation and public engagement techniques. I am always on the lookout for how planners and other folks do this sort of work and what I can learn from them. When you get down to it what it really taught me was the value of listening. People value knowing they have been heard and understood.

The last formative experience for me would be getting involved in the American Planning Association (APA). The first two planning directors I worked for, Dee Blackwell of the Western Piedmont Council of Governments and Bill McNeil in High Point, North Carolina, were both very encouraging about my getting involved with the North Carolina chapter of APA as they had been. Becoming involved early in my career gave me exposure to a lot of other planners and planning approaches and set me on a path that led to holding national offices. All the people I have worked for in Greensboro have also been extremely supportive, but Dee and Bill started me off in that direction.

Is there one project you have found particularly challenging?

❭ As project manager for our Southside Redevelopment Area, I have had the rare position of working on a project from its initial kernel of

Planners sometimes lament that there is too little to show for our efforts at the end of the day or year. But planners who facilitate development decisions can often point to aspects of the built environment that they influenced. Sue Schwartz explains how an alley came to be named for her: "I don't think it was intentional; the builder and developer were arguing about names in a meeting we were in (they were college classmates and argue like brothers) when I snapped, 'Damn it, just name it Sues Blues because that is what you two do to me.' The developer absentmindedly wrote 'Sues Blues' in pencil on the site plan, and it got recorded that way. A few people know that's me, I think it's pretty cool since until we redeveloped it the unofficial name was 'Crack Alley' due to the drug activity there." MIKE COWHIG.

an idea through the planning process and now implementation. The planning process was long and difficult with a disparate group of stakeholders. The issues were tough: neighborhood decay, major drug and prostitution issues, the desire for historic preservation, and downtown revitalization.

An advantage of working in the public sector is the opportunity to stick with a particular project for a long time and see tangible results. Sue Schwartz was project manager for the Southside Redevelopment Area in Greensboro, North Carolina, from the earliest planning stages in 1992 through implementation efforts that continued for over a decade. This is a view of the live/work units and townhouses that line Martin Luther King Jr. Drive, which is the major spine of Southside and a key entrance route to downtown Greensboro. MIKE COWHIG.

The resulting plan was complex and the implementation tasks involved were daunting. The city had never attempted some of the things called for in the plan before. It also called for work across city department lines—something that was not so common in the mid-1990s. I learned a lot of technical things about development and reinvestment, but the biggest challenge (which ultimately led to the biggest reward) was learning how to break down those complex tasks into more manageable bites and get the tasks done in a way that built momentum for the project.

What are the most satisfying parts of your job?

❯ The most satisfying part of my job is going through a planning process with a neighborhood and watching neighbors take ownership of the plan and its implementation. To me, there is no feeling like the one you get when you see a community become strong advocates not just for their neighborhood but also for good planning and responsible government.

Equally satisfying to me is mentoring the next generation of planners. I was very fortunate early in my career to have a number of people I learned from who also inspired me. Whether it is being involved with new planners through APA or in our organization, I enjoy their energy and enthusiasm.

And the least?

❯ The least satisfying aspect of my job is when we have to justify our existence (as a profession and an important part of city government) over and over.

Bridging Rural and Urban Areas

ELIZABETH "BOO" THOMAS, ASLA

President and CEO, Center for Planning Excellence

Baton Rouge, Louisiana

What is the Center for Planning Excellence and what role does it play in local planning in Louisiana?

❯ The Center for Planning Excellence (CPEX) is a nonprofit organization that coordinates urban and rural planning efforts in Louisiana. We provide best-practice planning models, innovative policy ideas, and technical assistance to individual communities that wish to create and enact master plans dealing with transportation and infrastructure needs, environmental issues, and quality design for the built environment.

CPEX's role is to bring community members and leaders together and then provide guidance as they work toward a shared vision for future growth and development. Through this collaboration, the community decides what type of planning would suit their needs.

What is your role with the organization?

❯ I interact with local elected officials, design professionals, neighborhood citizens, and community leaders about planning issues. Of course, I work with my very talented and brilliant staff to guide them in fulfilling the mission of the Center for Planning Excellence dealing with local planning issues, development projects, parishwide issues, or regional planning.

How does CPEX function within Louisiana?

❯ In the wake of hurricanes Rita and Katrina, CPEX partnered with the Louisiana Recovery Authority to create a comprehensive regional plan for South Louisiana: Louisiana Speaks Regional Plan. The

Planning practices have evolved with technology to enable the inclusion of many more people in the planning process. Though public meetings remain a staple of good planning, websites and online surveys now allow people who are unable to attend meetings to have a chance to add their voice to the process. Boo Thomas helped lead the development of a regional plan for a large portion of south Louisiana in the wake of Hurricane Katrina, a process that reflects the input of 27,000 voices. DENNISE RENO, FOR LOUISIANA SPEAKS, INC.

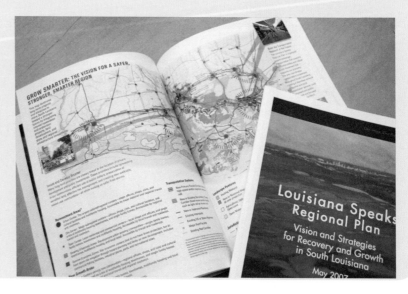

plan is unprecedented in its geographical scope (35 parishes), level of citizen participation (27,000 citizens), and the range of issues it addresses. These issues include transportation, coastal restoration, risk management, community growth, and economic development.

Now in the immediate aftermath of Hurricanes Gustav and Ike, the Louisiana Speaks Plan is even more important because it provides the roadmap for recovery and illustrates the opportunities for rebuilding "safer, stronger, and smarter!"

What experiences have shaped your vision of planning?

❭ Being asked to lead the first neighborhood redevelopment project in Baton Rouge was a daunting experience. Although I had concentrated on urban planning projects in graduate school, nothing could really prepare me for the overwhelming assignment to try to transform a failing neighborhood. I quickly learned that I needed to involve as many players and stakeholders in this effort as possible. I laid out an ambitious schedule of public meetings, living room

meetings, business owner meetings, and church meetings. Being willing to meet with anyone and everyone who was interested in or threatened by this effort enabled me to gain the confidence, trust, and support of the residents, property owners, business owners, and community leaders.

What are the most satisfying parts of your job?

❭ Working with the committed and concerned citizens that are committed to improving their neighborhoods, cities, and region. When we are doing a neighborhood revitalization plan, and then see it to implementation, it is very rewarding for me to see the satisfaction and triumph on the neighbors' faces! They understand that their efforts were the reason for the success, and I understand that the Plan enabled that to happen!

And the least?

❭ The regular conflicts that occur when codes are violated, when citizens don't get their projects approved, and when we are not able to deliver on some aspects of the plan.

Large public meetings, such as this one during a neighborhood revitalization effort in Old South Baton Rouge, Louisiana, are one of the many ways that planners can inform and involve stakeholders in the planning process. CENTER FOR PLANNING EXCELLENCE.

Planning in a Midsized City

BRAD STEINKE

Director of Development Services

City of Apache Junction, Arizona

What does your job involve?

❯ I am responsible for managing the short-term planning, long-range planning, building permits, code enforcement, and revenue development (grants).

Some community plans utilize a conceptualized approach to land use planning, painting broad brush strokes to describe desired future conditions rather than detailed, parcel-by-parcel future land use designations. This Development Plan for Apache Junction, Arizona, uses such an approach. Although the level of detail and the terminology differs, this is only a slight variation on the "comprehensive plan," as it is more commonly known. CITY OF APACHE JUNCTION.

DEVELOPMENT PLAN

Do you have a daily routine?

❭ It seems that the more years you log, the less true planning you do. I spend most of my time administering the department (working on the budget, personnel, going to outside meetings, being the department spokesperson) and very little time rolling up my sleeves and working with development proposals and long-range planning tasks.

Part of a planner's job is being a regulator. Are you comfortable with that?

❭ We are in the business of being regulators whether we like it or not. We regulate how other people live and we exercise authority over other people's money.

The planning office is a regulatory body, and some planners earn their stripes by saying no. There's a potential for confrontation every day.

How do you deal with that?

❭ I think it's important to argue issues, not personalities. You have to be respectful of the person on the other side of the public counter. They are your client, essentially. You have to put yourself in a position where you don't dictate to them, you have to act as a facilitator. And then you have to make a decision. In that situation, you need to communicate to the person and help them understand why you're doing what you're doing. And, for you as a planner, you want to leave the conversation knowing that they may not like the law or the policy that you're discussing, but that doesn't mean they don't like you as a person.

Nine of ten people will leave the office and understand what you did and respect why you're doing it. The other one in ten is a mutant case. There is no way of resolving those situations, and you'll just have to live with it.

Is that a difficult transition?

❭ I think planners have to realize that we are in the business of public service. Planning is not all high-level thinking. Most planners go into the profession at the bottom rung and have to deal with some unseemly sides of planning. Zoning administration, for example. I think everyone who goes into planning should have to do zoning review for a season. It's part of how we make sure our plans are implemented and are sustained over time.

As a planner, you have to learn how to communicate, mediate, and facilitate. If you're not comfortable with any of those things, you need to learn how to do them or look at another career.

How much of this is learned on the job?

❭ I hope medical school provides doctors with many more tools to use on the job. Planning school really teaches you to think in the manner of a planner. But you will not learn everything you need to learn in the classroom. School is not going to give you a toolkit, or allow you to understand everything that goes into a planner's day. It's not that type of profession, and it can be tough to get that message across to students and someone looking at planning as a career.

Given all that you've said, you still mostly enjoy working with the public.

❭ I learned very early in my career that I like to deal with people on a daily basis. When I went into the private sector for a time, I lost that interaction. I like the "edge" of having to solve problems every day.

What is your biggest challenge?

❭ The ongoing challenge for most of us is probably the lack of resources to do the "best" plan. I learned early that a planner who cannot compromise and gain consensus will probably not be effective. This took a few years for me to work out.

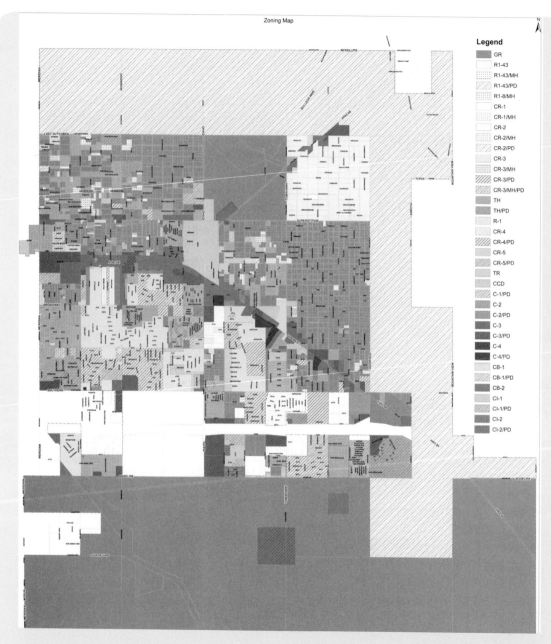

Whereas future land use maps may be intentionally vague as to the locations of boundaries separating different uses, zoning maps must be much more specific about the location of parcel boundaries and zoning designations. Zoning is a legal mechanism by which limits on land use are made part of the local municipal codebook. Even a relatively small community like Apache Junction, Arizona (with a population of 31,800 in the year 2000), may utilize dozens of unique zoning districts to define the various legal parameters on development in the city. CITY OF APACHE JUNCTION.

If you want to, you can set off on a path from a job as Planner I to Planner II to Planner III to planning manager to planning director. Some people want to move beyond that, to become city manager, the main cog in the wheel in local government, where you're in charge of personnel, budgeting, and the management of the city. I knew I would be very, very unhappy with those additional responsibilities.

There is a question that most planners eventually ask themselves: Is there one rung in the organization that you would be most happy with? You may know planners who love their current positions, as an assistant planner or Planner III. They like what they do and what they get out of the job.

I manage 20 people in my position, so I am removed from a lot of the day-to-day planning work. Every once in a while, I will stick my nose in our planning supervisor's office just to stay sane.

Planners aren't trained as managers, so we have to learn on the job. Some planning directors may have taken a management class, but, by and large, it's not what we're trained to do, and it's not what most of us do well, either.

Becoming a Planning Director

The "planning director" in a city or regional planning office or in a consulting firm is one of the highest positions that a planner can achieve. Becoming a planning director is definitely not for everyone. The planning director is in the political hot seat. Many times, unlike the planners who work under the director, the planning director can be dismissed for no reason at all. In addition, the planning director has management responsibilities—managing the planning office budget, managing people, and managing the office's time.

RICHARD BERNHARDT, FAICP

Executive Director, Metropolitan Nashville-Davidson County Planning Department

Nashville, Tennessee

Why did you decide to become a planner?

❭ I was always interested in cities and urban design, even as a teenager in junior high school. I determined that a career as a planner suited my needs. Later, in college, I went to architecture school at Auburn University, but once I began, I realized that architecture wasn't the background I needed unless I planned on becoming an architect. At the time, planning was becoming more of a social science field than a design field, so I changed majors and got a degree in economics with a minor in political science.

After college, I got a job at Metro (the Metropolitan Planning Commission for Nashville and Davidson County, Tennessee) and through an education program, I had an opportunity to attend graduate school in planning at Ohio State. I came back to Metro, but after working here a couple of years, I came to the realization that I was most interested in

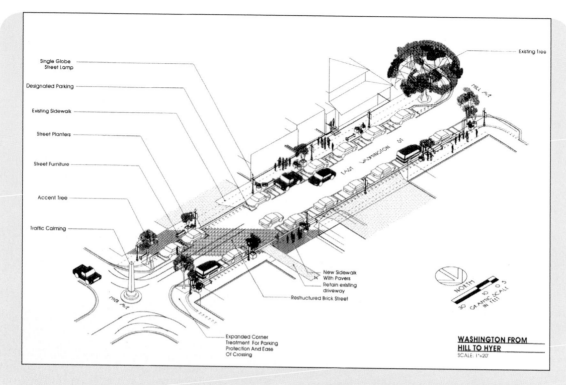

Single Globe
Street Lamp

Designated Parking

Existing Sidewalk

Street Planters

Street Furniture

Accent Tree

Traffic Calming

Existing Tree

HILL AVE.

EAST WASHINGTON ST

HILL AVE.

New Sidewalk
With Pavers

Retain existing
driveway

Restructured Brick Street

Expanded Corner
Treatment For Parking
Protection And Ease
Of Crossing

NORTH

30   10   0   5
GRAPHIC SCALE
IN FEET

**WASHINGTON FROM
HILL TO HYER**
SCALE: 1"=20'

making a difference in a community, and to do that, I thought I needed to be a planning director.

I left Nashville and I took a job as director of Hopkinsville-Christian County, Kentucky, an area of about 70,000 people, and after three years there, moved to become planning director in Gainesville, Florida. I worked there another three years before I was appointed the director of planning at the Orlando Planning and Development Department, where I oversaw the whole range of development in the city. I ended up staying in Orlando 17 years, then had the opportunity to work for EDAW as the director of their town planning studio. I enjoyed that job but found that I missed the public sector. Around that time, the job in Nashville opened up. I was convinced that they were interested in a proactive planning agenda, so I applied for the job and was hired in 2000, and I've been here ever since.

▲ Effective planning for urban streets sometimes requires detailed, three-dimensional illustration such as this to convey the desired outcome. This sketch for a single block in Nashville, Tennessee, describes the specific location of street lights, trees, planters, parking, and pavement types. CRAIG OWENSBY/METRO NASHVILLE PLANNING DEPARTMENT.

Although you're not a designer, urban design has been central to your career.

❯ The design of cities and placemaking were always interesting to me, even before I knew what a planner was. I was always interested in how places came together and how successful downtowns developed.

I'm still interested in the design component, which is why a lot of the work I've done has been around the principles of New Urbanism, traditional design, and form-based planning.

Although I am not a designer, I have learned through study and experience enough about basic

Planners in leadership roles need not be urban designers themselves to establish high standards for urban design in a community. By valuing urban design and hiring other planners with expertise in design, a planning director like Rick Bernhardt can help to ensure that new development is properly planned and critiqued before approval. Though very close to the street, the townhomes pictured here utilize landscaping and a raised first floor to create an effective transition from the public zone of the street to the private zone of the home. CRAIG OWENSBY/METRO NASHVILLE PLANNING DEPARTMENT.

urban design to be able to critique things and provide leadership, and in every place I've worked, I've tried to build a strong design studio.

Why is that important to you?

❭ Two reasons. The design studio is here to assist developers in interpreting zoning codes and offering design assistance. They also work with our community and land development planners when we do detailed neighborhood plans that address basic urban design issues. The designers also help to lead the development of form-based codes. This is of critical importance because the built environment is at the core of what a city is, and understanding how the built environment impacts communities is extremely important.

In every place I've worked, I have reallocated resources to create a design studio and help it function.

Why was it important to you to become a planning director?

❭ I realized early on that a planning director had an opportunity to set a planning department's program, to interact with elected officials to help set a community's priorities, and to educate the community about these priorities and the alternatives they have to achieve their goals. I like the process of expanding

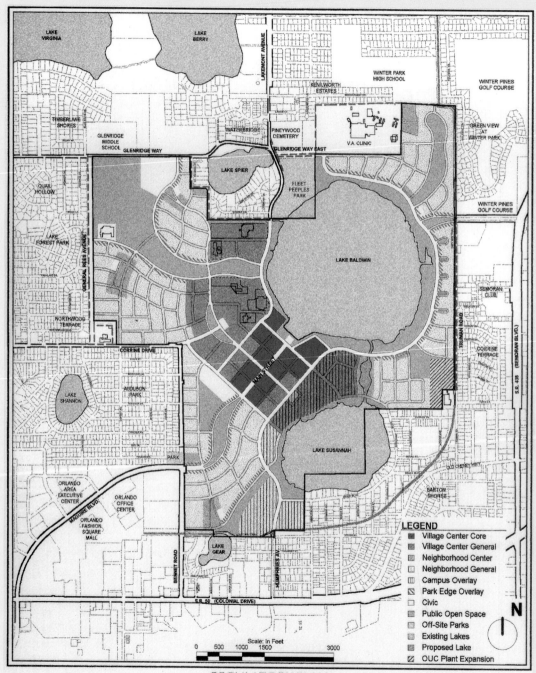

REGULATORY PLAN

Empowering residents to take ownership in the planning process requires face-to-face discussions and the sharing of information in ways that allow residents to quickly learn about the issues at hand. Maps are a great tool to get people talking and asking questions about the planning process. CRAIG OWENSBY/METRO NASHVILLE PLANNING DEPARTMENT.

the options perceived by the community to consider more livable and sustainable alternatives.

The development tone of a community often reflects the leadership of a planning director. Personally, I have always been more of a proactive planner. You have planning directors who are more comfortable in an administrative role. This type of director is usually willing to go along with the inherent direction of the politicians and elected officials.

◀ Communities sometimes utilize regulatory plans to define the desired building design and format in a very specific way. The regulatory plan is different from zoning in that it is usually less focused on land use but provides detailed design guidelines for a range of design parameters. This regulatory plan for Baldwin Park, a neighborhood in Nashville, Tennessee complements a separate zoning map for the same area. CRAIG OWENSBY/METRO NASHVILLE PLANNING DEPARTMENT.

I want planning to be out in front. As a planner, I think you have to be willing to interact and lead. The planning director has the ability to engage or exclude the community from the planning process.

Today, Nashville's planning process is citizen-driven in terms of how we engage the community. Historically, the department did planning by steering committee. There was little opportunity for unconnected citizen involvement and no design studio, so I reallocated our resources to provide more meaningful opportunities for citizens to be involved.

What does a planner need to know and do to become a planning director?

❯ Part of it is a willingness to continually learn and be open to new ideas. I have always been heavily involved in APA. I have served as chapter president and been on the board of APA. I also have been involved in the Congress for the New Urbanism since the beginning.

When I first took a job as planning director, I took a pay cut because I thought it was more important to gain skills and function in a significantly higher administrative and political environment than to make a little more money. The agency didn't have a lot of resources, so I had to figure out how we could fully function as a planning agency. This experience was very valuable to me as I moved forward in my career.

Why did you decide to leave Kentucky and move to Florida?

❯ I got all that I could out of that job, and at some point, I looked for additional challenges and moved on.

What happens as planning director is that you move from making a difference in how you structure a department and work with the community and evolve into the maintenance of your program. Once you get into maintenance mode, the job becomes much less satisfying to me.

I want to work with a community that wants to change and get it the tools that enable it to grow. After 17 years in Orlando, I had hit the maintenance mode, so it was time to move on.

What is your approach as planning director?

❯ My objectives are building a livable community through a planning program focused on empowering citizens into owning the planning process, then providing the community the tools and techniques to make a difference. In Nashville, when we go out and start a plan, we tell the community, we want them involved. This is not going to be my plan or the mayor's plan. And if the plan reflects the community's values, after we create it together, you have to be the one defending it to the city council.

The first question I ask myself when I start working in a community is: do we have a planning infrastructure in place that supports this approach? Once we have that structure in place—and it took awhile to get to that point here in Nashville—then we can educate people as to what the implications of their choices are. We can get into issues of urban design, mixed use communities, multi-modal transportation systems, those kinds of elements.

Our job as planners is to educate people into making better choices. We constantly need to understand our role. Certainly, there are times when planners need to take a different position from the community, but throughout the process, our job is to set the stage for the community to develop an effective plan, educating them as to what their alternatives are.

Charting Another Path to Planning Director

RONALD BAILEY, AICP

Executive Director, Chester County, Pennsylvania Planning Commission

West Chester, Pennsylvania

Why did you become a planner?

❭ I began my career working for the U.S. Forest Service at the time in the late 1960s when NEPA (National Environmental Protection Act) was first affecting federal agencies. Absent other staff with an environmental background, I was assigned to prepare master plans and environmental impact statements. Unfortunately, the agency had not yet recognized the need for planners and permanent positions were limited to foresters, civil engineers, and landscape architects.

In 1973, the State of Oregon passed SB 100, the Oregon Land Use Law. As a result of this legislation, all counties had to hire a planner. I was appointed the planning director of a county in Oregon.

What was it like to transition from federal into local planning?

❭ It was not difficult. I started with the federal government when NEPA was brand new. Agencies were scrambling to prepare the required EIS documents and to institutionalize the environmental review process. I was at the right place at the right time to learn the environmental review process as it evolved.

The passage of the Oregon Comprehensive Planning Act in 1973 envisioned preparation of comprehensive plans by the state's local govern-

ments that contained extensive data and analysis similar to an EIS. My skills in meeting facilitation, demographic and environmental analysis, and report writing were readily transferable to preparing comprehensive plans for counties in Oregon.

What I had to learn quickly was planning law in Oregon, but since the enabling legislation was brand new, I was learning along with every other planning official in the state. In fact the statewide planning goals that were adopted by the Oregon Land Conservation and Development Commission to serve as the standards and requirements of county and municipal planning were formulated in 1974, which enabled me to witness and participate in the law's evolution.

Case law also changed rapidly in 1973 and 1974, particularly with the landmark case of Fasano v. Board of County Commissioners of Washington County, which mandated consistency between comprehensive plans and implementing ordinances. The Oregon Bar Association conducted numerous continuing education classes on the new Oregon laws, which I attended whenever I could. I also took classes at Portland State University that were taught by the attorney who had won the Fazano case.

You left Oregon and later became planning director in Lancaster County, Pennsylvania, before moving to Chester County. What are your duties today as executive director?

❭ I am responsible for overseeing the development and implementation of the county's comprehensive plan. I also administer a staff that provides consulting assistance to municipal governments in the county,

▲ In Chester County, Pennsylvania, planners developed future growth scenarios to illustrate how the rural county would appear if development continues at low densities. This scenario, based on trends, shows the potential outcome of uncontrolled, low-density development. CHESTER COUNTY PLANNING COMMISSION.

reviews all land developments and subdivisions in the county, and works with regional planning agencies to program transportation improvements.

I am responsible for staffing the Chester County Planning Commission and implementing the Commission's work program, and I coordinate the work of the commission and my staff with a variety of agencies and organizations.

What does your job involve?

❯ Much of my daily work involves administration—developing and executing the departmental budget, supervising employees, managing work programs and project timelines, writing and re-sponding to letters and emails, and reviewing and editing documents and reports.

My job also involves setting the direction for planning. On a day-to-day basis, I may not be developing the models or the analysis that results in a plan, but I have assistants working for me who do. I also serve as a member of the Pennsylvania State Planning Board and, in that capacity, I work on policy recommendations to the legislature and governor.

▲ Another growth scenario illustrated the county's vision of clustered development designed to preserve and enhance the rural landscape. This vision, drawn so the public could understand the benefits of controlling growth, was enacted as part of the county's comprehensive plan. CHESTER COUNTY PLANNING COMMISSION.

What are some of the experiences that have shaped your ideas of planning and how you approach the projects on which you work?

❯ Planning is a collaborative process. To be successful, plans have to be negotiated with the community. I came to Pennsylvania in 1988 because of the opportunity to do good planning in Lancaster County. The county has some of the finest farmland in the world, unique and historic commu-

nities, a diverse economy, and was experiencing sprawl development.

In the late 1980s, the debate over Lancaster County's future had become divisive, with one faction being pro-growth and the other no-growth. Despite such conflict, however, there was a tremendous opportunity to create a new vision for the future by negotiating with both factions. We negotiated a premise that parts of Lancaster County were appropriate for development and parts were not. The result was a comprehensive plan that directed growth to existing communities and protected large areas of agricultural land.

Consistency of proposed development to Landscapes

2007 Proposed Subdivision Activity

Consistent Plans
(Size relative to number of units or square feet)

Not Consistent Plans
(Size relative to number of units or square feet)

Livable Landscapes

rural

rural center

suburban

suburban center

urban

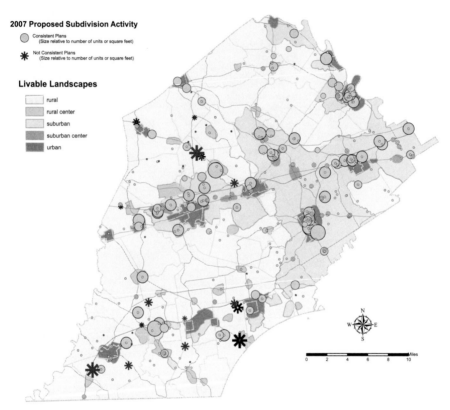

In 2007, the suburban landscape received the highest number of proposed new lots/units (over 1,300) followed by rural and the urban landscape. Approximately 75 percent of the new lots/units proposed during 2007 were considered consistent with the policies defined in Landscapes. Most of these plans represent proposals at locations in the urban, suburban and suburban center landscapes. Development proposals in the rural landscape accounted for the largest disparity, in terms of consistency with Landscapes. Approximately 80 percent of the proposed new lots/units that were located in the rural landscape were designated as inconsistent.

Consistency with Landscapes

	Reviews		Lots/units		Structure sq. footage	
	yes	no	yes	no	yes	no
Rural	94	32	242	928	325,691	333,708
Rural center	15	2	100	9	99,984	488,316
Suburban	120	0	1,331	0	1,595,720	0
Suburban center	20	0	187	0	393,837	0
Urban	78	0	1,057	0	1,230,724	0
Total	327	34	2,917	937	3,645,956	822,024

If someone aspires to be a planning director, how do you advise them to proceed?

❭ To become a planning director requires building a resume with experience in several areas of planning. I think it is important for planners to have experience in both preparing comprehensive plans and in preparing and administering zoning and subdivision ordinances.

Sometimes individuals think of comprehensive planning as "pure" planning, while ordinance administration is some kind of lesser activity. It is the ordinance, however, that determines how the land is developed. A planning director who does not have an understanding of what it takes to review subdivisions or to stand at a counter and enforce a zoning ordinance may be handicapped in knowing how to balance programs.

I should mention, however, that becoming a planning director should not necessarily be a universal ambition. A person who excels as a planner—who enjoys using technology and analytical techniques, and who

◀ In the years since the Landscapes plan was adopted, Chester County has monitored the implementation of the comprehensive plan by summarizing proposed subdivision and land development activity in monthly and annual reports. CHESTER COUNTY PLANNING COMMISSION.

really likes to work on plans that create meaningful change—many derive the most satisfaction from an ongoing career as a journeyman planner.

Most planning directors do very little planning themselves. Instead, they largely deal with politics, budgets, personnel management, and administrative matters, not with the plans that are created in their jurisdiction.

Being a planner can be an excellent springboard to a career as an administrator of planning programs, but planning and administration are different fields. In fact, a planner who wants to become a planning director should take coursework in management, either as a supplement to their academic achievements or by pursuing a master's degree in public administration or in a planning field with a strong concentration of administration and management courses.

I would also suggest that any planner who aspires to be a planning director should obtain membership in the American Institute of Certified Planners. While AICP is rarely a condition of qualification for a position, more and more employers are looking for candidates who are certified. AICP membership can be the distinguishing factor in a group of applicants.

Merging Regional and Local Planning

JOHN FREGONESE

President, Fregonese Associates

Portland, Oregon

What was your career path?

❭ As a young person, I was interested in geography and earth science. I went to Oregon State, but not in the planning school. I was focused on cartography and geomorphology, so I could be a water resources manager, managing dams and working on water resources issues, technical stuff really, far away from planning.

While at Oregon State, I took a class in land use planning and found it fascinating. At the time, in the mid-1970s, there weren't a lot of job opportunities, so I stayed in school to get my graduate degree in planning, and, while I was there, I took classes in law and economics. The more I studied planning, the more I saw the connections with urban geography.

When I got out of college, Woodburn, Oregon, needed someone to put together a comprehensive plan. I was hired as planning director, and that became my first planning job. Woodburn had a limit on sewer extensions, so I developed a sewage and growth allocation program that got me noticed. A few years later, I got a job as planning director in Ashland, Oregon. It was a great move for me. I was 28, and Ashland was a great place to be a planner. The local government was progressive. We had 20 percent of the population who walked to work. It was a great place to be. I ended up staying for 13 years.

It was only when Ashland got content and an anti-growth faction took hold that I began to look elsewhere. Metro Portland (the regional government) needed a planning director and it was another great opportunity. The agency had a great GIS system, so I had great tools at my disposal. We were able to build land use models and test scenarios with land use transportation metrics. We used that as the basis for Metro 2040, a regional growth concept.

How was the transition from local to regional planning?

❭ I was an opportunist in some sense. I had been a planning director for a small Oregon city for 13 years and worked in small cities for 16 years, so I worked on a lot of issues where the city and county worked at cross-purposes.

I was also interested in bigger issues and doing something different, so when the opportunity came to lead the Metro 2040 project, I decided to do it. It was my introduction to regional planning, and I found it took a lot of my skill set to do that.

Because of my background as a geographer, I was well adapted to set up a system to do regional modeling and scenarios. And because of my experience as a local planner, I had the skills needed to implement it and communicate with local planners on what needed to be done. I had a lot of experience in local government, so it turned out to be a good opportunity for me.

After five years at Metro, I had a lot of experience doing regional planning and large-scale planning, but I also had opportunities to do the small-scale work on downtown and area plans.

You left Metro to start your own firm. Now you integrate regional planning with small-scale area plans. How does that work?

❯ We've used my background as a small city planner and as a large regional planner to focus on large regions and the interactions within these regions, to understand the driving forces of change within these areas.

For a planner who wants to work at the large scale, it helps to have experience at both ends of the telescope. You need a really large zoom lens to look at issues from a regional perspective, but then you also need to zoom down to the local level and see what's happening there. So you need a lens that gives you resolution at all levels.

We ask everyone in our office to work at both scales. Fortunately, we have the advantage of be-

ing a very computerized shop. Without high-tech tools, planning in this manner is very difficult. If you look at plans from the 1970s, you see a lot of fuzzy blob maps of corridors and wedges. Those were great concepts, but they had a lot less connection to what was happening on the ground. Today, we can do much more specific work with our regional modeling tools.

We want to set plans in a regional context but also at the human scale. If you lose the human scale, you can forget who the client is. When you look at a region from a god's-eye view, people look like ants. So you always want to make sure you understand the human scale.

▼ John Fregonese's approach to regional planning focuses on small areas to illustrate how redevelopment will appear on the ground. FREGONESE ASSOCIATES, INC.

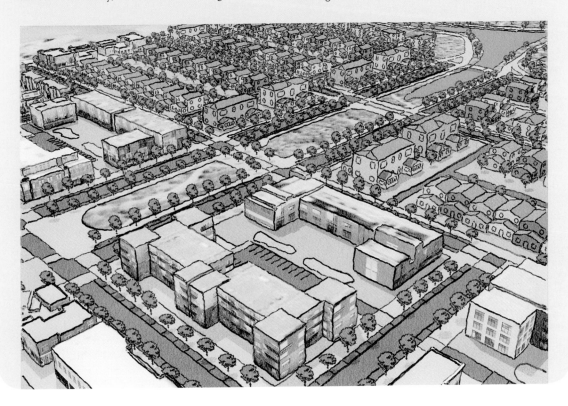

How do you do that?

❯ We do a lot of small-scale modeling and visualization. We used to have to draw watercolor sketches to illustrate these concepts; today, we can use SketchUp software to do that. We build scenarios at a fine-grained scale using GIS and link these to the transportation model.

If you want a different kind of community than you have today, you have to understand how the market works and how developers operate, and create incentives for developers to implement your vision. If you have regional policies that have no anchor in reality, they won't be implemented. All change happens at the local level, and the plan should be the guide for that change.

Why is there so much emphasis on the local scale in your work?

❯ If you can't describe what you're planning, people imagine the worst. They fill in an unknown future with a very negative view of what might happen, almost what you see in a science fiction movie, with vermin-infested infill slums.

So we take specific small areas and illustrate what can happen there. We pick a few stations and show what transit station infill areas and transit-oriented development would look like and how the policies would be implemented. We want to provide information for the public to assimilate at a level they can understand.

What advice would you give a young planner or planner-to-be who wants to do this kind of work?

❯ Be a generalist. And don't be afraid of math. Try to understand the technical side, not just the policy side. And hone your communication skills. Be prepared to learn your whole life. What we will be planning for in 20 years is not what we're dealing with today. It's a rapidly changing field.

Many public meetings and charrettes conclude with reports from planners about the key discussion points and views expressed by participants. Often these comments are recorded on maps and documented in the meeting minutes for later reference. FREGONESE ASSOCIATES, INC.

Planning at the Regional Scale

JOHN HODGES-COPPLE

Regional Planning Director

Triangle J Council of Governments

Durham, North Carolina

▼ In the Raleigh area, two Metropolitan Planning Organizations (MPOs) created a single regional transportation plan. The transit component connects five regional centers to one another and to communities throughout the region. TRIANGLE J COUNCIL OF GOVERNMENTS.

What does your job entail?

❯ I manage the regional council's work related to land use, transportation, and the environment. I am responsible for overall management of the program (including the staff and budget), as well as the day-to-day execution of projects, mostly related to the intersection of land use, transportation, and air quality, including transportation–air quality conformity for the region.

I am heavily involved in the region's transportation demand management (TDM) program, a recent

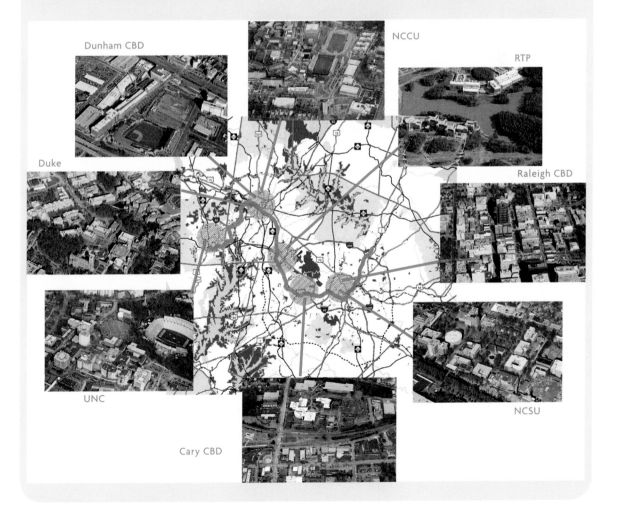

Dunham CBD

NCCU

RTP

Duke

Raleigh CBD

UNC

NCSU

Cary CBD

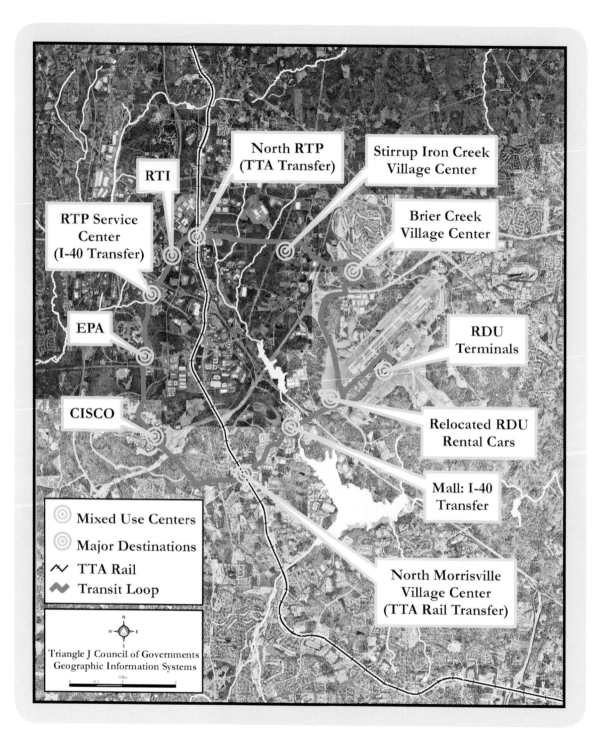

North RTP
(TTA Transfer)

Stirrup Iron Creek
Village Center

RTI

Brier Creek
Village Center

RTP Service
Center
(I-40 Transfer)

RDU
Terminals

EPA

Relocated RDU
Rental Cars

CISCO

Mall: I-40
Transfer

Mixed Use Centers

Major Destinations

TTA Rail

Transit Loop

North Morrisville
Village Center
(TTA Rail Transfer)

Triangle J Council of Governments
Geographic Information Systems

special advisory commission on transit, a new development and infrastructure partnership, and with other issues where cooperative efforts are required between the region's two metropolitan planning organizations, the state department of transportation, and the regional transit authority.

Do you have a typical day?

❭ No, and each project I have can involve vastly different tasks. Some typical things I do include establishing and facilitating partnerships, which essentially involves managing collaborative processes with technical staff from a variety of local, regional, state, and federal agencies; researching issues and synthesizing their results into written documents; and administering programs and projects, including developing project/program proposals, securing funding, managing the budget and staff efforts.

How is this job different from the other jobs you've had as a planner?

❭ No two jobs I've had have been the same. This job combines several aspects I want in any job: a sustained connection to a specific place (as contrasted with a consulting job, where each project is independent and is located in a variety of places), at a scale where activities can be meaningful, and in a setting not too buffeted by the politics of the moment and where longer-term issues could be addressed.

◀ The Center of the Region Enterprise helps to coordinate planning among six local governments and the Research Triangle Park in North Carolina. One strategy is a transit loop that would link the Research Triangle Park and Raleigh-Durham Airport to nearby development and a planned rail line. TRIANGLE J COUNCIL OF GOVERNMENTS.

What is your biggest challenge?

❭ Sustaining ongoing cooperation among diverse interests within a voluntary regional framework to achieve meaningful results to guide development in ways that are best for mobility and environmental protection is very challenging.

Regional planning agencies have basically no power. Does that make a regional planner's work more difficult?

❭ It's just a different set of challenges. The implementation of what you come up with happens through other agencies. If you work on a local plan, you need to work with local agencies to implement it and you need to set up a mechanism to make that happen.

In some ways, it's easier because you've removed the difficulty of people worrying that you're going to bring the regulatory hammer down on them. But it's more challenging in the sense that you have to get a whole bunch of different actors moving in the same direction.

Is there a particular type of planner or personality type best suited for regional planning?

❭ I think a generalist will do better in these positions than a specialist because you have to have an understanding and be able to work with a lot of very different personalities. It's not a job where you sit down and do a design for a neighborhood or write a regulation.

It also takes patience. I don't think a person who's impatient would enjoy this work or be very successful. If anyone walks away from a project, it can torpedo the process. But, generally, I think this work would appeal to a variety of folks who understand what the job involves.

Planning at the State Level

BRAD BARBER

Barber Consulting/Former State Planning Coordinator, Utah Governor's Office of Planning and Budget

Salt Lake City, Utah

Why did you become a planner?

❯ I became interested in planning while an undergraduate economics major at Weber State University in the early 1970s. I saw the work of the Utah State Planning Coordinator's Office and saw how they incorporated good substantial economic analysis in their planning efforts and how this was leading to very good decisions in big picture planning efforts at the state level.

At that point I realized this is what I wanted to do: mix my economics degree with urban and regional planning, and I set my professional goal to work in the Utah State Planning Coordinator's Office and eventually become the Utah State Planning Coordinator.

I continued my education at Weber State University in economics and took all the planning courses I could. I went to graduate school at the University of Utah, and I chose this institution as they would allow me to mix relevant planning courses with my master's program in urban and regional economics. At the same time I received graduate certification in urban and regional planning.

You eventually achieved your goal. How did you set about to do it?

❯ I started working at the regional level. I was not as much interested in zoning and design as I was with

the regional and state-level planning initiatives that were taking place: energy development, transportation issues, and large-scale land use planning. Utah was forecast to grow by two million people, and I saw that we were going to have several large-scale issues to grapple with.

I worked for five years as an economist and planner for the Wasatch Front Regional Council, doing economic analysis for long-range transportation planning projects and evaluating transit scenarios. From there, my career took off and I joined the state.

The state's high growth rate caused local leaders to organize an initiative that came to be known as Envision Utah. You helped to shepherd a key component of Envision Utah, the Quality Growth Strategy, into place. What was your role?

❯ In 1995, Governor Michael Leavitt sponsored a growth summit. We held town meetings all over the state, linked by computers and satellite. It was a huge production aimed at getting a focus on issues of land conservation, air quality, water, and roads and, eventually, it led to the creation of Envision Utah.

It was the state's role, and my role as state planning coordinator, to be the organizer of the process. We set up and orchestrated the meetings and provided the technical support. We did a lot of the number crunching. We did the analysis for the effort: the transportation modeling, the air quality analysis, and the GIS work.

When the report rolled off the presses in 1999, as the Quality Growth Strategy, the state was an equal partner in the process.

ENVISION UTAH
QUALITY GROWTH STRATEGY
AND TECHNICAL REVIEW

January 2000

ENVISION UTAH
A Partnership for Quality Growth

Keeping Utah Beautiful, Prosperous, and Neighborly for Future Generations

Envision Utah • P.O. Box 30901
Salt Lake City, UT 84130
801-973-3307
www.envisionutah.org

Sponsored by Coalition for Utah's Future

Envision Utah was a statewide effort bringing together public agencies and private organizations to create a Quality Growth Strategy that seeks to protect the state's environment, economy, and quality of life. State planners led the analysis of growth scenarios, did detailed research, and facilitated public involvement, in an effort to preserve critical lands, promote water conservation and clean air, improve transportation systems, and provide more and better housing options. ENVISION UTAH.

Did you like the job?

❯ Being state planning coordinator was the job I enjoyed the most. It was also the most challenging because of the high level of politics that was involved: dealing with legislators, high-level federal officials, mayors, department heads, and so on.

It was also challenging to manage a large staff with all of the personnel issues involved. But the job was immensely rewarding, as I had the ability to affect major planning decisions involving transportation, smart growth, and federal land policy.

Envision Utah was innovative in that it brought together state, regional, and local governments to create a framework for walkable communities, transit-oriented development, and coordinated transportation improvements. How did it come together?

❯ The growth challenges were so severe that we needed to do something. The idea we had was to do this cooperatively with local communities without a regulatory framework of state law. People were ready for that, but it still was a long battle to bring everybody on board. It took years for us to build confidence and credibility among the public and local elected officials. It was a long road.

My role was to bring the governor on board, first and foremost. I needed to make sure the governor believed in it, was confident in it, and that we would do it in the right way. His confidence grew over time, and he became a great spokesman and warrior to get it done. To get everybody else in the state involved, including the Department of Transportation to do all the modeling and analysis, was really tough. A lot of people were asking why should we be doing this, but, eventually, it all came together.

What skills do planners need in this type of job?

❯ I think a combination of political, people, and technical skills are important, because without the political persuasion, nothing is going to happen. You have to sell the idea. But equally important was, if we didn't have good numbers, the thing was not going to fly. So you have to make sure the technical work is going to stand up to scrutiny.

Leading a State Planning Agency

RICHARD EBERHARDT HALL, AICP

Secretary of Planning, State of Maryland

Baltimore, Maryland

Why did you become a planner?

❯ I grew up along the Wicomico River (in the Salisbury area) on the Lower Eastern Shore of Maryland. I spent a lot of time on the river and saw sprawl while also seeing that some of that growth could have been located in Salisbury.

I was also shaped by the fact that my mother was a social worker and my father a soil scientist. I think much of planning is the midpoint of these two professions.

As I pursued planning in college, it became clear that it was something that fit my interests: analysis and science, politics, community service, need for local knowledge, public policy, and the goal of making our communities and environment better.

How did you make it back to Maryland?

❯ I have a traditional planning background in land use and environmental issues. I went to school in Chapel Hill and worked in local government in North Carolina before moving back to Maryland.

I had a job for three years in Harford County, where I worked on critical area issues, stream buffers and watershed issues. Then I came to MDP in the early 1990s to work on the Patuxent Watershed Demonstration Project, which addressed watershed issues affecting the Chesapeake Bay.

Later I developed a growth model from scratch, working internally within MDP and local governments. We still use the model now. However, my current job as secretary of the Maryland Department of Planning is truly the most challenging, and I am enjoying it, too.

What about working in state planning appealed to you?

❯ While I do miss local government work at times, I really do like planning at the state level, especially for Maryland. I am a native Marylander and I think it is a great state in which to do planning. Maryland has a rich history of planning. You have the Chesapeake Bay and the environmental planning issues associated with that. There is Baltimore City and its planning challenges and opportunities, all of the interesting things other local governments are doing, BRAC, smart growth, economic development, transportation, and historic and cultural resources. You have all of these issues playing out in a state that some refer to as "America in Miniature."

I make the analogy of state planning being at the 30,000-foot level. We are in the crow's nest. Few organizations in the country have the mission that we do. While the work of local governments is critical, generally I think planning across the country could benefit from more people taking the 30,000-foot view of things. This would better enable people to synthesize issues across jurisdictions, regions, and states.

How does this work contrast with local government planning?

❯ When you work in local government, you can zero in on specific areas, but our focus is the entire state. At times, our efforts can seem a bit removed or diluted, and progress can be slow. You can't always see the cause and effect of your work. Still,

I like it, although at times I miss the hands-on environment of local government work.

One thing that helps me is that I cut my teeth at the local government level. I try to be in close contact with local government planners and the development community. We try to be careful with the policies we develop. We realize that local planners are dealing with issues on a day-to-day basis, and they have developers screaming at them at the front counters of planning offices. We mostly have the privilege of being spared that.

What we do sometimes is to highlight gaps in how policies are implemented. We try to make some links across jurisdictional boundaries, and when we look at them, we may point out a gap in how policies are implemented, what in our view needs attention.

One thing that is helpful to planning in Maryland and binds people together is the Chesapeake Bay. Ninety-five percent of the state drains to the bay and it shapes the state physically and mentally. It's a very helpful issue to have when you talk about growth issues statewide.

What are your duties as planning secretary?

❭ I run the agency, serve as an advisor to the governor on planning issues, coordinate with our sister agencies, and work with the General Assembly, local governments, and other stakeholders.

Does your job have a typical day?

❭ It is highly variable. Some days are focused on hearings and work related to the General Assembly while they are in session. Other times I am meeting with task forces, committees, local governments, smart growth advocates, and other stakeholders.

I also spend a fair amount of time with my staff and sister agencies. Sometimes I am working on memos, analysis (although not as much as I used to), presentations, and so on.

As a native Marylander, I think I know the state pretty well, but I'm always learning. If you look at my resume, it has planning nerd written all over it. But to my mind, this job is a perfect fit for me. That doesn't mean from time to time that I don't wish we could do more.

What advice do you have for planners interested in state government?

❭ While I don't think it's an absolute requirement, I think having experience in local government first helps a lot. It gives you a grounding in how things work and can help you later on.

I remember working as a local government planner and getting critical comments back from the state on a project I worked on. No one wants to be criticized. It was hard reading them, and I still remember it.

It's helpful to know how the development process works, how land is zoned, and how preliminary subdivision plans come in. It's been a while since I've put a scale on a site plan, but having that background is key.

It also helps to have strong GIS and analytical skills. You need to be good at communication and public outreach. So much of what we do in state planning is being a salesman. State planning laws provide guidance, but they're really built on local policies and programs. You have to be patient and politely persistent in this job and do more to influence local officials than tell them what to do. If not, you're going to be frustrated in this job.

Planning in the Federal Government

RICHARD SUSSMAN

Former Chief, Planning and Compliance Division, National Park Service, Southeast Regional Office

Atlanta, Georgia

Your first planning job was with the Bureau of Outdoor Recreation, which at the time was an agency within the U.S. Department of the Interior. Tell me about that job and how it led to your current position within the National Park Service.

❯ I started out working on outdoor recreation plans and that got me into natural resource planning. When the agency moved into the Heritage Conservation and Recreation Service (during the late 1970s), I went with it and started working on natural heritage programs in a lot of different states in the southeast. When the National Park Service absorbed the agency, I changed jobs and started to do general management plans for NPS.

How has the planning within the National Park Service changed during that time?

❯ The mission doesn't change because of the mission of the National Park Service doesn't change, but the way we do planning changes somewhat. The director's orders change. Planning standards change in the parks. The basic NEPA laws are the same, but how the laws are interpreted changes, so it's an evolving process. But we're always using the same basic planning principles.

Over the years, general management plans have become less site specific and more attuned to desired future conditions. We used to do more development concept plans than we do today. Policies change. But

general management plans are still the basis for how a park is managed for the next 15 to 20 years.

Local planners work with local residents. Who do NPS park planners work with?

❯ The park is our primary client, and the public at large is our client. And we have stakeholder groups in each park. Some are more engaged than others. And, of course, we work with Congress.

Most people who want to work in the National Park Service know something about the Park Service and have a visceral desire to work here. Seldom do we get people who are foreign to our mission. They usually come to the job with an interest in doing national park planning.

What do you need to do to be successful planning in the federal government?

❯ Patience. Lots of it. You need a willingness to work with a range of stakeholders and an ability to process a wide range of information and synthesize that information in the context of a host of options or alternatives. You need to have a vision to get to an outcome. There are various ways to manage a park, not just one answer or one way to get to an outcome. You have to be open to ideas and be able to communicate in a way that's understandable to a broad range of interests.

Planners have quite a bit of public interaction and a lot of public meetings. At least three or four times during the planning process, we like to sit down with the public, from scoping to reviewing the preliminary alternatives to the final alternatives. We make every attempt possible for the public to understand our proposed actions, so you have to be a good public speaker.

Wright Brothers National Memorial

Kill Devil Hills, North Carolina

General Management Plan Environmental Assessment

August 1997

National Park Service
Southeast Support Office
Atlanta, Georgia

A General Management Plan is a National Park Service document that addresses major issues facing a national park. Alternatives are based on a park's mission and goals. The plan identifies the programs, actions, and facilities that are needed to manage the park's resources and support the visitor experience. COURTESY OF THE NATIONAL PARK SERVICE.

A lot of people love a park the way it is and don't understand the need to change. Sometimes there is tension among the users of a park, whether it's the environmentalists, a recreational user group, a boating group, or a fishing group. The planning decisions we make are about how to manage the park's resources and provide for the visitor experience. The planning process is all about facilitating the answers to these questions.

What are some of the challenges particular to doing planning projects for the National Park Service in particular and the federal government in general?

❯ Limited funding and staff resources often lengthen a project for too many years. Also, balancing the many viewpoints of stakeholders and being flexible to work within different environments shaped by different administrations is a challenge.

Scheduling is always a challenge. You have to coordinate with the planning team, the Denver Service Center (where the National Park Service has a concentration of planning staff who work on projects nationally), and park staff. The busy time for each of these groups varies, so the schedule has to be worked out ahead of time, and there's a lot of coordination and tracking of projects that is necessary.

What are the most satisfying parts of the job?

❯ Working with a team on a project that will guide a park's actions over the next 15–20 years, establishing new boundaries for a park, or guiding a study that will form the basis for establishing a new unit of the National Park System.

Also, being able to work on international assignments. The National Park Service has the reputation as being one of the leaders in conservation worldwide. As a result, I was afforded the opportunity to work on park projects in Nigeria, Thailand, and Cambodia. The Cambodian experience was particularly satisfying. I was part of a team of experts representing seven countries providing advice on the nomination of a site to the World Heritage list.

Are their particular attributes or characteristics in a planner that you think are key to someone being successful in planning federal projects?

❯ Being able to work with a multitude of constituents and stakeholders; a keen knowledge of the policies and laws of the agency and appreciation for the mission of other agencies.

Consulting for the Federal Government

ALYSE GETTY

Project Manager, Parsons Infrastructure and Technology, Inc.

Norcross, Georgia

Alyse Getty's work is national in scope, working on contracts for the federal government, but regional in scale, working on specific park regions in the country.

What are your primary responsibilities and duties in your current position?

〉 I am a program manager and a project manager for Parsons, working in the federal sector. I am responsible for a multi-year planning and compliance contract with the National Park Service, Southeast Region. I am managing park management plans and environmental impact studies for several parks in the region, including Virgin Islands National Park, Virgin Islands Coral Reef National Monument, Buck Island Reef National Monument, and Chattahoochee River National Recreation Area.

What is your educational background and training?

〉 I have a bachelor's degree in Environmental Science and Political Science from Alfred University in New York.

I have certifications in wetland delineation, project management, health and safety/40-hour OSHA, wetland education training (both projects WET and WILD), Dale Carnegie management training, trail design, construction, and maintenance.

My career experience includes consulting positions over the past 28 years, the majority of which are with Parsons here in Georgia.

What are some of the experiences that have shaped your ideas of planning and how you approach the projects on which you work?

〉 I have been incredibly fortunate to have worked on a wide variety of projects over the years for a variety of different types of clients in different arenas including: transportation, wastewater, drinking water, recreation, defense, park management, and utilities.

Early in my career I worked for the National Park Service both as a volunteer and as a seasonal employee. I worked directly with the public as an interpreter and understand the power of education and sharing information as the cornerstone of stewardship and caring. I spent my first few years doing aquatic resources research and permitting for small consulting firms, and performing a variety of compliance, permitting, and planning projects. Even though the projects and nature of the clients have varied tremendously, there is a common thread among many . . . the importance of public involvement, early input, and honest dialogue.

How do you spend your work time?

〉 Meeting with clients either in person or having planning team conference calls, monitoring progress on projects in terms of team assignments, reviewing drafts of planning documents, tracking budgets and schedules, research, and technical writing. As a project manager, in general, I manage the scope, budget, and schedule for each my projects.

What are some of the challenges particular to doing planning projects for the federal government?

❯ Each project has its own unique set of circumstances and challenges. Depending on the branch of government you are working for, you have different policies to meet requirements, and sometimes these change midstream.

You have to be flexible and realistic about what can be accomplished within a fixed budget and schedule. Given today's dollars and how stretched they are, full funding on a project is not always possible. This causes starts and stops that create frustrations for the public and the project team alike. It is often difficult to maintain schedules due to limitations in funding. Other challenges are posed by the nature of the agency, with staff changes likely during the course of a project. New team members bring new expectations that require open communication to avoid problems interpreting a project scope.

What does it take to be successful in planning federal projects?

❯ Flexibility, because no two projects are alike. If you go into a project thinking it will go from A to B to C, you will be frustrated and totally disillusioned because you may find yourself going through several different directions before you get to the end. What works on one project may not work on another. If you're very inflexible, you're not going to be happy in this arena.

How do you deal with that?

❯ You have to enjoy problem solving and work with the client to find solutions to problems. You have to be willing to see beyond today to potential solutions and not hit the wall every time. You always need to look for creative ways to solve issues.

That's the fun part. If every project was the same, you wouldn't have many people in this business.

What Planning Topics Interest You?

Many planners describe themselves a "generalists," and it is not necessary to select a specialization as a planner. However, many do specialize, and some subfields of planning require as much training and specialized experience for the specialty as for the general training in planning. Here, planners in 11 subfields of planning describe their work.

Perhaps the most important thing that can be said about this group of profiles of planning specialists is that it only scratches the surface. Many other specialties exist. This collection represents some of the more common ways that planners delve deep into a particular field of expertise.

URBAN DESIGN

Like a prehistoric species still alive among younger evolutionary offspring, urban design is the profession that spawned urban planning in all its contemporary variety. Planned cities using grid systems date back thousands of years. Architects designed grand radial boulevards with monumental vistas in the Renaissance, designs that influenced Pierre Charles L'Enfant's plan for Washington, DC, in the 1790s and Baron Haussmann's transformation of Paris in the 1850s. Urban planning and urban design were one and the same in the early twentieth century, but the advent of the automobile age and the growth of the planning profession we know today coincided with a decline in urban design as a focus of the profession. In the embrace of cars, commerce, and zoning laws, planners forgot their professional heritage and abandoned their focus on physical design in favor of efficiency and safety. The result was a bumper crop of forlorn urban spaces and, by the 1990s, a renewed embrace of urban design as a central function of the profession.

The urban designer is a designer of space. Urban designers are usually brought into a project when the objective is to create spaces, especially commercial districts, that attract people. Designers use buildings to define space and give it character and comfort. Setbacks, heights, materials, proportion, transparency—all are essential variables that influence how a space feels. Street trees and other landscaping, lighting, signage, and sidewalk design are also key considerations. By manipulating these characteristics the designer can create a unique character for a place and can influence the type and timing of activity that occurs.

Urban designers are typically trained both in planning and architecture or landscape architecture. They speak the language of architecture and are often skilled in visual representations of design ideas, but they are also familiar with planning concepts and policies. Whereas architects design buildings in their entirety, urban designers are concerned primarily with the exterior details of key facades and how the buildings will be used. The urban designer must understand and accommodate various transportation needs, including walking, biking, driving, parking, and public transit.

Though some communities have urban designers on staff, most are employed as private consultants and are hired by communities or developers for specific projects. In some cases, the public or private client is seeking a vision for how a space can be developed or redeveloped. This task requires graphic rendering skills, either by hand or by computer. In many cases the urban designer is instead creating a regulatory framework of guidelines or standards within which property owners will commission designs for specific buildings and sites. This task requires knowledge of how such regulatory mechanisms function. Both activities require an understanding of why good public spaces work.

Designing Places

JOE BERRIDGE

Partner, Urban Strategies, Inc.

Toronto, Ontario, Canada

Why did you become a planner?

❭ I think that being a planner is all I ever wanted to be. As a kid I was fascinated with maps, with the evolving landscape of the part of England I grew up in, from the Neolithic age, through the Romans, the Saxons, the Normans, the railway age—all of whose footprints were still visible on the ground. And I remember with embarrassed hindsight writing letters to the local paper while in high school protesting the proposed city center redevelopment. So who knows why, but I was programmed early.

I was very lucky to have joined the City of Toronto Planning Department in the early seventies at a time when some amazing people worked there and a new young mayor, David Crombie (himself an urban studies lecturer), created the space for a whole new

▼ Urban designers developed a gateway concept for the University of Waterloo in Ontario. This concept sought to improve the way people enter and exit the campus, by foot, bicycle, and motor vehicle. © URBAN STRATEGIES INC®.

way of planning the city which laid the basis for Toronto's current success. That gang from City Hall went on to build World Financial Center in New York City and Canary Wharf in London, and have a huge impact on the evolution of Vancouver and other cities. It was the best possible grad school.

How did you choose a school for your planning degree?

❭ I went to the University of Sussex for my bachelor's degree because at the time it was the newest, most exciting, innovative university in the UK and reputedly had the prettiest girls in largest numbers. I later did my master's in Urban Geography at the University of Toronto, which I chose after deciding I wanted to spend a couple of years in North America and of all the places I applied, they offered the most generous teaching and research associateships. Somehow after that I never returned to the UK.

What does your job involve?

❭ I am one of eight partners in my firm, Urban Strategies, Inc. Being a partner means having to bring in about a million dollars of work a year, so that is job one. But new work only comes in if you do the best work possible, so I have to both ensure

An urban design plan for derelict docklands in Cork, Ireland, involved recognizing the unique character of the historic city and accommodating twenty-first century uses and activities. The close grain and mix of uses of the plan area would open up the waterfront and set a standard for sustainability and high-quality urban design. © URBAN STRATEGIES INC®.

that everything that comes out of the office is as good as it can be and chase new prospects as hard as I can. We expect a lot of our staff and so they expect a lot of the partners—so I have to work really hard and try and stay ahead of them both in the quality of the work and the relationship with clients. Our firm's philosophy has been simplified to this—do the best work, make money, have fun. A partner's job is to manage the tensions and enjoy the delights of trying to resolve those three goals.

About a half of the firm's work is at the end of a plane ride in the U.S., Canada, and the UK. I have the primary responsibility for the UK work.

Do you have a typical day?

❯ Very few days are alike, which is great. I travel a lot, going to the UK once or twice a month, and even in Toronto I am out at the clients' offices a lot. I am responsible at any one time for perhaps 15 to 20 projects, but usually about half a dozen are hot and require my attention.

I set the overall direction for a project, lead the in-house work team, manage the relationship with the client, and worry about money. Much of my job is in fact what I call anxiety transfer, making sure the staff are worrying about everything, so I don't have to. Their job is to make me redundant

▶ In 1996, a bomb exploded in Manchester, England, destroying more than 1.5 million square feet of retail and office space in the city center. The disaster spurred the city to sponsor an international urban design competition for the reconstruction plan. © URBAN STRATEGIES INC®.

▼ Urban designers functioned as master plan advisors to the elected officials in Manchester and chaired design juries that evaluated potential redevelopment projects. The rebuilt center has helped to transform the national and global image of Manchester. © URBAN STRATEGIES INC®.

by being able to deal with the client, do first-class work, and not blow the budget. My job is to get them there, at which point they can become a partner.

What are some of the experiences that have shaped your ideas of planning and how you approach the projects on which you work?

❭ I think my basic ideas of the potential of planning were forged in those early years at the City of Toronto. A conscious decision was made by the city government and citizenry that they did not want Toronto to go the way of U.S. cities. So what on the face appeared a much more restrictive planning regime was introduced, requiring housing at the expense of commercial development downtown and protecting inner city neighborhoods from both public and private sector redevelopment pressures. In fact this market intervention created value, as well as a great central city.

But that experience also showed the limits to planning. Too much faith in the power of community neglected the needs of the city as a whole. Toronto was the adopted home of Jane Jacobs—she lived around the corner and was a good friend—but her views were hardened by Nimbyists into an extreme localism that devalued any citywide initiative.

I went into private practice frustrated by such process planning and was lucky enough to be retained extensively by Olympia and York, probably in the 1980s the world's most powerful downtown developer and a firm with an extraordinary culture of excellence. We worked with them in New York, London, Boston, San Francisco, and Moscow, which gave our firm the basis for its global reach.

What they taught me is that planning is only real if it is implemented and built. Everything else is just paper and talk. But to build things in either the public or private sector requires a skill set, an organization, an energy, and an appetite for risk that is rarely found in the planning profession. That's why the UDCs [urban development corporations, known in the U.S. as community development corporations] in the U.S. and the UK for whom we do much of our work today are such important and interesting creations, trying to translate the public interest through private sector mechanisms into actions on the ground.

The project that has been for me the most satisfying—that brought together everything I had thought and learned about planning—was the reconstruction of the center of Manchester, UK, after a devastating IRA bombing in 1996. The bomb destroyed an area about a kilometer in diameter right in the heart of the city.

I was asked to be the strategic planning advisor a few days after the blast and for the next three years helped set the direction and design of the rebuilding. It has been an amazing success, achieved as it had to be in record time and, while all the statutory planning and public procurement rules were effectively bent or set aside, the public interest has been hugely well served. Frankly, I thought after that project that I could have happily retired.

What has been your greatest challenge as a planner?

❭ Reading all the repetitive prose that planners write. Excavating purpose from process. Persuading people that planning is a content discipline, that should be based on analysis and outcome, rather than the sum of collective opinion. The unbelievably slow speed at which government operates.

What are the most satisfying parts of your job?

❯ I love going to a new city, with a new problem, and understanding the way the place works and figuring out what to do and, eventually, having the client agree. I love trying to distill analysis and process into action. I love the bright young people who come into my office and work their butts off with such intelligence and good humor—and who eventually teach me as much as I teach them. I love real urban professionals, engineers, architects, civil servants, politicians, who answer to the higher calling. I love the smell of fresh concrete in the morning.

And the least?

❯ Reading those endless, sleep-inducing reports that could have been written about any project anywhere. Bone-wearying travel. The passive-aggressive behavior that is seemingly the default affect for too many public sector planners in every city in the world. Words, meetings, words, meetings, words, meetings. And no action. Self-righteous citizens wrapping themselves in Jane Jacobs—if only they knew what she was really like. Engineers with asphalt for hearts and tape measures for brains. Do-nothing environmentalists.

Using Urban Design to Create Consensus

CRAIG WATSON, RLA

Principal, Urban Design, Planning and Landscape Architecture Studio Director

SmithGroup/JJR

Washington, DC

How did you become an urban designer?

❯ When I was 18, I left the Midwest and moved to San Francisco and, later, Seattle. Living there, I developed a passion for cities and their complexity. I was drawn to how intricate, animated, and diverse urban life can be. Cities are always changing. They're never static.

After a few years of living on my own, I went back to the Midwest to attend Michigan State, where I graduated with a degree in landscape architecture. Upon my graduation, I had the opportunity to meet with a firm, LDR, whose founders years earlier had moved from the Midwest to Maryland to help developer James Rouse design the new town, Columbia.

I was offered a job and immediately began working on new towns and residential golf course communities, two concepts that were popular in the 1980s, before a downturn in the economy late in the decade.

While the U.S. was mired in a recession, I had an opportunity to move to England for four years, as the firm branched into planning internationally. This gave me a chance to work in city centers in the UK, Northern Ireland, and many cities throughout Europe. It was there where I turned away, professionally, from land development and land planning and into urban design. I decided I would focus, from then on, on economic development and urban generation, looking at cities holistically and addressing the challenges created by urban sprawl.

COLUMBIA ROAD NORTH CONCEPT PLAN

LEGEND
- Sidewalk improvement, as necessary
- Street tree
- Lane demarcation
- Roadway divider
- Crosswalk
- Bus station

Bus Station
- Introduce Metro identity to promote and market transit
- Facilitate and promote transfers
- Consolidate bus stops
- Iconic architecture

Columbia Promenade
- Increase public space
- Shorten pedestrian crossing distance
- Calm traffic
- Reinforce pedestrian priority
- Increase linear planting area

Green Space
- Close Harvard Street slip lane
- Provide plantings

Master Meter
- Increase payment options
- Reduce sidewalk clutter
- Variable rates
- Cheaper installation and maintenance

Site Furnishings
- Furnishings to reflect character of Columbia Road

Loading Zone
- 2–3 hour periods
- Parking at other times
- More spaces, less time
- Specific locations to be determined

Separate Bicycle Lane
- Remove center lane
- Provide continuous bicycle lanes

Pocket Park
- Close Euclid Street
- Expand public space
- Create adjacent promenade

HNTB
September 2005

Corridor plans are a cornerstone of planning and urban design. In Washington, DC, planners teamed with urban designers and transportation engineers to address issues of pedestrian flow and environment, on- and off-street parking, safety, transit, bicycle activity, and traffic operations and capacity. CRAIG WATSON/HNTB CORPORATION.

What is your definition of urban design?

❯ One definition of urban design would be as town planning—the arrangement, appearance, and function of towns and hamlets to metropolitan centers.

Design focuses on aesthetics and the shaping and use of the public and urban realm. It embodies many core disciplines: urban planning, landscape architecture, architecture, and engineering. Our European forefathers mastered this connection, as did Pierre L'Enfant, Kevin Lynch, and Frederick Law Olmsted.

Over the past four decades, urban regeneration and revitalization have been a primary focus throughout the world. The possibilities are endless. Just look at what has happened to urban landscapes in London, Berlin, Vancouver, and Washington, DC, as just a few examples.

Urban design is a process. Master plans evolve and economies change, but guiding growth, applying smart growth principles with new technologies, implementing transit, and supporting ecological and sustainable initiatives are always needed and are always evolving.

What are some of the experiences that have shaped your ideas of planning and how you approach the projects on which you work?

❭ Living in England influenced my passion for cities. Cy Paumier of LDR was a key mentor to me during this period.

In the early 1990s, traditional town planning as practiced in the UK was predominately influenced by architects who were using processes that were long established and took a long time to complete.

Our approach, by contrast, was quick and involved lots of graphics and charrettes, as well as total stakeholder involvement, multiple concepts, and a holistic focus. Compared to the other approach, ours was different and we were very successful. We made significant impact in cities like Liverpool, Birmingham, Manchester, and Belfast.

More recently, I have had the opportunity to guide a city in Maryland through a five-year process of creating the largest urban park in the community, an investment of tens of millions of dollars.

In this city, the community embraced the process, a vision and supported an aggressive implementation program that other, even larger, cities would have been reluctant to tackle. The market has responded, and the area has exploded with office, residential, and mixed-use development and redevelopment, all based on the city's commitment to this public realm investment.

Throughout the project, we listened to and engaged the community at all levels. At the end, it was not our project, it was everyone's.

What, in particular, did you learn from this project?

❭ We always need to remember that our clients are communities, not faceless entities. They are groups of people, and, ideally, we want to engage them at all levels.

Thirty years ago, public participation was very limited. Since then, as urban designers, we've all become more responsive and responsible, and this is critical on projects where public dollars are spent.

The true art of being a consultant is being able to orchestrate and guide a process where you take a vision generated by the community and develop it into a concept that is ultimately accepted by the community. You want to develop that concept together—I hesitate to use the word "sell"—so it's a transparent process, not top down.

We have to be educators in a subtle and sensitive way, without being condescending. That's why we use examples and best practices to illustrate a concept. Whether it's the cliché that "a picture says a thousand words," or something similar, you have to remember that, for most projects, this is not the first time this problem has been addressed. So we try to show our clients examples and then help them build their own futures.

It's an educational process, and when it works best, you will make them think and get them outside of their comfort zone.

What is the future of urban design?

❭ I think implementing smart growth, transit-oriented development, and urban revitalization and reinventing our urban suburban cores are the next hurdles. The United States has had such a disposable mentality. Sprawl has led us to new growth areas without anyone taking responsibility for recycling existing urban areas. That inevitably leads to decline, and the public sector has not been able to hold the private sector accountable.

I know it's a cliché, but we need to continue to think outside the box to challenge, inform, and impassion the public and elected officials. Planners are so caught up in numbers and the particular requirements of the zoning ordinance that they're not able to think strategically about development. And they're afraid or intimidated by the private sector.

Our European neighbors have gotten it forever. Why do you think their towns have been able to thrive? Because they're not allowed to sprawl. Therefore, a rural landscape exists and transit has been successful. Until we get it, we're not going to make our cities what they can and should be.

▼ J-Town is a proposed mixed-use project of offices, shops, apartments, hotels, and recreational facilities at the Jemulpo metro station in Incheon, South Korea. Urban designers worked closely with architects and planners and the client to develop a concept to maximize land value and create a vibrant mixed-use neighborhood. Green spaces link activity centers within the site and to the surrounding urban fabric. CRAIG WATSON/HNTB CORPORATION.

What is the importance of mentoring?

❭ You can only learn so much in school. School will teach you the basics, and it's important to have those basics under your belt, but once you get into the profession, you need to build on those skills and apply them to your work.

No one is in this profession alone. So I would begin to think about mentoring and nurturing your skills from the earliest days of your career. Take time out of your schedule and talk to the senior staff in your group, develop a relationship with them and ask questions. And then, as you progress up the ladder, continue to do that and take time with younger staff. There is room for mentoring at all levels. It can help you learn how to be a good project man-

ager, and later, once you're a principal or partner, it's essential that you be exposed to new ideas, and mentoring is one way to do that.

I see a difference between my generation and young professionals who are just out of college. When I was younger, it seemed like I and the people I came into the firm with were always asking for more opportunities. Consequently, we were given opportunities we might not otherwise have received. I don't always see self-initiative among younger planners, but such an approach will help you get ahead. Otherwise, it will take longer and longer to get to the pinnacle of your career.

What advice do you have for young planners and urban designers?

❭ Understand corporate protocol and how your firm does things. If you work for an organization that embodies your values, you will be successful.

Networking is also important. Be visible in the local arena. In the long-term, it's important to be recognized for your good work and to develop a name. That can help you market yourself and bring in the next project, whether that's marketing to outside clients or working in your company, because that will give you a base of clients to work from, as opposed to having to start from scratch every time.

HOUSING PLANNING AND POLICY

Most planners spend at least a portion of their time and careers planning for housing. Housing is the dominant urban land use throughout the country and the largest single expense for most Americans. The protection of residential property values is important not only to protect the financial well-being of homeowners but also to safeguard public revenues—municipalities typically rely on property taxes as the primary source of public revenue to build and maintain essential public services such as schools and transportation facilities.

Housing policy has far-reaching impacts on other aspects of our communities and lives. Policies regulating the density of housing affect demand for transportation options and public open space and parks. Policies regulating the types of housing that may be built (e.g., single-family homes versus multifamily apartments) and the location of those types (e.g., interspersed or segregated) affect affordability and social diversity in a community.

Planners who focus on housing are usually engaged in efforts to ensure that all members of a community have access to safe, affordable housing. Through a combination of regulation and financial assistance, housing planners may help renters become owners, help owners maintain their properties, and assist those people who might otherwise be homeless. The federal government has had a role in these efforts since the creation of the Federal Housing Administration in 1934, now part of the Department of Housing and Urban Development (HUD).

Housing specialists are usually implementing programs funded, at least in part, by HUD. These specialists may administer a program that subsidizes rent payments, known as Section 8 vouchers, for qualified low-income residents. Or they may help to establish and administer public housing units. Some communities have attempted to manage affordability by requiring the construction of private units that

Nonprofit organizations are supporting green buildings and neighborhoods across the nation. The Enterprise Foundation's Green Communities Initiative provided more than half the funding to develop affordable cottage-style apartments around a preserved wetland. ENTERPRISE COMMUNITY PARTNERS.

can be purchased or rented by people earning less than the local median income. Though many housing planners work for local or county government, private, nonprofit organizations are also involved in efforts to provide affordable housing. Housing planners may also work as consultants, even in the administration of federally funded voucher programs.

Housing planners need basic math skills and an understanding of financing tools such as mortgages. They also need an appreciation for the diverse needs and challenges people face in their efforts to find housing, including income limitations, physical handicaps requiring accessible design, transportation requirements, and the unique needs of families with children.

Filling Housing Needs

AMY MENZER

Executive Director, Dundalk Renaissance Corporation

Dundalk, Maryland

Tell us about your job in community development.

❯ I am executive director of the Dundalk Renaissance Corporation. We are a small nonprofit community development corporation and community-based membership organization. We were born out of a larger-scale community planning process, an Urban Design Assistance Team (UDAT), in 2001. This week-long charrette brought in outside planners and architects to help the Dundalk community, a working-class, older industrial suburb of Baltimore City, reimagine its future.

I do everything from raising funds to developing our business plan to supervising house renovations to developing membership drives to fielding random community inquiries to making sure our Internet is functioning properly and that we have enough toilet paper. That is both the beauty and the curse of being head of a small nonprofit organization.

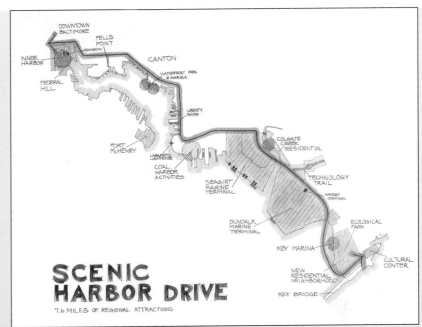

SCENIC HARBOR DRIVE
7.6 MILES OF REGIONAL ATTRACTIONS

▶ The American Institute of Architects has convened Urban Design Assistance Teams (UDATs) of architects and planners since the 1960s to work with local communities in week-long workshops. A team in suburban Baltimore developed design concepts to link the community of Dundalk with downtown Baltimore. DUNDALK RENAISSANCE CORP.

◀ Façade improvements are supported by local organizations to encourage reinvestment in older neighborhoods. Programs can be aimed at residential or commercial properties. DUNDALK RENAISSANCE CORP.

The most important thing I do right now is manage our house renovations, because these will produce developer fees that enable us to expand our staffing and increase our volume of renovations. When we have more staff, I expect to spend more time on fundraising, program development, board development, and neighborhood marketing.

Being director gives me the opportunity to grow the organization and shape the direction of our efforts to revitalize Dundalk. I like that broad-scale perspective and the organizational development aspects. But our housing work is fairly targeted geographically, and with just me working on housing, what we do is more limited than I'd like.

What's your typical day like?

❯ It can vary tremendously. There is usually some paperwork related to grant applications or reports, construction loans, construction management, paying bills, and so on that takes up as much as 20 percent of my time. Supervising our house renovations currently absorbs about half of my time (in field inspections, progress meetings, gathering materials, preparing scopes and drawings, troubleshooting) Supervising our Main Street manager and attending events organized either by us or by the county or another organization absorbs another 10 percent of my time.

There is a fair amount of consensus-building with board members and funders that must occur for any major change such as hiring, but there are other decisions I am at greater liberty to make as needed such as whether to make an offer on a specific house (if it's in our board-approved target area). I spend some time every day fielding random inquiries from the community. Some days I may spend almost entirely on preparing a mailing, designing our annual report, decorating our storefront windows, or preparing budgets.

Given your interest in urban issues, what is it like to work in a suburban community?

❯ Older suburban communities are really at a crossroads. They are not urban, so the strategies that might work, say, in downtown Baltimore may not apply. They are places that are less dense to begin with, so thinking about what Smart Growth means in older suburban areas is a bit of a question mark.

Dundalk is a walkable place. It was built from a plan created in the 1920s, so it has "great bones" and a legacy to build upon.

Our job is to promote what we have here. There's a lesson in the complexity of real life. We don't market Dundalk as a place to live, work, and shop. That's not realistic for most people. Dundalk already has people who live in the low-income spectrum, so for us, diversity means attracting higher-

Decorative signage is often used at entry points or gateways to reinforce a community's identity. Installing these improvements often signals a milestone in community revitalization efforts. DUNDALK RENAISSANCE CORP.

income households, but the money that supports our programs is aimed at creating affordable housing. That creates some challenges for us, which I find intellectually and practically challenging, as well as worthwhile and worth talking about.

What characterizes community development in suburban areas, as opposed to more urbanized areas?

❯ Wealth creation as a community development goal is highlighted by the potential for homeownership to create wealth for people, and it is this country's major means of wealth creation. Because older suburbs tend to be populated by the first tier of working-class homeowners, older suburban decline means that those who can least afford to have their home values decline (with few other ways to create wealth) and the ones most likely to experience the problem. In my dissertation (and in some grant applications), I have argued that this is an important social equity issue.

While older suburbs tend not to be the places that are the absolute worst off in the region, there are nonetheless social equity dimensions to their situation, (Older thinking focused just on helping the poorest of the poor as the highest and most noble form of work, for charity purposes or planning. I disagree.)

Equity planners have tended to emphasize how their efforts can help those who are worst off, and working as an "equity" planner in an older suburb would force some modification of this approach based on the issues I raised above.

Finally, in Essex–Middle River and in Dundalk, some of what we have felt necessary to do to revitalize these areas is actually de-densify by demolishing very dense, World War II–era apartment buildings to make way for a wider range of housing types that make the communities more economically diverse. So, while counterintuitive, smart growth in an older suburb may involve some de-densification.

ECONOMIC DEVELOPMENT PLANNING

A typical week as a public-sector community and economic development planner might include meeting with several local businesses to hear about their current needs and concerns, attending a meeting of a downtown business owners association to discuss progress toward a planned downtown street improvement project, and working on a promotional brochure that highlights the advantages of living and doing business in the local community.

Economic development planners work with communities and businesses to promote a balanced, stable local economy. Most economic development efforts seek growth that creates new jobs, especially jobs that pay well enough to support families living in the community. These efforts usually require the collaboration of public officials with private business owners and are focused on projects that make the community more attractive to businesses and their employees.

Economic development became a focus of the planning profession in the Great Depression, as government took on a more active role in regulating and promoting the economy. The Tennessee Valley Authority and the network of hydroelectric dams that it created intended to bring electrical infrastructure to Appalachia in order to encourage employers to locate to this deeply impoverished area. In the industrial boom following World War II, the emphasis was on improvements to the transportation network to facilitate the efficient flow of materials and products. Though some of these efforts occurred at a national level—consider the postwar development of the interstate freeway system—economic development programs have been, and continue to be, grassroots affairs, conceived and managed at the local or regional level.

The components of local economic success have evolved over the decades and centuries. Throughout the industrial age cities thrived on access to natural resources and access to vital transportation corridors (first rivers and oceans, later railroads, then highways and airports). These remain important today, but in the post-industrial American economy, the most important resource is people, and success in the global economy is dependent on the attractiveness of the community to highly skilled employees who have many options in the job market. Consequently, economic development efforts today often focus on improving those attributes that make a community attractive as a place to live, including good schools, a variety of attractive restaurants and shops, recreational opportunities, and cultural activities.

In some communities, especially those that have undergone the loss of a major employer, workforce development is the focus of economic development. The community may target certain industrial sectors and work with local educational institutions to provide training programs to prepare local workers for jobs in those industries. Increasingly, communities are seeking to diversify the range of industries operating in their community in order to reduce the community's dependence on a single industry and buffer the community from the ups and downs in the economic cycle.

Economic development planners are sometimes employed by consulting firms that prepare studies and plans for communities. However, because successful economic development planning often relies on the development of relationships with business and elected leaders, most economic development planners are employed by local municipalities and economic development corporations.

Planning for employment uses is an important land use consideration in both local comprehensive plans and economic development efforts. In many places, employment uses are concentrated in business parks and campuses. JASON VALERIUS.

Partnerships with private businesses are crucial to success in economic development planning. Business owners in a community understand the challenges they face in their attempts to compete and grow, and their involvement in planning and development initiatives is key. The economic development planner must be a good communicator who can relate to those business owners and their needs and concerns.

Important skills include strong interpersonal communication, clear writing, an understanding of economic trends and forces, and capacity with basic math to calculate trends and estimate the impact of proposed programs or projects.

Planning for Economic Development: Public Sector

WILLIAM ANDERSON, FAICP

Director of City Planning & Community Investment

City of San Diego, California

Why did you decide to focus your career on economic development?

❯ Most planning concerns have their roots in economic development—the quality of jobs; people's ability to afford adequate housing; quality public facilities and services; merchants' ability to maintain competitive commercial districts; coordination with environmental protection; and the region's economic base and structure. These factors profoundly affect how cities evolve—socially and physically.

I've participated in planning as a consultant, a community activist, a planning commissioner, and, now, as a planning director.

My first planning job was with a national planning and development economics consulting firm called Economics Research Associates (ERA). They were a California-based firm with a Boston office, where I

started. Each year was like a new job since what you did varied by your assignments. I enjoyed the topical and geographic variety.

I ended up spending 23 years at ERA, eventually becoming a senior vice president, starting with a couple of years in Boston focused on projects in the Northeast, then transferring to the Los Angeles headquarters, and then starting a small office in San Diego, back in my home town.

About 70 percent of my clients were government agencies and 30 percent were private developers or property owners. I think I ended up working in over 30 states and 8 foreign countries on urban planning assignments, usually focusing on the urban economic aspects and feasibility assessments as part of multidisciplinary planning teams.

What are some of the experiences that have shaped your ideas of planning and how you approach the projects on which you work?

❯ After 27 years in the field, I've had a lot of experiences which have influenced my thoughts about city planning, but one that I've always remembered, early in my career, was a particular day of contrasts. I was working on two assignments—

San Diego's City Heights Community Center, part of the City Heights Revitalization Plan, opened in 1998 as a recreation component of an urban village that includes a library, community college, gymnasium, and police station. CITY OF SAN DIEGO.

one was a specific plan for thousands of acres in San Diego County that was surrounded by some of the highest-income communities in the nation; the other was a concept plan for a mixed-use district in San Diego's barrio. I had a morning meeting with the land owners who were funding the specific plan in the county. The clients expressed their strong concern about a proposed open space system which would have public trails passing next to their planned gated communities, bringing the public too close. That afternoon, I had a community meeting in the barrio. We spent much of the meeting discussing with residents their simple need for a grocery store in their poor community and a place that would bring people together. I realized planning and its tools can be used to maintain exclusivity or to address basic needs and foster inclusivity. I try to focus my career on the latter.

Because of my experience in so many different places with different traditions, I have the opinion

that there are many different ways to plan and build cities, and that the right approach must be crafted for the particular economic, physical, environmental, historical, and cultural context. I don't subscribe to normative standards.

While I like many of the principles embodied in certain planning standards, I believe formulaic planning can suppress creativity, and eventually cultural development. The most interesting cities are organic. I prefer establishing the goals and objectives that represent a particular region's, city's, and community's values, then crafting the right planning approach for the given context to meet those objectives and achieve those goals.

What does your current job involve?

❯ I oversee four major divisions—community planning, urban form, redevelopment, and economic development, as well as public facilities financing, in the City Planning & Community Investment Department.

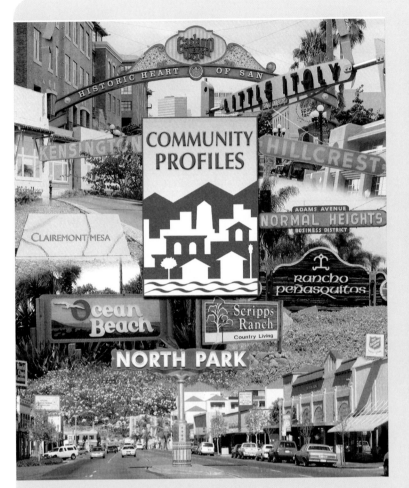

San Diego is composed of many distinct communities, each with a unique identity.
CITY OF SAN DIEGO.

The department is responsible for implementing the General Plan, preparing community plans, reviewing major plan amendment proposals, urban design review, park and open space planning, habitat planning, historic resources, redevelopment activities, management of the Community Development Block Grant program, small business assistance programs, special districts such as business improvement districts and parking districts, and public facilities financing.

What does a typical day include?

❯ Meetings with staff, other departments, constituents, Council members, the chief operating officer, and the mayor to address specific issues; directing my deputy directors; responding to emails; field work; coordination with other agencies; and reading background material and drafts.

Planning for Economic Development: Consulting

ELAINE VAN S. CARMICHAEL, AICP

President, Economic Stewardship, Inc.

Sturgeon Bay, Wisconsin

How did you become a planner?

❯ I grew up in the 1960s having no idea what people did for a living, beyond understanding classic archetypes involving uniforms (doctor, firefighter, letter carrier). Since I was raised in a built-out Boston suburb, which only hired a planner in about 2000, I never thought about the profession at all.

However, when I think about my childhood, my plannerly outlook makes sense. I was always interested in using my brother's toys to build cityscapes. I worked on the landscape for his model train set and lay in bed thinking about underground people mover systems. We also played "Explorer," usually separately, which entailed riding our bikes as far as possible in half the time available, with the explicit intent of getting lost. The fun came from finding the way home and telling each other about our adventures; later I used cars.

In seventh grade, an art teacher asked us to "draw where we want to live." Every other kid came back with house plans and eagerly showed off where to find the hot tub, the home theatre, etc. I created a plan for a city, complete with Central Business District, transit system, parks, schools. Mortification about "misunderstanding" the assignment ensued, but the incident pleases me now.

And last, but not least, my scientist father taught me how to use numbers to tell a story while my mother, a community activist, taught me how to get along with practically anyone.

In college I found myself one class short and discovered Study of the City, a survey course taught by Alex Garvin, then a planning consultant and commissioner in New York City. Since class met only once a week and most of the grade depended on a single paper, it was perfect for my needs. The first lecture, as was traditional during Yale's "shopping period," provided an overview of the entire course to help students choose well. When I walked into class, Garvin had a two-carousel slide show going with an aerial of Radburn, New Jersey, on the left and Columbia, Maryland, on the right. I just stood there while he compared and contrasted them, alluding to Ebenezer Howard and the Garden Cities movement. Classmates had to tell me to sit down because I was so absolutely gobsmacked.

I walked out of that lecture having found my calling. Within 24 hours I went from being completely unaware that the field existed to telling everyone that I was going to be a city planner some day.

What motivated you to start your own firm?

❯ I gave up a partnership at one of the field's preeminent firms because I had risen to the point where I mostly managed others instead of actually doing the work. My time in the sweet spot—talented enough to do the work and make the presentations, but inexpensive enough to make the projects profitable—was over.

The projects could not support my billing rate and so my involvement shrank to showing up, making speeches, and supervising the young-uns' work. I was getting into trouble, either wrecking project budgets by being overinvolved or ruining my life by working after hours to avoid billing against them. Having my own firm made the economics work again.

In my experience, being a consultant and, especially, having your own firm is like moving to a big bed. After sleeping happily with your partner in a full, when you finally get a queen (let alone a king) bed, the full in your friend's guest room seems unbearably constricting. You can't go back.

What do you mean by "economic stewardship"?

❯ We are land use economists with a heart. We offer a blend of market analysis, financial feasibility, impact analysis, and strategic planning, and the largest of these is the strategic thinking. We try to focus on what is distinctive about a place's character, what makes it competitive.

When we work with a community, we try to understand the economy as a system, analogous to any complex ecology. There are behavioral factors as well as economic factors at play. Large-scale changes can result from small interactions between individuals, ideas, companies, and community. New ideas create disequilibrium that can accelerate growth or launch a downward spiral; we're trying to identify opportunities where small strategic interventions can yield big results.

What this means is working with all economic actors; it's a "hydra" of organizations, businesses, and other entities that span the public, private, and nonprofit sectors. We pay attention to all of an area's component parts, much like gears. You want gears fitting together so they function well: no grinding, no sand. When you understand these relationships, which takes a lot of time so you can develop mutual trust, you can see where the impediments to smooth interactions lie. It's looking at how to improve the linkages, rather than relying on a silver bullet approach.

Depending on how you approach a community, you get very different answers on how they define the issues. I think our approach has more salience for local people than, say, an economic cluster analysis, which often seems somewhat like a black box. We try to meld the technical work—and we are rigorous about methodology—with a deep investigation into what makes a community tick.

In most communities, some problems or choices reduce easily to numbers, but not all. There's always opportunities that can never be fully expressed in dollars and cents. So we try to get a hold on both of these factors. You won't get the best answer by evaluating things solely in terms of dollars and market support, just as you can't move forward just by acting on things that are warm and fuzzy.

For many communities, the fact of having hired a firm to look at something caps a long process. Often it means it's safe to look at a particular issue. But often somebody needs to come in and help tease out the real story. . . . what's really going on underneath the apparent issues, what it takes an outsider to say out loud.

Is there a lot of demand for this type of work?

❯ This kind of work is expanding, in part, because people are now able to work where they want to live, as opposed to living where they can find work. There's more and more free agency and a greater interest in knowing how to have it all. Another thing that's contributing to this is the work of Richard Florida, who helped people understand the relationship between being a good place to live and business formation. Similarly, from my point of view, good places to live are good places to visit. They're also good places to invest time and money, whether it's where to spend a vacation, raise a family, retire, or start a business.

The work we've done in Breckenridge, Colorado, is on point. The town wanted to figure out how to help its various heritage attractions achieve more attendance. Instead we found a way for people to commemorate the 150-year anniversary of the town as an economic development venture.

The project evolved from one thing to something completely different, which often happens in our work. The reason we can support this is by having a small firm that's flexible, where we can do what needs to be done without being as sensitive to budget as larger firms must be.

I like that about having my own firm, although it's definitely not the path to create wealth through consulting.

What are some of the experiences that have shaped your ideas of planning and how you approach the projects on which you work?

❯ For me it's hard to separate ideas about planning from ideas about what serving as a consultant means. As a consultant, it's much easier to talk to a community about difficulties it's facing, and helping it choose to address problems and understand what challenges lie ahead. It's really important to leverage one's out-of-town status to:

■ tell the truth

■ push for decisiveness

■ distinguish between any individual example and community-wide policies

■ broker deals and vet decisions with those responsible for implementation

■ represent private sector, landowner, and developer interests to planner—and vice versa—to improve the quality of the work and, similarly, stand in for perspectives that are missing from the debate

■ keep capacity issues in perspective

■ examine the system as much as whatever the engagement is supposed to be addressing

■ call attention to non-obvious things that make their community special

It's absolutely necessary to find some way to fall in love with some aspect of the client community, its people or its problems, to do good work and ensure that you avoid becoming moralistic (as, say, historic preservationists, New Urbanists, and property rights advocates all tend to do), trust the clients' ability to be as progressive (or not) as their communities can tolerate, stay resilient and empathetic to work through (or squelch) feelings of resentment that emerge when things aren't going well.

HISTORIC PRESERVATION PLANNING

Most cities are in a state of continuous reinvention and redevelopment. New projects often result in the alteration or removal of existing buildings, bridges, or other human creations that make up the urban fabric. Sometimes it is clear which buildings are historic and deserving of protection and which are not, but a vast gray area exists between the abandoned 1970s car wash and the lovingly maintained 1890s Victorian mansion. Even the car wash may merit preservation because it was designed by a famous architect and is favored by residents as a unique landmark. Preservation planning is about evaluating the history of our built environment and engaging stakeholders in conversations about preserving that history.

Supporting the restoration of historic housing stock is a key component of historic preservation efforts. In the Southside neighborhood of Greensboro, North Carolina, historic houses were restored after being in jeopardy of demolition. MIKE COWHIG.

The number of full-time historic preservation planners in America is rather small. These planners are generally employed by large cities or state or federal agencies such as the National Park Service. More common are generalist planners, usually public sector employees, who are occasionally engaged in historic preservation planning. Planners who work for or with Main Street programs often spend much of their time working on historic preservation by working with property owners to restore the historic facades on main street buildings.

Historic preservation efforts are often led by citizens passionate about a place and interested in its protection. The planner's role is to help answer questions and facilitate discussion. Was the building designed by a famous architect? Is it in good condition? Is it part of a district of buildings that merit protection as a group? Or conversely, is it a rare specimen of a particular architectural style?

Historic designation can be contentious and controversial. On one side are those members of the community who are passionate about conserving the heritage and character of a place. On the other side are people who are just as passionate about bringing in a new business or new housing that is slated to occupy the site of the historic feature. Creative planners may be able to help reach a compromise that protects some aspects of the historic site (for example, an arch or a smaller section of a building that was built in stages), while allowing others to be replaced.

Discussion is often necessary because people disagree about the value of historic structures and because that value must be weighed against the benefit of redevelopment, or highway expansion, or open space creation, or whatever the project may be.

Historic preservation planners need some architectural knowledge and should be familiar with both national and local history. They need to be familiar with the guidelines for historic designation at the local, state, and federal level, and also with grant programs available to help fund protection.

Protecting, Preserving, and Planning for Historic and Cultural Resources

PETER BENTON, AIA

Principal Preservation Planner

Heritage Strategies LLC

Sugarloaf, PA

You were trained as an architect. How did you make the transition to ecological and historic preservation planning?

❯ When I was designing buildings, I found myself growing more and more dissatisfied with architecture as a profession. I felt the buildings we were designing were self-centered and shallow and were aimed mainly at the architects and not at the users.

First, I abandoned architecture to pursue ecological planning and, second, I became a historic preservation planner, and through that, I was able to address the things that interested me.

I went to work for a firm and became exposed to landscape and ecological planning. The principals there taught me how to read a landscape. You can really drop yourself anywhere, look at the landscape around you and understand what has happened there over whatever timeframe you choose. By looking at the geology, the plant communities, and other materials, you can piece together the history of the place.

Then you can look at signs of the landscape and see the hand of man. Look at landforms and remnant features in the landscape and figure out what people were doing there. You may find stone walls in the woods that were once dwellings and discover areas that were once agricultural lands by looking at the plants. By evaluating all of this information, you can tell how the landscape has evolved, what has been disturbed by human intervention and figure out how it has changed over time.

Preservation planners assisted in the reconstruction of Erie Canal Harbor in Buffalo. As the western terminus of the Erie Canal, the site transformed the city and the nation during the nineteenth century. A downtown waterfront park is being created to represent and interpret the site's history.
JOHN MILNER ASSOCIATES, INC.

You can do the same thing in built communities. When you work with historic villages and communities, there is less of a natural environment and more of a human involvement and an interplay between human design and the evolution of the landscape. It's really intriguing to see and to study, because you can see it in so many different places.

What do you enjoy about this type of planning?

❭ The real pleasure I get is going in and learning about a place. The satisfaction I get, once a project has begun, is making a difference in a community, and that has to do with helping people understand what they have in front of them. Many people are living too close to the landscape to recognize it. They need fresh eyes.

Second, I try to give communities a broader philosophical perspective on how to view the landscapes around them and how to help them understand the dynamics of change. Third, I give them tools to use to effect change in the way they want it to happen, and that gives me great satisfaction, especially when communities use these tools to actually do something.

Do historic preservation planners only work in historic communities?

❭ No. Every community is historic, and this work can be done at any scale. We do planning for historic communities, but we also do comprehensive plans, preservation plans, revitalization plans, and design tools. As a preservation planner, I use every planning tool available, and I encourage my clients to use every tool. Whether that is traffic planning, zoning ordinances, or other conventional planning tool, I think any tool available to move a community toward its goals is game.

How are these tools applied?

❭ We look at broad cultural landscapes, community landscapes, regional landscapes, and how they are changing. We look at how to enhance their character and accommodate new change.

We're also working with historic properties. These can vary from a historic house to a neighborhood to a park. We do a lot of work with historic battlefields. These are historic properties that cross large areas, and the issues involved with them can be quite enormous.

What about planning for heritage areas?

❭ Heritage area planning is a term and discipline that has developed during the past 15 to 20 years. State heritage area programs address regions with a common historic theme. The goal is to bring together the resources, sites, and communities that have relationships across a common set of historic themes to improve the quality of life in these areas and to attract visitors. These plans have an economic development component, a stewardship component, an education component, and an interpretation component.

What outcomes do these plans generate?

❭ We will develop recommendations to coordinate stewardship and the preservation of historic landscapes. Plans will address recreation and trails, way-finding signage, and education and assist historic sites to develop interpretive exhibits.

Heritage plans are designed to take advantage of an area's historic character to revitalize it.

What do planners need to learn to do this type ecological and preservation planning?

❭ I think my career path indicates that you can move step by step toward your interests from

The Shenandoah Valley in Virginia includes several historic downtowns that served as the basis for a heritage plan. JOHN MILNER ASSOCIATES, INC.

almost anywhere. Geography is central, as is the study of cultural landscapes and historic preservation planning. But knowledge of traditional urban planning is also critical.

You want to avoid being pigeonholed as a preservation planner, so you need a firm grasp of the traditional planning tools. If you go to school solely for preservation planning, you can be limited. So if you do that, make sure you get a graduate degree in urban and regional planning with a specialization in historic preservation. Then a lot depends upon seeking out and working for the right firm and professionals.

I would recommend earning your AICP certification. You want to be seen as more than just a historic preservation planner who develops historic districts. We need to break out of that mold and look at the broader landscape.

It's important to me to work collaboratively with other people. So I work a lot with landscape architects, architects, and planners and try to bridge all four disciplines.

How do you see your work changing in the future?

❯ Actually, I see it as the future, especially as the population increases and development pressures continue to increase. If you look out 100 years, then look back, the change in 100 years is hard to imagine, but I think it's going to be intense. How are people going to handle that? The field of sustainability is going to be central to how we adapt and change.

If you look at the sustainability movement and the green building movement, they were basically developed by the building products industry to build new, less wasteful development in more efficient ways. But the most efficient pattern is not to build new and abandon our inner cities. I think that's being recognized now by everybody.

Moving forward, I think the sustainability movement is going to be oriented toward revitalizing and reusing historic communities. The challenge is enormous.

Because of the link between historic preservation and the creation of an interesting shopping area, historic preservation is often an element of local economic development. Many communities, especially in regions dominated by rural landscapes, have used the Main Street program as a model for local economic development blended with historic preservation.

The National Trust for Historic Preservation pioneered the Main Street approach in the 1970s. Today, the Trust boasts over 1200 Main Street programs nationally. The trust calls its approach "preservation-based revitalization," focusing on older, traditional business districts. For more information on Main Streets, visit http://www.mainstreet.org/

In both economic development planning and heritage planning, tourism can be an important element of the approach to generating jobs, increasing sales by local businesses, and preserving the historical qualities of an area. Williamsburg, Virginia, is perhaps the preeminent example of a place where historic preservation has generated an enormous economic engine driver.

Lancaster County, Pennsylvania, has also taken this approach. Lancaster County created a Heritage Planning Division in 2003 that connects Lancaster's efforts to preserve its Amish heritage with its tourism program. Tourism can generate funds that are subsequently reinvested in programs that help to preserve an area's heritage and historic character.

COMMUNITY ENGAGEMENT AND EMPOWERMENT

The early history of urban planning and urban design is dominated by iconic individuals—Baron Haussmann, Pierre Charles L'Enfant, Sir Ebenezer Howard, Daniel Burnham—men who designed cities according to their professional vision for the space. Men of enormous self-confidence, they showed no concern for understanding what the public wanted or needed. To this day, legal requirements to give regular folks a voice in the planning process are weak. Most plan adoptions and land use decisions can be made with only a single public hearing, a meeting at which anyone may voice an opinion about the decision at hand and be heard by the decision makers—and then be ignored.

But while the laws have changed little, society has changed significantly over the past century. Trust in public officials waned dramatically in the 1960s and 1970s, and citizen activists began pushing for the chance to actively participate in planning processes. Today, most planners embrace public involvement as an essential aspect of the job.

Planners face many challenges in their efforts to achieve effective public engagement in the planning process. First, people must be involved early enough to have a genuine opportunity to influence the process. Waiting too long to get input from stakeholders can result in angry residents and a plan that doesn't meet the needs of the community. Ironically, people are often not interested in getting involved until there is an immediate threat to the status quo, such as a proposed development project that could remove a cherished open space.

Planners need to rely on a variety of methods for seeking public input and building consensus. Some people are not comfortable speaking in public meetings, while others are unwilling or unable to respond in a written format. Some people want a seat at the table to help work through the issues and have the time to do so, while others are able to devote only a small amount of time to learn about the project and express an opinion. A single planning process can incorporate multiple approaches to engage ordinary people—a specially appointed task force representing various constituencies, focus group meetings, online surveys, a multiday design charrette, and a series of public information meetings.

Planners must be strong communicators, both in writing and when speaking, to engage the public effectively. Clear and concise written documents are essential. Planners should also practice patience and empathy, especially when confronted with frustrated stakeholders. People who disagree with the direction of a plan for one reason or another can become very emotional and blame the planner for everything they dislike about the plan and past interactions with city government. Stakeholders should

Public meetings are a staple of a planner's work in all types of jobs and specialties. CRAIG OWENSBY/METRO NASHVILLE PLANNING DEPARTMENT.

Residents of a neighborhood in Hampton, Virginia, celebrate the grand opening of the Kenneth Wallace Neighborhood Resource Center, named after a policeman who was killed in the line of duty. The city's innovative neighborhood program enabled the community to transform the tragedy into something that made the neighborhood safe (the building includes a police substation) and provided a resource (computers/meeting space) to make neighborhoods better. CITY OF HAMPTON NEIGHBORHOOD OFFICE.

be given the opportunity to share their opinions, but the planner also needs to find ways to defuse the occasional angry outburst and keep control of the meeting when tempers flare.

While most planners engage in public involvement activities as just a portion of their duties, some people choose to make this the central focus of their work. Planners who specialize in public participation spend much of their time learning about the people in the community who need to be included if the planning process is to be successful. Often, their work focuses specifically on building agreement, or consensus, about the right way forward for a community. Planners who focus on public participation may seek specialized certification in public participation. The International Association for Public Participation (IAP2), for example, provides courses leading to a certification as a public participation professional.

Another specialization area related to public participation in planning is community organizing. Community organizers work to empower people in all aspects of the communities, including planning activities. Community organizers usually work in parts of the city where residents have often been ignored or treated unfairly in the past. Community organizers may work with people from racial and ethnic minorities, the poor, the homeless, immigrants, the handicapped, crime victims, and many others. The organizer's goal is not merely to achieve social justice but to build up the capacity of the residents to meet their own needs and to demand fair treatment from government.

Community empowerment efforts are sometimes led by planners, and sometimes by people of other backgrounds, such as social work, public health, religion, or even business. Community organizers may work for government agencies, but often they are employed by nonprofit organizations funded by foundations.

Engaging Neighborhoods

JOAN KENNEDY

Former Planning Director and Neighborhood Office Director

City of Hampton, Virginia

Why and how did you become an urban planner?

❯ I actually started out in architecture school. I had never heard of urban planning when I was applying to college in 1969.

By my fourth year, I had completed most of my coursework for a B.S. in architecture and was accepted into a "university year for action" program. This was a federal initiative coming out of the Action Agency (the agency that then sponsored the Peace Corps and VISTA). Their hope was to interest college students in public service. My assignment was to work for the Charlottesville, Virginia, Planning Department doing a housing needs study under the supervision of a graduate planning student. I did extremely well on the project and even wrote a long feature article for the local newspaper on the work we did. This was my first exposure to planning.

I was the first woman to graduate from the University of Virginia architecture school after attending all four years. Upon graduation, I went out to New Mexico as an architect in the VISTA Program and worked in an urban design studio affiliated with the University of New Mexico. Following that, I worked as a program officer for ACTION helping nonprofits in New Mexico with program planning and proposal writing.

Upon my return to the East Coast, a job recession was in full swing and architecture jobs were

scarce. I accepted a job as an urban designer in Hampton—having been warned by contacts in the architectural field that doing so would "turn me into a planner," and that is exactly what happened. As the urban design work became limited in the office, I started doing planning assignments and discovered that this was where my natural talents and interests were best aligned.

What were those early experiences like at UVa and in Hampton?

❯ I was raised in a big Catholic family with seven girls and one boy. From the time I was 12 or 14 years old, I was coached by my family on career development. It had never occurred to me that I would be held back because I was a female.

I was in the first year of women admitted to the University of Virginia. Throughout that process, I think the dean of admissions got to know us better than our parents knew us, because he was looking for people with grit, women who would not be fazed by the fact that they were in the minority. They did not make any special accommodations for us. We just went about our business and worked hard. I was lucky in that I had the kind of personality where those kinds of issues didn't bother me very much.

When I started in planning in Hampton I was the only professional female in the planning department, and when I became planning director I was working in a male-dominated profession that interfaced with the male-dominated development community.

In Hampton, many of the developers and builders were uncomfortable working with a woman. Being taken seriously by the developers while not taking myself too seriously was a challenging balance. Sometimes I would ask the assistant planning director (a male) to take the lead on a project if that would get us the result we needed.

Today this is not relevant. It's not a big deal now because it's not a male-dominated profession anymore. But some people made a big deal about it then.

In Hampton, you led an initiative to engage citizens in planning, which later gained national attention as a model program. What sparked your interest in this work?

❯ My first jobs were with community groups and then later I interfaced more with developers. I found great wisdom and hope in the general public that was an important balance to the often profit motivated plans of developers. I came to honestly believe that plans are better plans when the public is involved, so I guess it is an interest that was sparked by an experiential belief. In neighborhoods

the formula is even more crucial because the residents are both the greatest stakeholders and the greatest investors.

You served as planning director for the city of Hampton, as well as the head of its Office of Neighborhoods. What did you learn about yourself in those positions, and how did your past experience help you when you started those posts?

❯ As planning director, I learned that I could relate to citizen interests better than development interests. That having been stated though, I learned that, with effort and patience, I could come to understand the point of view of almost everyone that I interfaced with. This was critical in crafting plans and solutions that did the most to meet the broadest needs of the community.

My tenure as planning director was marked by an emphasis on citizen involvement in planning. This was really difficult at first because I was ac-

Joan Kennedy and the neighborhood staff in Hampton, Virginia, created Neighborhood Month to celebrate citizen involvement in the city's neighborhoods. Hundreds of events have taken place in the years since the program began. CITY OF HAMPTON NEIGHBORHOOD OFFICE.

customed to associating value with efficiency and technical competence. The slow messiness of citizen involvement really challenged my sense of professional competence. Over time, though, I came to trust the value of good process in cultivating good planning with strong citizen involvement. Then, I ended up making this trust into a career move into the Neighborhood Office. I learned there that this community work (facilitation, involving a broad base of stakeholders, building community vision and relationships) was probably my vocation all along; it just took me a while to recognize it.

Another challenge was balancing what you learn in the textbooks and the best practices in the field, with the realities of meeting community needs and priorities. A purist stance tends to get one discounted as not credible. A lax professional stance does not give the community what they are paying for in a professional planner. Again, this is a difficult balance to discover and hold.

What have been the most and least satisfying parts of your job?

❯ Most satisfying is working with the community to help them discover and achieve a greater vision. Least satisfying is managing the politics.

What traits were you looking for in the planners you hired?

❯ I never wanted to hire somebody who hadn't done a minimum wage job in their career. My experience was that, when someone felt there wasn't any job that was beneath them, they would be able to get along with people from every level of society.

Whatever job needs to be done, you need to go out there and do it.

I would also advise planners not to take yourself too seriously. Try to focus on what's really important and don't sweat the details. And the ability to get along with other people and work in teams is important.

What about the future of citizen-based planning?

❯ In citizen-based planning, there's a tendency to do whatever the citizens want to do. If you're not careful, you can kick the professionals to the curb. Sometimes planners don't want to engage the community because they're afraid that citizens are going to politicize technical decisions. Others don't want to spend the time necessary to become good citizen planners.

I think citizen-based planning will continue to be very important, and the cities that embrace it will benefit. But it's important not just to write down what citizens have to say and assume that it's the right course. Communities that have done that have found that the process has boomeranged back on them, and in response, they move back to a situation where they don't want to involve citizens at all. So it needs to be done carefully.

Overall, though, I see the neighborhoods movement picking up steam. I'm invited all over the country to talk about how to set up a program. It's becoming standard practice in most cities in the United States. Whatever the future brings, I think bringing citizens into the process is something that will continue, too.

Listening to People

CORINNA MOEBIUS

Bordercross Consulting Group

Miami, Florida

Why and how did you choose the career path you've taken?

❯ A catalyst for my career path was "Environmental Perception & Spatial Behavior," a geography class taught by Dr. Richard Wilkie, at the University of Massachusetts, Amherst. As an undergraduate, I was thrilled to learn that research existed on "spirit of place" and perception of the environment. Still, I had no idea about careers in public participation and civic engagement. I thought my future was a career writing for *National Geographic*!

In fact, I kept changing my major because I didn't know where I fit; I just knew what interested me. At first I was a sociology major, then an anthropology major, then an anthropology/journalism double major, then an anthropology/geography double major. When I wanted to be a "triple" major, I suddenly discovered a bachelor's degree with an individual concentration option. I was the most "last minute" person to be accepted in the program, and received my "BDIC" in Communications and Anthropology, with a minor in Geography. My major focused on "how people perceive and communicate about their environment."

From Dr. Wilkie's class, I confirmed that I wanted to learn how people relate to place—including the neighborhoods and cities or towns where they live, and I started my investigation into the politics and control of public space, migration and displacement, safe havens, and community identity. My

learning over the years did not take place solely in the classroom. For instance, during the eight years when I lived in Washington, DC, I played cowbell with the djembe and conga drummers who gathered in Malcolm X/Meridian Hill Park every Sunday when the weather was warm. Drummers, most of African descent, had gathered there for the past 30 years. In 1999, complaints from residents of new condominiums adjacent to the park forced the drummers and dancers to move to new territory in the park, just as the gentrification of surrounding neighborhoods was forcing many low-income residents to move to other parts of the city. Nonetheless, even individuals who'd had to move away still returned to the park on Sundays. The drummers felt the circle reconnected them to their old neighborhood, or their country/city of origin, or the home of their ancestors: Africa.

So in my fascination with place, I always wanted to know: who is part of the decisions that affect these gathering places? How can we ensure that residents of all backgrounds have a say in the places that have so much meaning to their lives? Together, how can we build inclusive communities?

Interestingly enough, one of the greatest opportunities that ever opened for me, career-wise, was on a bus ride back home after attending a transportation forum in DC. I was on the crowded 17 bus, standing in the aisle, when a stranger said, "Didn't I just see you at the forum?" We struck up a conversation, and it turned out he worked in DC's transportation department. I told him that I was currently an Internet consultant, but that I wanted to shift my career, so I could get back to my interest in nonvirtual communities. He asked me to email him my resume and he would forward it to public participation consultants who might want someone with strong Internet skills. (Of course, this is yet another reason for using public transportation!)

He was the one who introduced me to Mencer (Don) Edwards, a top public participation consultant in DC, and immediately I was able to start working with Don. Eventually, Don and I were members of the five-person consulting team that defined the planning and public participation strategy for Washington, DC's new Comprehensive Plan. As the proposal stated, our goal was "developing a Comprehensive Plan development strategy that is inclusive and stresses the relationship between community, place and identity." What more could I ask for?

Why and how did you choose which school to attend for your degree?

❭ I received my undergraduate degree from the University of Massachusetts, in my hometown of Amherst. And I originally chose UMass because my father was a professor there, and I could get a college education for free. Specific courses such as Cartography, Land Use Law, and Environmental Perception and Spatial Behavior helped me delve further into the relationship between place, community, and identity.

For graduate school, I chose California State University, Northridge. I could have applied to much more prestigious schools, considering my grades and other academic and non-academic achievements. But I chose CSUN because it had an excellent Communications department and was the perfect setting for me to learn about diverse communities, since not a single racial/ethnic group dominated the student population. CSUN also had a history of student activism.

At CSUN, I was able to specialize in critical theory, cultural studies, and community studies. I did my thesis on place, community, and identity. I examined the significance of the question "Where are you from?" in that the answer isn't just about where one lives but is a signifier of a particular identity we want to present. The fact is, we human beings judge people based on where they are from. Our identity is wrapped up in place, whether we like it or not, so we're strategic in how we answer that question.

You work in civic engagement, public participation, and policy development. What is it about this work that interests you and drew you to it?

❭ I am interested in civic engagement, public participation, and policy development because I believe in a participatory democracy. I believe that residents and other stakeholders should have a say in the future of a place. I really like the following statement from the philosopher John Stuart Mill: "If all of mankind minus one were of one opinion, and only one person were of the contrary opinion, mankind would be no more justified in silencing that one person, than he, if he had the power, would be justified in silencing mankind."

Unfortunately, I have seen the impact of exclusion from the decision-making processes regarding place. I have witnessed people grieve over the loss of a favorite gathering place. I met a taxi driver who gave an elderly woman a ride across a busy street because she felt it was too dangerous to cross, the result of poor transportation planning. I have heard the stories of people in DC and Miami who were displaced during "Urban Renewal."

We live in increasingly diverse communities. I believe that through effective communication and public participation processes, we can work

Civic networking describes the process of building relationships among citizens to strengthen community involvement, civic engagement, and social trust. Civic networking can take place online and face to face and be designed to serve the collective goal of bettering a community. © GOVERNMENT OF THE DISTRICT OF COLUMBIA, 2006.

together for inclusive and equitable communities—and places that are sustainable, healthy, and safe for everyone—including kids, elderly folks, and people with disabilities. When we listen—truly listen—to each other, and value the perspectives of stakeholders (residents, small business people, bicyclists, and others who live and work in a place), we are more likely to build better policies and better communities. We can engage in placemaking. (Learn more about placemaking from one of my favorite organizations, Project for Public Spaces, at www.pps.org.)

When people love a place, truly love it, the way I have loved the neighborhoods where I have lived, they become better stewards and caretakers of the place—and act more neighborly. When they love a place, they consider staying, and perhaps raising kids there . . . and then they start to think about what kind of place this will be for the next generation, and the next, and the next.

People who work in public participation and civic engagement have a role in building democracy, and in building communities that work for the people who live there—now and in the future.

What is the connection between your work and planning?

❯ Throughout most of my career, I have engaged in work that has an impact on communities and place.

Before I moved to Miami, I worked closely with urban planners. As a public participation specialist, I helped develop the strategies and plans for how to bring diverse stakeholders into the planning process. I had to think about every possible way to build access to the process and remove barriers. For instance, many people need to understand why it even matters to participate: "How does this impact my life?" Others want answers to basic questions: "Is the public meeting accessible to people with disabilities?" "Can I get there by bus?" Others want the details: "How will we know that our comments will actually be read, or will inform the plan?"

Public participation specialists also have a role in helping urban planners know how to build par-

how **YOU** can get more involved

Joining this workshop is an important step in the Comp Plan revision process. There are many more ways you can stay involved:

1. ATTEND PUBLIC WORKSHOPS AND JOIN IN THE DISCUSSIONS
This week's workshops are the first in a series. Follow-up workshops are planned for June 2005 and January 2006. These later workshops will provide a continued forum for discussing proposed policies and actions as the Comp Plan is developed.

2. LOG ON TO WWW.INCLUSIVECITY.ORG
The inclusivecity.org website is full of information about the Comp Plan revision, including: background information, a schedule of Comp Plan events, and online comment forms. Once registered, you will be able to submit feedback and sign up for an email notice of all relevant Comp Plan events and workshops. Registering is the best way to stay informed!

3. HELP US REACH, EDUCATE AND ENGAGE THE COMMUNITY
Help build an inclusive city by educating and engaging DC residents of all backgrounds and all parts of the city, so everyone can participate in the Comp Plan's revision in the way that is most comfortable for them. To assist those who want to help with civic engagement, we've created a series of Quick Guides customized for specific types of organizations and institutions, as well as individual activists, publishers of online content and business owners. Each guide lists quick and easy ways for groups and individuals to help. To download the Quick Guides, see the How to Participate section on inclusivecity.org.

continued from front page

Why is the Comp Plan Being Revised?

DC's current Comp Plan was adopted in 1984. Although it has been amended several times, the Plan does not reflect the realities and challenges of today's DC. The "future"—as envisioned by our 1984 Comprehensive Plan—is already history. In 2003, a Citizens' Task Force, appointed by the Mayor and City Council, recommended that the Comp Plan be thoroughly revised, not just amended. The Task Force found that the existing plan was outdated, difficult to read and understand, lacked adequate maps and graphics, and did not provide the direction needed to address the tough issues facing our city today.

How is the Comp Plan Being Revised?

The Comp Plan revision has already begun. More than 3,000 residents participated in the Mayor's Citizens Summit III and helped to outline a vision for DC's future. One of the important outcomes of the Summit and the neighborhood meetings that followed was a commitment to grow inclusively. This commitment means that we need to work harder to heal the divisions in our city, to retain existing residents as we attract new residents, and to ensure that growth benefits all Washingtonians and not just a few. It also means listening. Through workshops and community meetings on the Comp Plan like these, residents will have an opportunity to voice their opinions on the issues that matter the most. By focusing the Comp Plan on these issues— and developing a realistic strategy for implementation—we can ensure that the revised Plan will have a real and lasting impact.

THE WASHINGTON, DC, COMPREHENSIVE PLAN

Your Voice Will Be Heard!

The Office of Planning will be collecting, documenting and sharing comments gathered from the workshops, the website and other community involvement avenues as OP develops the Plan.

- From Workshops & Discussions (booths, comment sheets, notes from session discussions, etc.)
- From online sources (inclusivecity.org website, listserves, blogs, etc.)
- From the Comp Plan Task Force meeting summaries
- From small group and other community meetings on the Comp Plan
- Other media sources (TV, radio, news, etc.)

The visual timeline in your packet shows how community input will be incorporated into the Comp Plan.

For more information on the Comp Plan, log on to www.inclusivecity.org, send an email to info@inclusivecity.org, or call the DC Office of Planning, at (202)442-8812.

---

growing an **INCLUSIVE** city
FROM VISION TO REALITY

THE WASHINGTON, DC, COMPREHENSIVE PLAN

do **YOU** have something to say
about DC's future? This is your opportunity.

Participation Materials

In your information packet, you will find:

- This Community Workshop Guide
- A visual timeline of the Comp Plan revision process, called "Working Together to Create the Next Generation of DC's Comp Plan."
- Summary sheets on the Four Challenges to be addressed at the workshop: Housing Choices, Transportation and Land Use, Environmental Quality and Access to Employment
- Comment Sheets on the challenges
- Workshop Evaluation Sheets

Se ofrece servicios de interpretación en español a los residentes del Distrito de Columbia que existan a este taller. Llamar al 202-442-8818 para mayor información y para pedir el servicio.

community workshop **guide**

As members of the DC community, we all have a vital interest in our city's future. The decisions we make now about how DC grows and develops will affect the look and feel of our city for generations to come. By participating in the Comprehensive Plan (Comp Plan) revision process, you are making a commitment to the city's future and helping to create a truly *inclusive city*.

DC Comp Plan Week

The District's Office of Planning is holding a series of public workshops between January 25 and January 29 throughout the city to involve the community in the revision of the city's Comp Plan.

The workshop's opening session will provide an overview of the Comp Plan revision process and outline four major challenges facing the district today. Participants will then join small, interactive workshops to discuss the challenges of most interest to them:

- Housing Choices
- Transportation and Land Use
- Environmental Quality
- Access to Employment

What Does the Comp Plan Do? How Does it Affect Us?

The Comp Plan is a legally required document that guides the city's growth and development. It includes maps showing the kinds of uses envisioned across the city, and policies and actions addressing important topics such as housing and land use. The Plan may affect the way key properties in your neighborhood are developed or redeveloped. It affects the way the city invests in new public facilities like recreation centers and libraries. It affects the location of new businesses, new parks and open spaces, new housing developments, and new transportation facilities. The focus of the Plan is on the long-term future of our physical environment—our streets, buildings, and open spaces—rather than city services and day-to-day operations.

continued on back page

COMMUNITY WORKSHOP GUIDE

Brochures, newsletters, and other types of informational materials are used to inform the public about plans and encourage participation at meetings. © GOVERNMENT OF THE DISTRICT OF COLUMBIA, 2006.

ticipatory processes. For instance, many folks feel uncomfortable asking questions in front of a small group, so when I was a consultant on the revision of the DC Comprehensive Plan, we designed public meetings to give residents plenty of opportunities to ask questions face to face with planners, informed by easy-to-understand fact sheets and maps. These details helped residents feel more comfortable sharing opinions, and planners had a greater opportunity to hear from residents who might not have spoken up otherwise. A public

participation specialist can help educate and build awareness among urban planners and policymakers as well as among residents and other stakeholders.

In my recent work as director of Imagine Miami, a countywide civic engagement and community building initiative based at the Human Services Coalition, I focused on cultivating a "civic network": a culture of civic engagement. I've learned that when people are aware that they are not alone in their commitment to community, they are more likely to stay involved. People become discouraged if they think they're the only one who cares, or if they don't know how to get involved. Imagine Miami helps people step into community involvement and civic engagement. And when people take these first steps, they're more likely to eventually attend a neighborhood or public meeting and become interested in community planning.

What has been your greatest challenge as a civic engagement specialist?

❯ My greatest challenge has been to choose what role I want to play in cultivating civic engagement. I've had moments when I've wanted to join activists on the front lines to advocate around a particular issue. I've desired to work within government so I can see with my own eyes how public comments are being incorporated into a plan. I've even thought about running for public office so I can take an even greater leadership role in policymaking. Often, I've longed to be more of a participant in the civic engagement processes I've helped host or facilitate.

My advice to others is to always be true to your integrity and to an ultimate goal of participatory democracy. I have often served as a "bridge" or ambassador between activists and planners, helping to break down the "us versus them" dynamic. It's not an easy role, but it's a vital role. Civic engagement specialists are connectors. We build collaboration, communication, and civic networks.

The Internet has become one of the most important tools for public engagement, participation, and education. Project websites have become increasingly common and allow for interaction between and among the public, stakeholders, and a project team. © GOVERNMENT OF THE DISTRICT OF COLUMBIA, 2006.

What are your primary responsibilities and duties in your current position?

❭ Currently, I am CEO of my own consulting business, Bordercross Consulting Group. Our team of consultants specializes in developing, launching, and advising on civic and cultural projects and events.

We focus on asset-based community development; arts and cultural development; urban gardening, civic engagement, and local economy initiatives; commercial and cultural district revitalization; and geotourism and destination development. We also design and facilitate participatory processes (such as World Cafe community dialogue), workshops, and training.

What does your job involve on a day-to-day basis?

❭ I am always aware of the need to be attentive, to listen, and to learn from those whose voices are often left out of planning processes. I learn by visiting and exploring particular places, observing how people interact in a place, and by talking to stakeholders from all walks of life. Sometimes the most important part of my job is to sit down and have a coffee (or cafe con leche) with a community member eager to share his or her insights or ideas about a neighborhood. For instance, barbershop owners are often incredibly knowledgeable about the dynamics of the neighborhood where their shop is based, especially if they've been there for a long while. The wisdom that a person may impart can be beneficial to many other neighborhoods as well.

What are the most satisfying parts of your job?

❭ Perhaps the least satisfying part of my job is the responsibility of finding new clients, and making sure that clients are timely about paying for our services.

The most satisfying part is knowing that I am having an impact on the lives of ordinary people, and even on future generations. I love seeing the spark in someone's eye when they "get" asset-based approaches and start thinking about their role as a community asset. I am excited when I see a business corridor transformed by a new level of collaboration between local business owners and nonprofits. At events that I have designed, I have witnessed an energy (it's almost magical!) among residents from diverse backgrounds who are jubilant about meeting each other and passionate about place. It is truly inspiring to see what happens when people express their love and caring about place, while discovering how interconnected they are with others. I personally believe that community involvement and civic engagement are good for the soul!

ENVIRONMENTAL AND NATURAL RESOURCES PLANNING

Planners who specialize in environmental protection and natural resources management are engaged in one of the youngest specialties in the profession. After centuries of growth in which the natural world was viewed as a hostile opponent to be conquered, American opinions began to shift toward preservation in the late 1800s. Most early preservation and conservation programs were focused on the effective management of our natural resources for continued economic benefit, such as forest for lumber, soil for farming, and scenic sites for recreation. Environmental planners today operate within a framework of federal environmental regulation spawned in the late 1960s by

Stormwater management is a key component of site design. Cleared and graded land allows rainfall to quickly run off the site, carrying sediment and pollutants with it, which in turn can degrade water quality in streams and lakes. Planners work with engineers to design stormwater detention and retention ponds as a way to control stormwater on site. JASON VALERIUS.

a combination of alarming examples of air and water pollution (e.g., the Cuyahoga River fire) and careful scientific documentation of the effects of pollution on ecosystems (e.g., Rachel Carson's *Silent Spring*). Ian McHarg is known as the father of modern environmental planning, publishing the now-classic *Design With Nature* in 1969.

Environmental and natural resource planners are engaged in a continuous search for appropriate compromise between protection and use. Almost all development has some negative impact on the natural environment—destruction of habitat, an increase in stormwater runoff to local waterways, or increased emissions of pollutants to the atmosphere. The environmental planner's role is to help communities and regions understand how to protect natural resources without saying "no" to all development. Some places are more sensitive than others. Some ways of developing are more damaging than others. Environmental planners use their understanding of natural systems to help communities find a reasonable balance between growth and preservation. Of course, where that balance is the "right balance" can be a matter of dispute. The environmental planner's role is to help the public and decision makers understand the environmental impacts so that they can be weighed against other benefits that may result.

A key challenge faced by environmental planners today is the cross-jurisdictional nature of the work. An effort to protect a river basin, for example, can require cooperation among multiple states and many cities within each state. This is an important reason that environmental regulations are predominantly federal programs, including the Clean Water Act, the Clean Air Act, and the Environmental Protection Agency. It also helps to explain why employment in this specialty is most likely to be in the public sector, either for the regulatory agencies themselves, for other state or federal agencies that must comply with the regulations in their own projects (e.g., state departments of transportation), or with publicly funded advocacy or watchdog groups (e.g., a public service commission).

Another key challenge environmental planners face is the shift of emphasis to addressing non-point-source pollution. The regulations of the 1970s were successful in correcting the most visible types of pollution from obvious point sources like factories. Many serious pollution problems remain today, but they are often harder to see and much harder to control because they come from many sources. Carbon dioxide emissions, for example, are a primary contributor to global warming, but carbon dioxide is invisible and there are many, many sources.

Most environmental planners are engaged in some combination of technical analyses and public education. The planner's responsibilities may include documentation of conditions in the field, the development of Geographic Information System (GIS) maps showing the location or distribution of important natural resources, statistical analyses of data, the preparation of reports to share findings, and presentations at public meetings to help stakeholders understand the findings and issues to be considered. Because of the contentious nature of many environmental issues, environmental planners also commonly specialize in public participation and consensus-building.

With the growing realization that global climate change requires dramatic changes in how cities think about their use of energy, environmental planning is likely to be a rapidly growing area within the planning field. Reducing a community's carbon footprint will engage planners in helping set priorities, preserving land for production of renewable energy, and establishing policies related to energy efficiency in the transportation and building sectors.

Increasingly, environmental planning is moving away from being a small and distinct specialization within planning to being an essential component of every planner's work. Later in this chapter, the Sustainability section features planners whose work foreshadows the way planners will be doing their jobs in the coming decades, integrating economic, social, and environmental planning under the umbrella of sustainability and, increasingly, resilience.

Advocating for Sustainability

JAMES SEGEDY, FAICP, AIA
Director of Community Planning
Pennsylvania Environmental Council
Pittsburgh, Pennsylvania

How did you become a planner?

❯ My path was somewhat roundabout. My career path had always been directed towards being a doctor, but my GPA took care of any hopes I had of going to medical school. I had always had an interest in environmental issues and large-scale systems, and certainly in good design of any type. After much soul searching and many conversations with a lot of folks, it became obvious to me that urban design and community planning would allow me to do the kinds of things I wanted to do.

I guess it's safe to say: fascination, insatiable curiosity and passion, and a regular dose of listening to Paul Spreiregen's* *Places for People* on the radio every Thursday morning set the stage.

How did you choose a school for your planning degree?

❯ There were a number of factors. I wanted both a practical education and one that would allow

---

*Paul Spreiregen trained as an architect in the United States, and through a Fulbright Scholarship in Europe came to learn more about urban planning as well. As a leading architect, he hosted a program on National Public Radio for 12 years, showcasing the value of good architecture and good planning. He was a pioneer in promoting sustainable design, especially passive solar design, in which large, south-facing windows capture the heat of the sun to warm buildings in cool weather. For more information on Paul Spreiregen, visit the MIT School of Architecture and Planning website, http://sap.mit.edu/resources/portfolio/spreiregen/.

me the opportunity to teach. That meant a solid master's degree from an accredited program and a Ph.D. program. Staying in-state was a plus. Fortunately, both Michigan and Michigan State offered the right opportunity and funding for the whole program. Since Michigan State was having problems in keeping their program open, I went with the University of Michigan.

Why and when did you decide to focus on environmental planning?

❯ It was my passion for all things environmental and energy-related that drove me into planning more than the other way around. I guess it could be said that I was an environmentalist first and realized that the tools that would give me the greatest opportunity to do something about it were to be found in the planning realm.

What does your job as an environmental planner involve?

❯ My primary responsibilities are to help communities understand the relationships—often cause and effect—between the traditional activities and opportunities found in any community and the natural environment. That often means developing new diagnostic and implementation tools for communities to utilize in aiding the decision-making process.

I also coordinate and facilitate community visioning processes in areas that have new environmental, natural resource, and recreation resources and very limited opportunities to do these on their own.

Pennsylvania was called "Penn's Woods" for good reason, and we still have the wild resources, beautiful vistas, and authentic communities with which people connect. But the livability and sustainability

Jim Segedy's passion for nature and protecting the environment allows him to do what he loves and get paid for it. Protecting water quality, providing quality habitat for fish, and creating places for anglers to enjoy are all part of the job for an environmental planner. ILLUSTRATION BY LOHREN DEEG.

of our communities and landscapes are at risk every day. We are one of the slowest growing states, but we consume our cherished farms and natural places faster than any state except Wyoming. Our communities and landscapes are threatened by the loss of thriving downtowns, open space, wildlife habitat, and connectivity between the places we live, work, and play. PEC has focused its expertise and experience into the Center of Excellence for Sustainable Communities, which addresses sustainable development, smart growth, land stewardship, and access to our resources.

Do you have a typical day?

❯ There is no "normal" or "routine" in my days (thankfully). On a regular basis I will be "in the field" working with local officials to help them assess their needs and options, or facilitating community visioning charrettes or other related activities. I also work on developing design and development

guidelines, model ordinances, and other tools for local municipalities.

Approximately 15 percent of my time is dedicated to developing self-help tools and "manuals" for local communities.

Approximately 10 percent of my time is dedicated to managing projects and contracts.

What are some of the experiences that have shaped your ideas of planning and how you approach the projects on which you work?

❯ For me, it was more the people who influenced how I approach planning and projects. Certainly my fascination and love for communities, especially the unique character and place of smaller communities (and visiting many of them on family vacations and visiting relatives while I was growing up) was an important factor, but primarily it was the influence of several people that led me to planning and through my planning education that has been the key.

Specializing in a Holistic Way

LISA HOLLINGSWORTH-SEGEDY

Associate Director for River Restoration, American Rivers

Pittsburgh, Pennsylvania

Why did you decide to focus on environmental planning?

❯ I simply matched my resources and needs: skills and experience (resource) with a closer job opportunity (need).

How did you become a planner?

❯ I backed into planning by serendipity. I was working as an environmental geologist and wanted a job with less out of town travel and a shorter commute to the office. There was a regional planning office within 30 minutes of my location, and so I changed my "environmental geologist" resume to an "environmental planner" and wrote a letter to the executive director of the regional planning agency explaining how his office couldn't possibly function without an environmental planner on his staff. It worked. I spent the next 14 years of my career there, advancing from basically entry level to senior planner and eventually to planning director.

Since you started as a geologist, how did you train to become a planner?

❯ My planning degree was from the University of OJT (On the Job Training). I did spend a year studying for the AICP exam and made a point of reading all the textbooks I would have used in a planning curriculum.

What does your job involve?

❯ I am involved in river restoration with the nonprofit organization American Rivers. My position is to help remove dams that are no longer used and are in poor condition to restore rivers to their original form and function. This provides water quality, aquatic habitat, riparian connection, natural flood protection, improved recreation, and community revitalization benefits. In many cases, removing dams also removes a safety hazard—it is often the death of a swimmer or boater who got caught in the hydraulic at the base of a dam that prompts interest in dam removal.

Do you have a typical day?

❯ Depends on the day! I do everything from evaluating the ecological benefits of removing a particular dam, to developing funding for dam removal projects, to providing organizational outreach, to recruiting new members and facilitating donations, to assisting the Pennsylvania Fish and Boat Commission in identifying potential new dam removal projects, to meeting with dam owners (public and private) to evaluate their own pros and cons in weighing their options of removing a dam, restoring a dam, or doing nothing, to coordinating with engineers for particular projects, to procuring engineering services, and even project management for dam removal projects that are under deconstruction.

What are some of the experiences that have shaped your ideas of planning and how you approach the projects on which you work?

❯ I have learned a lot of lessons the hard way, and I think as planners we all do that, regardless of our education. In working with local government elected officials and staff, I have come by several approaches that have given me some measure of success.

First, don't assume that the most obvious solution will interest everyone. Second, when you ask for someone's input, don't give them a blank page because it intimidates them. Instead, give them something to react to and they'll always find something to say about it. Third, it is almost always the economics that will drive any decision. Fourth, the way for planners to effect change is to "dig the hole in front of them and wait for them to fall into it"—in other words, make the decision makers think it was actually their idea. And finally, a good story is a better tool than all the statistics in the world when it comes to influencing people.

What advice do you have for someone interested in environmental planning as a career?

❯ My work is a multidisciplinary effort. I work with people who are engineers, biologists, fisher-ies managers, finance people, as well as folks in local government, state, the federal government, and everywhere in between. I think it's helpful to have as broad an understanding of all the areas of sciences as possible, in other words, be "multilin-gual" in the sense of being able to communicate with everybody involved in a project, regardless of their role and training.

As a planner, we are taught how to identify the links between things. In my work, I evaluate those links and find ways to work together with other professionals to build on those connections.

GEOGRAPHIC INFORMATION SYSTEMS

Geographic Information Systems refers to the combining of digital map data with geographically "coded" information about people, places, or other characteristics of things on the land. The map data can include the location of streets, underground pipes, and streams. The map data can include both physical features and social features. The map can show the physical street, from curb to curb, but it may also show the right-of-way lines that do not physically show up on the landscape but are essential information for a property owner who wants to build a new building.

GIS professionals are able to add multiple "layers" and, because it is digital, turn the layers on and off at will. For example, a planner might want to know where the vacant parcels are in a particu-lar neighborhood. Through GIS, a map could be created that showed the vacant lots' property lines. Then, the planner might decide that it would be helpful to know what the zoning of those parcels is. A click of the mouse, and a new map would appear with each different kind of land use (residential, commercial, industrial, park land, etc.) appearing in a different color. Finally, the planner realizes that only parcels of 5 acres or larger and in an industrial zone are really of interest. Another click, and only the relevant parcels appear in color.

GIS is a skill that almost all planners are familiar with. Land use planners, economic develop-ment planners, transportation planners, environmental planners, housing planners—even public participation planners, all use GIS to understand the characteristics of the places where they are producing or implementing plans. Because of the high degree of technical skill needed to produce complex maps using data from multiple sources, planning departments usually work with GIS spe-cialists, many of whom are also trained as planners but with advanced skills in GIS.

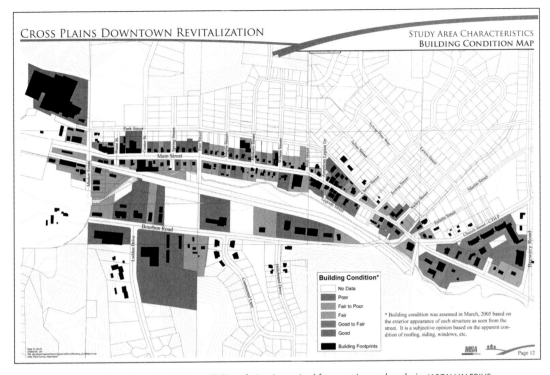

Planners use Geographic Information Systems (GIS) as their primary tool for mapping and analysis. JASON VALERIUS.

Specializing in GIS

PAUL SUCKOW

Senior Planner and GIS Coordinator, Harris County, Texas

Houston, Texas

What was your first experience with GIS?

❭ I was first exposed to GIS in 1989 when I was a city planner in Muskegon Heights, Michigan. Everyone in the department had the desire to create computer-based maps, so the first time I got my hands on the software—a version of Atlas GIS for DOS—I ran it right away. We all thought it was the coolest thing ever. We got data from the county and were able to map 911 call information for a large area around Muskegon and Muskegon Heights. Throughout that year and into 1990 and 1991, we used GIS to track the calls and then used the data to support a grant application for more police funding.

In 1992, after President Clinton was elected, the re-inventing government movement took hold and Al Gore made the point that every government entity should be using GIS. The city obtained MapInfo software, and I used it to make reports to meet the requirements of HUD. It was the first time that the city had used software out of the box to do GIS.

About that time, we started talking about integrating GIS with information technology, but it's taken a long time to get to that point.

When did you decide to focus your career on GIS?

❯ The year 1995 was a pivot point for me. I was working as a community development specialist at the City of Pontiac, Michigan, and applied for a senior planner position with the City of Detroit. At that point, I thought I might spend the rest of my

▼ This map shows the urbanized areas and the rural parts of a region. Understanding where development has occurred at "urban densities" is one of the first tasks in putting together a land use plan. Often, planners use the availability of "urban services" in an area to determine whether to mark it as urban or non-urban. Urban services are city water and sewer. Areas served by water would be one GIS layer and areas served by sewer would be a second GIS layer. The major roads shown in this map would be a third layer. And the city names superimposed over the map would be a fourth layer of information. A Geographic Information System can include hundreds of layers, which can be turned on and off to create the specific maps and analyses a planner needs. PAUL M. SUCKOW, SENIOR PLANNER, HARRIS COUNTY COMMUNITY SERVICES DEPARTMENT WWW.CSD.HCTX.NET.

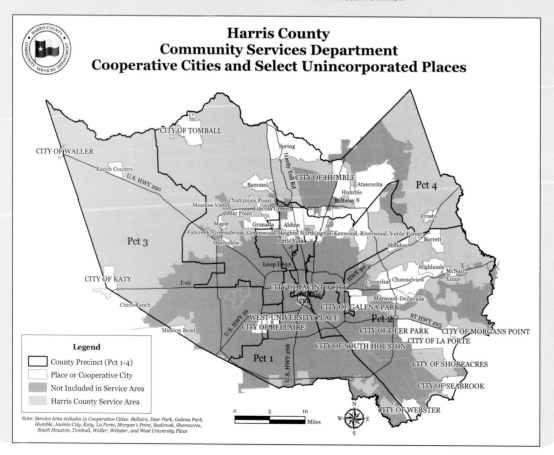

Harris County Community Services Department Cooperative Cities and Select Unincorporated Places

Note: Service Area includes 15 Cooperative Cities: Bellaire, Deer Park, Galena Park, Humble, Jacinto City, Katy, La Porte, Morgan's Point, Seabrook, Shoreacres, South Houston, Tomball, Waller, Webster, and West University Place

career in Detroit city government. After taking the exam, though, the job didn't feel right for me.

About the same time, my wife saw an ad in the newspaper for something called a GIS coordinator for Little Caesar Enterprises in their real estate department. They were looking for someone to use GIS in their site location research. They offered the job to somebody else, but they weren't able to come to terms and ended up offering the job to me. It was a lucky break.

I worked at Little Caesars for two years, mainly doing "ring" (or buffer) analysis, drawing 1-, 3-, and 5-mile radii around potential restaurant locations nationwide. It was the first time the company had invested in GIS, and compared to today, the tools were rudimentary. The software package we used had a text interface, but it had a pretty decent geocoder attached to it.

After a few years, a headhunter contacted me and we moved to Houston so I could work on GIS for a big oil company. I stayed in the private sector till 9/11. After that, I had a more civic-minded mentality and went back into the public sector.

What does your job involve?

❯ This agency has about 100 people in community development. We're the think tank of the group, trying to keep everything coordinated.

I fulfill map requests for the housing rehabilitation staff and for people who work in our housing assistance program. Map making takes up a fair portion of my time, but I'm also the person who manages and coordinates the GIS system for our department. The GIS system we have is stand-alone. It's separated from the main IT department of the county, so I maintain it.

LAND USE PLANNING, LAW, AND CODE ENFORCEMENT

To many people, land use planning and code enforcement is at the heart of what planning is.

One of the maxims in planning is "First plan; then do." This means that before planners enact regulations, they should first engage in planning to understand the area's needs and opportunities, to integrate actions across different sectors of activity (environment, housing, economic development, and transportation), and only then to fashion regulations to implement the plan. This process, called comprehensive planning, leads to a wide range of implementation actions, only one of which is new land use regulations.

Yet, because the profession grew out of early efforts to regulate land use, the identification between planning and land use regulation is firmly entrenched.

The first zoning ordinance was adopted by New York City in 1916 in an effort to curtail conditions deemed unpleasant and unsafe. By 1930, 47 states had adopted legislation enabling local governments to enact zoning. A zoning ordinance divides the community into a variety of districts, or zones, and within each zone it sets limits on the uses permitted, the density or intensity of those uses, and the bulk and location of the associated buildings. Subdivision ordinances play a complementary role, regulating the process by which land is divided into smaller lots. These ordinances ensure that the lots meet the minimum dimensional standards, provide adequate stormwater drainage, and are serviced by proper public improvements such as street access, sewer, and electricity.

Zoning is just one regulatory tool that planners use. In recent decades many communities have revised the zoning ordinance to allow planned unit developments (PUDs). The PUD approach allows for greater flexibility regarding the mix of uses, the placement of buildings, and the arrangement of lots. In exchange for this flexibility the developer agrees to an approval process that is more like a negotiation than the traditional approve/deny ruling. This approach was developed in reaction to criticism that traditional zoning too often resulted in boring, lifeless neighborhoods.

In an attempt to deal with rapid growth, many communities also use regulatory approaches to control the timing of new development and to manage the way that the community is growing. The growth management movement is revived every time the real estate market goes on a rampage.

One aspect of managing growth is placing controls on the design of new buildings. The failure of zoning ordinances to protect against bad design has led to experimentation with other approaches. Design guidelines are sometimes added as an additional layer of regulation in certain areas, especially downtown settings, establishing more detailed rules about materials, proportion, signage, lighting, landscaping, and even sometimes requiring specific architectural styles. A recent trend is "form-based codes." In this variation on traditional zoning, the emphasis of regulation is building form rather than just use and placement on the lot. Form-based code has emerged as a tool for creating engaging places and public spaces.

The proliferation of development regulations has necessitated two additional specializations in planning, code enforcement and code development.

Though most often provided by public sector municipal planners, code enforcement is also provided as a contract service by consultants. Small communities may have a "planner of record," a consultant on whom they rely for occasional, as-needed assistance. In all cases the planner's duty is to evaluate the proposal against existing plans and ordinances and prepare a report, usually for the Plan Commission, explaining how a proposal does or does not meet the regulations. The planner is often expected to report to decision makers in person as well and respond to questions as they arise. In most cases the planner interacts directly with the applicant at some point in the review process to explain and discuss the regulations and to ensure the submittal of all requisite elements. These planners should have strong written and verbal communication skills and should be able to communicate planning principles to nonplanners with ease.

While planners receive some training in planning law and most can write a first draft of a new ordinance, many communities prefer to refer their code development activities to an expert in the law, in this case, an expert in planning and municipal law.

Finally, land use regulations and decisions have wide-ranging impacts on a community, including fiscal impacts. Some planners specialize in advising cities on the impact that land use regulations will have on the tax base and, simultaneously, on the costs of providing services in a community. If the increase in taxes is offset by substantial increases in the costs of providing services, a policy promoting "growth" could actually promote decline as it triggers a cascade of budget cuts or tax increases that eventually eat away at the community's desirability as a place to settle.

Bridging Technical Disciplines

LANE KENDIG

Strategic Advisor and Former President, Kendig/Keast Collaborative

Former Planning Director, Lake County, Illinois

Sturgeon Bay, Wisconsin

Why and how did you become a planner?

❯ I became fascinated with architecture in grammar school and got a degree in architecture from the University of Michigan. I went into the Navy after school and as I reached the end of my tour, it was obvious that I was way behind all of my classmates.

I spent part of my tour in Vietnam as construction advisor to the Vietnamese and later selected and designed five naval bases for U.S. forces. I decided to apply for a graduate degree in city planning and was accepted at the University of North Carolina. In those days, it was a quite natural transition from architecture to city planning.

Why and how did you choose which school to attend for your planning degree?

❯ I was in Vietnam when I was making applications, and, at the time, I believe there were less than 20 schools that offered city planning. I was initially biased by looking at schools that had sprung from architecture; my first list was Yale where Paul Rudolf was head of the school, Cal Berkeley, and MIT.

With a classic Big Ten–Northern bias I rejected all the southern schools. I wrote the dean at Michigan who I had had several classes with and greatly respected. I gave a sharp critique, and he strongly recommended North Carolina, who he felt had the

best program. I applied there and I can no longer remember where else and was accepted.

What are some of the experiences that have shaped your ideas of planning and how you approach the projects on which you work?

❯ I owe a great deal to my training as an architect. First, one learns to defend one's opinions at the juries used to review projects and this sharpened my skills in the area of design. Even as a local government planner, one is asked to make decisions about what a developer's project will do—for or against the community.

Too many planners today have no clue as to how to evaluate or improve a developer's plan. NIMBYs push to shut development down, and planners do not have the skill set to improve the project and simply cut some dwelling units out to attempt to palliate the natives. My design training allowed me to draft zoning that encourages good design.

In graduate school I heard Ian McCarg give a presentation and took ecology against the dean's recommendations. That proved to be a wise move. A sizable part of the firm's practice has been built upon my ability to understand local environments from the Florida Keys to Teton County, Wyoming, and a number of communities with karst environments.

The third major experience was working in Bucks County, Pennsylvania, for a planning director named Franklin Wood. Franklin ran a unique planning operation. He kept looking for bright young people with the latest planning knowledge and then let them have their head.

As a result, Bucks County initiated one of the nation's first growth management programs. I was allowed to shape my tasks, resulting in one of the first computer planning efforts and performance zoning. Franklin ran political cover for the agency and planners did good planning and were not forced to produce plans reviews or other information to conform to a political agenda. That idea of standing up and fighting for good planning has proven to be excellent. I was able to maintain that same approach as planning director for Lake County, Illinois.

What has been your greatest challenge as a planner?

❭ Planning is a very technical profession with one major area of expertise being design and the others being environment, transportation, economics, or other fields. In order to really do our job of planning for the future, we must somehow bring these complex technical elements into plans and regulations. At all levels, professionals are forced to make their expertise heard over the clamor of residents who want nothing changed in their neighborhoods.

A very simple case is what is known as connectivity, making sure that local streets are well connected so that people may go from one development to another. Stub streets are required to provide for future connections. Time after time despite the planner, engineer, fire, and police advocating, the residents of the first subdivision fight successfully against making the connection, resulting in potential losses of safety and increasing congestion on major roads.

What motivated you to start your own firm?

❭ I had reached the point where as planning director in Lake County, I was increasingly spending most of my time holding hands of the County Board chairman and the administrator and doing less and less planning. I looked at other counties.

I had written *Performance Zoning*, and some of the lawyers I knew urged me to go into consulting. Looking at some of the places to go and having been offered a job in Pueblo, Colorado, I could see that I would go back to ground zero and repeat the successes in Bucks and Lake, but never really advance. As a start-up consultant about all I did was plan.

You have written development codes and developed comprehensive and master plans. Is it difficult to do both?

❭ A lot of people become specialized in one or the other, and a number of consulting firms are heavily specialized. I have one competitor who does nothing but development codes, but a number of us do both. My personal strength has been my broad depth of knowledge, from codes to plans. I have even written a Planners Advisory Report on transportation plans for rural areas, and a lot of my recent work has focused on environmentally sensitive areas. I feel comfortable in both of these areas.

A lot of planners in my class at North Carolina had undergraduate training as engineers, architects, and landscape architects. I think this kind of training gave you far more incentive to learn the technical aspects of planning. After my class, more planners entered graduate school with liberal arts degrees, and, as a consequence, more planners became generalists.

This is one of the dynamics in planning today, and I think it's a core problem we have as planners, at least in public agencies. Some planners reviewing site plans don't know anything about what they're looking it, and so they have no ability to give guidance to the client.

When I was a planning director, I always hired architects and landscape architects as current planners because I knew I could count on them to be able to review site plans.

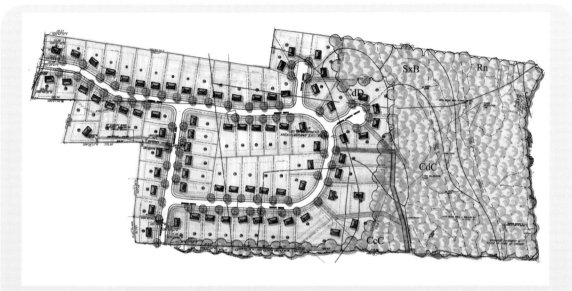

This design for the layout of a new subdivision clusters the homes at one end of the lot in a fairly traditional subdivision layout. The other end of the site is preserved as open space. Clustering homes in this way is recommended by many planners as a way of protecting some lands in rural areas from being covered with homes and lawns. LANE KENDIG.

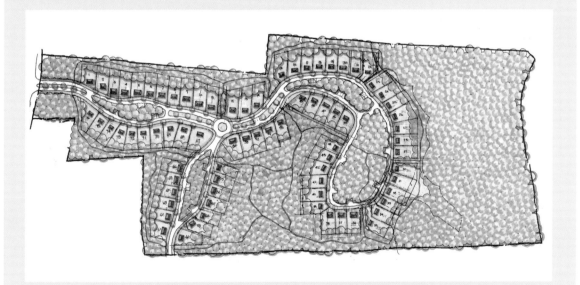

This subdivision design includes the same number of lots as in the previous figure, but this design affords a greater number of homeowners views and physical access to the preserved open space. Although the lots are smaller in this design, the residents would have a sense of living in a rural setting. Lane Kendig, who worked on these design alternatives, was greatly influenced by Ian McHarg, known for his seminal book, *Design With Nature*. LANE KENDIG.

You recently retired after 41 years as a planner. What was your role as the leader of your firm?

❯ For most of my consulting career, I was the only senior planner in the firm, and made the plans and codes and used junior staff to help. My role was as the creative, strategic, and tactical practitioner. The challenge is to push or educate the client to really do something special, to advance the state of the art. It is sad, the vast majority of communities are not doing anything better than Bucks County was achieving in the early 1970s.

Growth management evolved as most communities struggled and failed to come to grips with the issue of impact fees and impact assessments. Today, the code words for this are smart growth and sustainable communities.

Increasingly, I was serving as a mentor to my partner and what is now a firm over twice the size it was until 2002. I was spending time assisting in bringing junior staff to understand the technical elements and trying to create new approaches to old problems.

To you, what are the most and least satisfying aspects of planning?

❯ I have never really enjoyed administration or competing for jobs. It is very easy for a planning director to simply be an administrator. While at times this means working with elected officials on real issues, one gets valued as an advisor and thus sits in on too many meetings most of which have little to do with planning. This is not planning. It is the technical aspects of planning I really like.

There are real planning issues that communities need to address. Getting them to do so is very satisfying. It often requires strategizing how to force the elected officials to deal with an issue. I also enjoy presenting and educating citizens to accept new ideas and concepts. In the area of current planning, working with developers to improve every project is very rewarding.

Specializing in Code Writing

LEE EINSWEILER, AICP

Principal, Code Studio

Austin, Texas

Why did you become a planner?

❯ I just drifted into it. My father was a planner and my mother had worked in a planning-related field throughout my teen years. I have always suggested I learned it at the dinner table.

I started my college career hoping to be a high school chemistry teacher, drifted through chemistry to biology to environmental planning and cartography at the bachelor's level.

Why did you decide to focus your career on development codes?

❯ I have worked with codes primarily since 1996, when I went to work for Duncan Associates in Austin. Jim Duncan, the founder of the firm, saw me as a perfect candidate to supplement Kirk Bishop, who had moved to Chicago.

Codes are a narrow industry, and my first 10 years working for a land use attorney gave me a unique perspective on codes and plan implementation. I'm no fan of plans for the shelf, and therefore zoning and form-based code work is very satisfying—it gets implemented immediately.

What types of clients do you work with?

❯ We work for cities and counties across the U.S. We do two primary things: prepare zoning and do small area planning combined with zoning or form-based code work.

While we are often the lead on large-scale zoning rewrites (as in Memphis and Denver), we also do special work such as mixed use districts (such as those in Dallas and Prince George's County, Maryland), and implement area plans prepared by other design firms (such as those in Asheville, North Carolina; Ithaca, New York; and Charleston, South Carolina). We also have a small specialization in residential infill (McMansion) standards (Boulder, Colorado, and West Palm Beach and Fort Lauderdale, Florida).

What are your responsibilities in your firm?

❯ I am in charge of client management, code strategy, some code writing, and marketing (especially interviews). I also do the bookkeeping and other functions of running a small business.

What are your days like?

❯ I do a lot of talking. I spend most of my time either in meetings or on the telephone during the business week. Drafting code language often occurs on weekends, as does bookkeeping.

What are some of the experiences that have shaped your ideas of planning and how you approach the projects on which you work?

❯ I have always worked with inspiring mentors. My first was Charlie Siemon, a brilliant land use attorney. The exciting locales of his projects, the respect of his peers, and the sheer enjoyment of the strategy component of our profession inspired me early on. I truly love each new place, finding out what is special there, and crafting unique solutions. That's what's inspired me.

Specializing in Land Use Law

S. MARK WHITE, AICP

Attorney, White and Smith Planning and Law Group

Kansas City, Missouri

As a practicing attorney with a planning degree, do you consider yourself a planner as well as an attorney?

❭ Yes. In fact, I think of myself as more of a planner than an attorney. Most of my practice involves the drafting of land development regulations. Very little involves litigation. I use my skills as a planner to build consensus and develop standards for development. However, because codes are legal documents, it is indispensable to know the law and to keep that knowledge current.

▼ Zoning and land development regulations are increasingly graphics-intensive. Property owners and developers can better understand the intent of regulations when illustrations show the character of development that the regulation is intended to promote. REPRINTED WITH PERMISSION OF MARK WHITE (WHITE & SMITH, LLC). ALL RIGHTS RESERVED.

Why and how did you become an attorney focused on land use, zoning, and other planning issues?

❭ My father was involved in the development and management of manufactured housing communities, where zoning and the need for affordable housing are always important industry issues. I also had a keen interest in politics.

I attended the University of North Carolina, Chapel Hill, which has a topnotch urban planning program. I enrolled in the law school, but after taking Judy Wegner's land use law class in my third year of the program, I developed an interest in land use law and decided to enroll in the regional planning program.

Tell me about your practice, the types of clients that you work with, and the types of planning issues that you address.

❭ Nearly all of our clients are public sector—local governments (cities and counties). Most of my work involves draft development codes, such as zoning, subdivision, and smart growth regulations. We also develop impact fees, and assist our clients with land use litigation where needed.

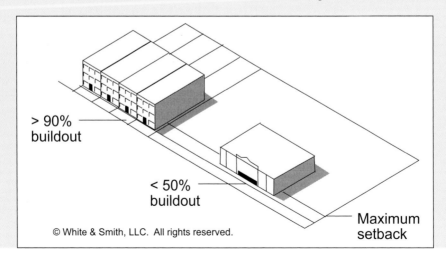

> 90% buildout

< 50% buildout

Maximum setback

© White & Smith, LLC. All rights reserved.

As a result of work with rural counties, I have developed and successfully defended regulations for concentrated animal feeding operations (CAFOs). I was also the board chair of a nonprofit CDC that built housing in an urban neighborhood of Kansas City for 10 years and have assisted local governments in developing inclusionary zoning and other programs to encourage the production of affordable housing.

What do planners most need to understand about the law?

❯ It is constantly changing. Changing the law can not only result in restrictions or conditions on how planning policies are implemented but also new opportunities. Many planners I work with are very conservative about legal restrictions, and unaware that the law may actually permit a broader range of techniques than they believe are possible.

It is also important to consult with experienced land use attorneys when developing or updating codes, or engaging in other actions that have legal consequences. This is a real specialty, and general practitioners normally lack the background to offer good alternatives.

It also concerns me that many planners without legal backgrounds engage in code drafting, which essentially takes them beyond their range of expertise. I have seen communities get into significant trouble because the code drafters failed to anticipate serious legal landmines.

What are some of the experiences that have shaped your ideas of planning and how you approach the projects on which you work?

❯ My experiences with affordable housing and community engagement profoundly shape my approach to code drafting. This is not an exercise that occurs in a vacuum. My most successful projects have involved significant stakeholder involvement, which builds trust and informs the end product.

My experience with affordable housing gave me insight into how the private development process works and the needs of the development community, and housing in particular. Planners should balance these needs with community design and environmental and infrastructure goals. They are all important.

What does your job involve on a day-to-day basis?

❯ A lot of client coordination (phone calls and online correspondence), research, and drafting. Our firm has a very large electronic and print library of planning resources, court cases and statutes, and development codes which I use extensively in developing my code products. Because almost all of my clients are out of state, I travel extensively for face-to-face meetings, focus groups, and public hearings.

What are the most satisfying parts of your job?

❯ The most satisfying is the intellectual stimulation and the fact that I get to make a living by doing the right thing. I also love my office, which is in an historic, downtown location and biking distance from my house. I have a variety of other professionals in my building, including an architect, an engineer, an employment consultant, and two attorneys with general practices. This gives me a variety of outlooks and people to discuss ideas with who have a "real world" perspective on the things I deal with.

The least?

❯ The least satisfying is having to spend time away from family while traveling (not to mention the hassle of dealing with airline travel these days), and dealing with limited budgets. There is often a significant gap between what a client expects and what

they are willing to pay for, especially with limited municipal budgets. This is just a fact of life that you have to deal with in this profession.

In the twentieth century, planners were silent partners in an insidious practice known as racial zoning. Racial zoning refers to zoning laws that specifically restricted African-Americans, Latinos, American Indians, and Asians from living in some areas of the city. Even after the U.S. Supreme Court declared racial zoning unconstitutional in 1927 (*Buchanan v. Warley*), zoning continued to be used as a way of segregating U.S. cities. Restrictions that increased the cost of building homes effectively restricted poor people, which, because of economic inequality, had a disproportionate effect on minorities' ability to live in large areas of many cities, especially in growing suburban areas. Again, too many planners acquiesced to communities that engaged in exclusionary zoning, and some planners undoubtedly advocated the practice.

Inclusionary zoning codes are an effort to reverse the longstanding injustices of racial zoning and exclusionary zoning. Many cities now require that all new housing developments of a certain size must include housing units affordable to those at the lower end of the income range in the county.

Assessing the Economic Impacts of Land Use Decisions

L. CARSON BISE II, AICP

President, TishlerBise

Bethesda, Maryland

How did you become a planner?

❭ I fell into planning by accident. As a freshman in college, I had declared a major in public relations and advertising. The second semester of my freshman year, I took an introduction to cultural geography as an elective. The second third of the course traced the evolution of the city, and I became fascinated with how and why cities developed the way they did.

I scheduled an appointment with the instructor, Dr. Michael Marchioni, to discuss the field of urban planning and the long-term career prospects. After our meeting, I quickly changed majors.

One of the reasons planning appealed to me was the fact that it was not a well-known profession. One of the themes of my life has been that I have not been one to jump on the bandwagon or follow trends. I've pretty much gone out of my way to differentiate myself. Although subconsciously in the beginning, I eventually learned this was an excellent way to create a niche for yourself professionally.

How did you choose a college for your degree?

❯ Since I am what you would call a nontraditional planner, I did not go receive a graduate degree in planning. Therefore, the reputation and/or perceived quality of a school's program did not factor into my decision.

My entree into planning was through my undergraduate degrees in geography and political science. Once I was working, I realized I would need a graduate degree. However, the idea of pursuing a graduate degree in a discipline I had already studied in undergraduate school did not appeal to me. Also, I quickly realized there was value to differentiating myself from the field, so to speak.

It had occurred to me as part of my internship as well as the initial days of my first job, that most planning directors had no idea how to manage an office, nor did they have any sense of business acumen. In other words, most were extremely talented planners who had had management responsibilities foisted upon them.

I also felt an understanding of economics, fiscal issues, and market analysis would be a good way to make myself stand out. Therefore, I took advantage of an employer-provided education program and enrolled in a local master of business administration program and eventually received an MBA with an economics concentration.

Why did you choose to work on the economics associated with planning?

❯ Again, this gets back to trying to differentiate myself from the traditional planner. I recognized early on in my first job that most planners did not have a complete understanding of how land use decisions affect a jurisdiction's bottom line in terms of costs and revenues. I also saw the need to incorporate market analysis into the comprehensive planning process.

So many of the future land use maps contained in the general plan have no grounding as it relates to the market for the different uses being contemplated. For example, if your community has too much retail, why are you drawing more regional retail on your future land use map?

What does your job involve on a day-to-day basis?

❯ My job involves quite a bit of multitasking and depends largely on whether I'm on the road. I am now on the road about three nights a week. On those days I'm usually meeting with a client to discuss issues related to policy or project management or have a presentation with the elected body.

Sometimes I am in town for a formal interview as part of the Request for Proposal process. Other times I am speaking at a national or state planning conference. When I'm in the office, I typically spend part of the day catching up with staff members on the progress of the various assignments they are working on in terms of deadlines being met, upcoming deliverables, or meetings.

There is also quite a bit of time spent preparing proposals in response to requests for proposals that have been issued. Finally, there is the day-to-day administration of the office, which includes making sure bills get paid, money is coming in, and the lights are kept on.

I don't consider myself a creative person, so I viewed taking a blank Excel spreadsheet and creating a complex fiscal model as quite a creative proposition. Initially, I also liked the idea that my compensation as a consultant was also directly linked to my output and relative value to the firm. This was not necessarily my experience in my three public sector jobs.

Example from Infrastructure Funding Strategy

	ROADS	SCHOOLS	PARKS	FIRE	EMS	LIBRARY
	TYPE OF INFRASTRUCTURE					
	GROSS FUNDING NEEDS					
	$253,924,000	$135,090,000	$56,279,330	$7,150,000	$600,000	$21,002,667
	LESS CURRENT FUNDING SOURCES					
Impact Fees	$38,885,529	$0	$13,458,312	$7,500,000	$0	$25,262,221
Unspent STIP Funds	$15,000,000	$0	$0	$0	$0	$0
New STIP Funds	$15,000,000	$0	$0	$0	$0	$0
Rural/Critical Lands			$5,000,000			
	EQUALS ESTIMATE OF FUNDING GAP					
NET FUNDING NEEDS	**($185,038,471)**	**($135,090,000)**	**($37,821,018)**	**$350,000**	**($600,000)**	**$4,259,554**
	POTENTIAL FUNDING OPTIONS TO MEET FUNDING NEEDS					
Revision to Existing Impact Fees	$45,000,000 ($1,200 per du)		$10,000,000 ($840 per du)	N/A		
Implementation of New Impact Fee				N/A	$600,000 ($20 per du)	
Local Option Sales Tax	$140,038,471 (15 years)		$27,821,018 (15 years)	N/A		$5,019,158 (15 years)
Bond Issue (backed by Property Tax)		$135,090,000 ($9.94 m/yr)		N/A		

Example from fiscal impact study

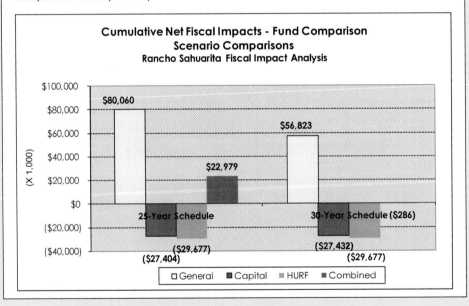

In rapidly growing areas, local officials need to keep a close eye on the relationship between spending on services to new residents and the amount of revenue generated by that development. Carson Bise specializes in gathering the cost and revenue data, analyzing it, and then presenting it visually so that decision makers can better understand the issues before deciding whether to raise fees or taxes. SOURCE: TISCHLERBISE, INC.

Now that I own the firm my day-to-day responsibilities are much different. I don't do as much actual "nuts and bolts" project work. My role is more of coaching and providing input on policy and so on. The part is day-to-day management of the firm as well as business development and marketing.

What are the greatest misconceptions about your work?

❭ The biggest misconception is one that I think quite a few consultants deal with. Many people I run into seem to think that a lot of consulting is simply boilerplate, or "cookie cutter," meaning that we simply take an existing study, change the name of the governmental entity, make a few edits, and we have a new study. This couldn't be further from the truth.

This perception is particularly true with our impact fee practice, as an impact fee study looks fairly simple when you read it. In essence, for each facility type the calculation seems relatively simple and straightforward. However, few people appreciate what went on behind the scenes to arrive at the calculation. This could include testing different methodologies/approaches in order to maximize revenue and/or achieve certain policy objectives.

What are the most satisfying parts of your job?

❭ Early on I was quite excited about the prospect of traveling to different parts of the country for a project. I had a somewhat naïve perception that it was quite a glamorous proposition. In reality, it turned out to be more difficult than I expected. However, I find it quite rewarding.

I really enjoy interacting with clients, seeing how organizational cultures varied by jurisdiction. I also love the challenge of creating and developing fiscal impact models for the assignments.

What are the greatest benefits?

❭ The greatest benefits are the sheer number of people I meet through my travels. I don't think local government planners receive the recognition they deserve. By and large, the people I have worked with are extremely bright and more importantly extremely dedicated to changing their community for the better. Unfortunately, most citizens do not have a true appreciation of the hours their planners put in or the sacrifices they make in order to make their communities a better place.

Another benefit is the travel. I've been to every state in the country with the exception of Hawaii and North Dakota. Most people don't get a chance to see all that our country has to offer, not only from a landscape perspective but also from a cultural perspective.

What do you like the least?

❭ I would say it is the administrative aspect. More specifically dealing with personnel issues and the paperwork required to operate a business on a daily basis, which can be quite time-consuming, even for a small consulting firm. All of this takes away from time that could be spent on projects, marketing, or strategic planning.

An impact fee is a tool that growing communities use to support the expansion of public facilities and services necessitated by the growth of the community. Impact fees are usually assessed on each housing unit in a new development or by the amount of square footage in a new commercial development.

New housing or new retail space requires additional capacity to provide police services, fire services, schools, parks, and so on. Eventually, an increased number police officers will need an expanded police station. An increase in public school students will require new classrooms.

TRANSPORTATION PLANNING

Whether crossing the street or crossing the country, travel is a necessary activity for most people. It is the job of the transportation planner to study these needs and help communities plan the facilities and services necessary to accommodate them. In many cases a transportation planner's work may influence the decisions of individual users, including not only how and when to travel but also where to live and work.

Transportation planning is one of the most technical subsets of the planning profession. Evaluating the supply and demand for transportation resources often requires the use of complex mathematical models that consider behavioral, economic, and land use variables at the same time. This complexity increases exponentially in urban areas where people have the ability to choose between multiple types of transportation. As population density increases it becomes possible for more people to meet their daily needs by walking or biking. These greater concentrations of users may also make public transit a viable option, including buses, trains, and subway systems. When planning for additional transportation resources to accommodate a growth area, planners must consider all available, or potentially available, transportation modes, and they must understand the users and their likely needs.

Transportation planners are employed in both the public sector and with private consulting firms. Public sector employers of transportation planners are usually large cities, counties, regional planning authorities, metropolitan planning organizations (MPOs), or state departments of transportation. Private employers range from large, international, multidisciplinary firms to small regional firms that focus exclusively on transportation planning.

"Most transportation planners are engaged, to some degree, in four basic tasks: (1) estimating future demand for transportation facilities or services, (2) proposing and evaluating alternative

This street in Fort Lauderdale, Florida, shows how even a modest investment, by providing special pavement striping for the bike lane, can create a visual cue to drivers that provides an added measure of safety for bike riders. Making transportation safer is one of the primary goals in transportation planning.
COURTESY OF DAN BURDEN, GLADDING JACKSON.

ways to respond, either by supplying more or different services or by attempting to modify demand, (3) calculating the costs of various responses or policies, using many definitions of cost, and (4) evaluating the options and recommending the solution most appropriate for the situation" (Hoch, Dalton, and So 2000).

The transportation planning specialty developed in the decades following World War II and was focused primarily on automobile transportation. This travel mode has become the preferred method of travel for most Americans. There are now more vehicles registered in the United States than drivers for those cars and trucks. Critics have charged that by focusing on safe and efficient automobile travel, transportation planners contributed to detrimental changes to cities throughout the country, including the destruction of neighborhoods, the decline of public transit systems, increased pollution and fossil fuel use, increased commute times, and the creation of new neighborhoods that discourage social interaction.

Contemporary transportation planners are much more likely to be asked, or required, to consider and account for all possible transportation modes and to encourage walking, biking, and public transit options as part of a balanced network of options. Increasing energy costs are driving public support for changes in land use planning to allow higher development densities so that alternatives to car travel are truly viable. These aspects of transportation planning will be presented in more detail in the next section on Sustainability Planning.

Developing Transportation Models

J. RICHARD KUZMYAK

Transportation Consultant, LLC

Silver Spring, Maryland

How did you become a transportation planner?

❯ My undergraduate degree was in civil engineering owing to my fascination with big public projects like bridges, buildings, and airports. However, I quickly tired of the engineering and construction aspects and became riveted with the more basic issues associated with planning and decision making.

This natural inclination was cemented by my first job out of engineering school when I worked with the Army Corps of Engineers in the early 1970s. It was coincidentally at the time that two things were happening: computers were beginning to force their way into old-line planning practices, and the 1969 National Environmental Policy Act had recently passed and the Corps found itself in the cross-hairs of the environmental movement. It was a massive institution that only knew how to do one thing, and that was to design and build major public works projects.

Two types of reactions ensued. Some engineers embraced the change, but many long-timers found it hard to accept that both the tools and the public sentiment were changing. The Corps was used to building dams or paving floodplains and being thanked for their work, and now their very existence was being challenged.

I personally found myself both admired and feared as a product of the new school of thinking and capabilities. Tedious drafting and computational tasks that earlier engineer trainees had been assigned to occupy their time were expected to take weeks to do. But with even a modicum of computer training, I was able to develop simple approaches that reduced these tasks to hours, as well as increasing accuracy, greatly increasing the ability to examine alternatives and their impacts. Many of the incumbent staff viewed these capabilities with uncertainty. It was a period of great change nationally.

What has been your greatest challenge as a planner?

❯ Trying to innovate as much as possible on projects when working against monetary and schedule constraints. Also, trying to understand how other professionals can be satisfied with and stand behind an answer that is convenient and profitable, but which they know is probably not correct or even ethical.

What are your primary responsibilities and duties in your current position?

❯ Since 1999, I have been self-employed in order to have maximum freedom to pick the assignments that are most meaningful to society and me. As a one-person operation, I must blend my pursuit of best practice and addressing important issues with the realities of keeping a backlog of work, meeting deadlines, being chief administrator and accountant and remaining fiscally sound.

How did you begin to work on issues related to transportation and land use?

❯ During my days with the Corps of Engineers, I became obsessed with the notion that the best answer to any given problem is not necessarily a major physical project and outlay of public resources, particularly without assessment of cheaper alternatives or consideration of the negative impacts of such a decision.

Prior to my land use focus, I challenged this type of conventional thinking in the transportation arena in such areas as transit investments, congestion management, travel demand management (TDM), air quality, and performance-based multimodal planning. With each of these important transportation policy issues, it became very clear to me that we were working at cross purposes— the private sector (in particular the development community) could influence local elected officials to advocate for projects that were clearly not going to be able to manage from a transportation efficiency standpoint.

The separation of land uses, along with low densities and associated transportation infrastructure design virtually ensured that more and more people would be dependent upon private automobiles for all their transportation needs. Transit would not work well in this environment, and even basic household needs—shopping, schools, recreation—would require a car trip. And then I also discovered that all the privilege in making these decisions about development patterns was located at the lowest levels of government, where local self-interest in economic development was most predictable and the accountability for the subsequent regional impacts was the least stringent.

In 1999, I felt sufficiently strongly about these imperfections in planning practice that I quit my job as a principal in a major consulting firm to be able to offer myself for service in my home state of Maryland to help it implement its Smart Growth law. My first job was working as a consultant for the state department of transportation—

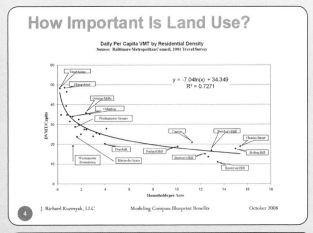

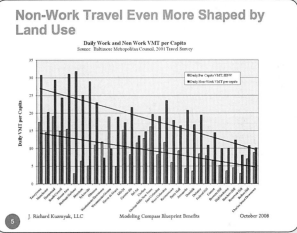

Good Land Use: More Than Density?

Explaining what matters through the "3Ds":

- **Density:** Easier to connect people with activities when they are closer together; also easier to serve with transit
- **Diversity:** Mixing of uses also puts people and activities closer together; Balance ensures that the right combinations are there
- **Design:** The manner in which the various land uses are arranged and presented affects how they are accessed and used: pedestrian travel is encouraged by orienting buildings to the street rather than parking lots, comprehensive sidewalk coverage and crossings, small blocks to enable direct paths
- **"4th D" = Destinations:** Nearness and abundance of opportunities outside the community and ease of access

6 J. Richard Kuzmyak, LLC Modeling Compass Blueprint Benefits October 2008

Planners spend much of their time delivering information to decision makers in order to help them understand the dynamics of their communities. In this case, transportation planner Richard Kuzmyak prepared these presentation slides to show decision makers in Baltimore how strongly density is related to the amount that people drive their cars. The more dense an area, the less people use cars for their daily travel. PROPERTY OF J. RICHARD KUZMYAK, TRANSPORTATION CONSULTANT, LLC.

the largest budgetary entity and major partner in development patterns—trying to help identify ways to inculcate the Smart Growth ideology into conventional, modal-oriented planning and programming.

What does your job involve on a day-to-day basis?

❯ I maintain a portfolio of projects, which I perform as a consultant. These projects range from front-end research efforts for organizations like the Transportation Research Board or U.S. Department of Transportation, to consulting assignments where I am working with a state or MPO (metropolitan planning organization) model or otherwise ascertaining the impact of a revolutionary approach to some aspect of planning or decision making, to supporting entities who are attempting to confront bad land use or transportation projects.

The work you do is highly technical. What type of skills should someone possess to do the type of work that you do?

❯ For me, the engineering foundation was essential to ensuring an objective, analytic, and quantitative view of each issue. The economics, statistics, and social science I received training in during graduate school provided key missing skills that most engineers are not fortunate enough to get in their education that might greatly widen their perspectives in defining appropriate responses to complex, multifaceted societal needs that are not often best addressed through construction. And finally, the training to work in multidisciplinary environments with intelligent and equally strong-willed peers I see as an essential way to both appreciate the multi-attribute nature of most public issues, as well as to develop the capability to listen, compromise, and take advantage of different skills in solving a problem most effectively.

A Metropolitan Planning Organization (MPO) is an organization designated by the federal government to do transportation planning in urbanized areas. MPOs are responsible for planning and coordinating federal highway and transit investments. MPOs are multi-jurisdictional in scope so that regional needs and connections can be addressed. For more information on MPOs, see Association of Metropolitan Planning Organizations, www.ampo.com.

Planning for Transit

NAT BOTTIGHEIMER

**Assistant General Manager for Planning
and Joint Development**

**Washington Metropolitan Area Transit
Authority**

Washington, DC

Why did you become a planner?

❯ I started my career completely haphazardly in
health care consulting. After three years of that, I
applied to a public policy program at UC Berkeley,
completely overlooking the planning program because I didn't really know what planning was.

Shortly after starting at the school of public policy,
I got an assignment on the topic of air quality as
a function of land use and transportation. I read
some materials by Peter Calthorpe and that was just
it. I knew that this was what I wanted to do.

I started working part-time in a local economics
planning and consulting firm, and I wrote my masters on policies that BART could establish to promote transit-oriented development. I took a number
of courses in transit and land use planning at the
College of Environmental Design in the planning
program, and professors Betty Deakin and Robert
Cervero were very influential in teaching courses
that encouraged and stimulated my interest.

Why did transit planning interest you?

❯ I was immediately captivated by all the things
that I remembered and loved about spending three
years in England growing up. I loved the buses. I
loved the trains. I loved being on public transit and
being with people. And I loved the urban settings
associated with transit and people. I loved that
there were environmental benefits from increased
transit use.

What are your job duties?

❯ I oversee our joint development program, long-
range and regional planning, capital planning, and
service planning and scheduling.

We do everything from regional planning with the
local council of governments to capital planning
and programming and station access planning, to
planning for bus bays, pedestrian bays, and parking service at transit stations and new bus service
planning, as well as joint development projects and
transit-oriented development.

What does your job involve day to day?

❯ Most days, I feel like a termite. I can see the vision
of building a majestic termite mound, but on any
given day I'm touching antennae with the other
termites, asking where there's good cellulose to be
had, schlepping to get it, putting it in place, answering questions from stakeholder termites about how
it's going, trying to motivate other termites, sharing
the vision of the mound, finding more termites to
work, etc.

It's chaotic, it's hard to see progress, you're constantly worried about big animals coming along
and tromping on the progress you've made, the
projects and goals take five years or more to come
to fruition, so on a day-to-day basis you need to
have a lot of faith that you're doing the right thing
and to stay energized, and you need to like the particular things you're doing. Which I generally do.

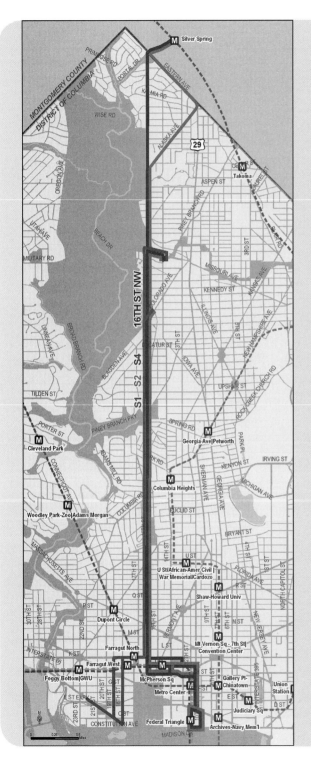

What are some of the experiences that have shaped your ideas of planning and how you approach the projects on which you work?

❯ I've been heavily influenced by the public policy analysis training I received at the Goldman School of Public Policy, and also very influenced by the economic analysis skills I gained working in consulting from 1992 to 2000.

As paradoxical as it may seem, some of the most influential work I did was in the late 1990s doing land use market forecasts in support of greenfield toll road traffic and revenue studies. I learned how metropolitan planning organizations forecast growth, I learned what Wall Street lenders expect in terms of documented analysis, and I learned a great deal about how to orient transportation infrastructure towards user groups who would pay to use the infrastructure.

I really didn't like working to promote toll roads that supported sprawling development, but I thought that the practice of preparing forecasts of population, employment, traffic, and revenue for investors who care about their money—and want to get it back—was a very disciplined type of analysis, and I wanted to bring those analytical skills to bear to promoting smart growth, transit-oriented development, and new transit systems.

The 16th Street bus line is included in Metrobus' Priority Corridor Network. The line (currently served by three routes) connects numerous activity centers and serves over 16,000 trips per day but is plagued by a high number of bus stop locations (more than 160) and excessive traffic congestion. Solutions involve a three-phase implementation plan, including skip stop service, branding, utilization of articulated buses, and adding supervisors in the first two phases, while the more politically sensitive and expensive options of implementing transit signal priority and peak hour transit-only lanes will be accomplished in the third phase. WMATA.

What has been your greatest challenge as a planner?

❭ Instead of asking, how much infrastructure do we need to accommodate the demand we forecast, I think we should be asking: What kind of infrastructure do we need to create the communities we want?

The analytical tools we use should be governed by the problems we want to solve, and I worry that we've been solving the problems we can with the tools we have. That's another way of saying that I think a lot of planning is technician-led rather than vision-led.

Another challenge is—it hardly warrants mentioning it's so big—the public decision-making environment that planning is in. I often worry that planners retreat to the technician mode because they are taught to leave politics to politicians, and that there is not a strong curriculum in how to be

staff—or even a consultant—and also facilitate and even promote decision making.

To be blunt, planning as a profession is at too great an arm's length from decision making, and because of how challenging local politics is, that's understandable. But somewhere along the way I think the planning profession has to more strongly inculcate a "wade in and engage" ethic and skill set.

What are the most satisfying aspects of your job?

❭ Day to day, I feel like my job is a small part of what's necessary to build a society that's more efficient, more environmentally conscious and respectful, and more humanly interactive. I love urban environments and I love clever design, and it's satisfying to work in an area that promotes the one and relies on the other.

Advocating for Transit and Transportation Improvements

OTIS ROLLEY III

President, Central Maryland Transportation Alliance

Former Planning Director, City of Baltimore, Maryland

How did you become a planner?

❭ I was studying international public policy with every intention of going to Africa after grad school. I was challenged by a professor not to "run away from the problems at home." So I shifted my focus from international public policy to domestic work, and planning was more attractive to me than domestic public policy work. I didn't want to just

write white papers that would be thoughtfully analyzed and often ignored. I wanted my work to be focused in crafting and helping to implement real plans for change in our urban centers. I saw urban planning as a way to do just that.

How did you choose a school for your planning degree?

❭ Once I decided that I wanted to do planning I researched which schools provided the strongest, most well-respected programs of study. MIT topped the list. Furthermore, the same professor who challenged me to use my skills and passion to focus on domestic issues told me that MIT was "too quantitative" for me and I wouldn't be able to handle it. So of course, more than ever, I wanted to go to MIT.

What are some of the experiences that have shaped your ideas of planning and how you approach the projects on which you work?

❯ I really believe my life experiences growing up have done the most to influence how I view planning and approach the projects I work on. My respect and appreciation for diversity comes from growing up in an extremely diverse city.

Jersey City, New Jersey, provided me with a view of America that was heterogeneous in every way. I saw that as strength, and I try to advance diversity in my work. There was a lot of inequity present in the inner city where I grew up that meant a lack of resources for human and physical development. Those realities help to push me toward seeking fairness and equity in my work.

What do you do as a transportation advocate?

❯ I am responsible for helping to shape and advocate for a rational and strategic transportation policy for the Central Maryland region. This includes Baltimore City and the five surrounding counties.

I lobby the state to make rational transportation decisions and to implement the projects that are impor-

▼ Planners bring many talents to advocacy organizations. Their ability to analyze different kinds of information and communicate clearly about alternatives makes planners a real asset to organizations whose mission is to educate and persuade. Advocacy planners can be found working in a number of different issue areas, including transportation, housing, and the environment. DAMIEN "CHIP" DIZARD, *ABSOLUTE PRESENCE* AND JUSTIN EYLER, *FLUID WEB SOLUTIONS*.

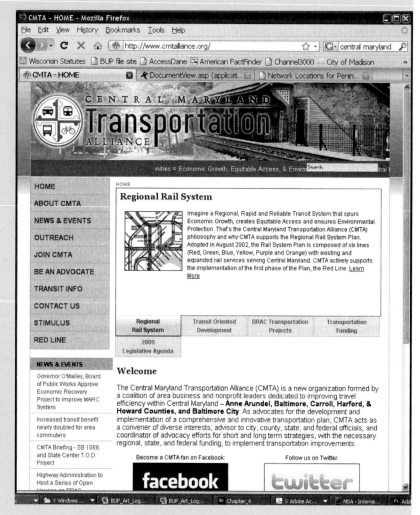

tant to our communities. I also lobby the federal government for funding to support these projects. I advise and harass the Maryland Transportation Administration to improve and expand service and get more ridership, and I work on education and advocacy, working with institutions of higher education and think tanks to improve our transportation plans and policies and fix our lack of adequate systems in our region. I also do a lot of fundraising.

What does that involve, day to day?

❯ I'm actively involved in a lot of reading, research, and review of transportation plans, projects, budgets, and legislation. I do outreach to various stakeholders and decision makers to educate them.

What does being a planner bring to your work?

❯ It's a huge benefit. I'm not looking at transit or transportation in isolation. I'm also looking at the issues of urban development and urban planning and trying to comprehensively connect all of them.

We have a saying that we use, R3 = E3. All of the projects that we support must be *regional*, *rapid*, and *reliable* transit and transportation initiatives that result in *economic* growth, *equitable* access, and *environmental* protection. So I need to draw upon all of my background and training in the planning field in this job.

Integrating Land Use and Transportation

TERRY MOORE, FAICP

Vice President and Senior Planner, ECONorthwest

Eugene, Oregon

What is your role at ECONorthwest?

❯ I manage research and public process for primarily public, but also private, clients. That position also means that a nontrivial part of my time is spent managing people.

Our mission statement is about applying microeconomic techniques to help our public and private sector clients make better decisions. Our projects are often about individual behavior and decision making in a context where government officials are making decisions about public policy. Since

microeconomics is about evaluating tradeoffs, and all public policy is about tradeoffs, we see every field open to us. Given my multidisciplinary background, I tend work on regional projects at the intersection of land use, economic development, public facilities (especially transportation), and environmental quality.

Do you consider yourself a regional planner?

❯ My degree is in regional and urban planning. I like working at the metropolitan level. Issues of transportation and land use are much bigger than the neighborhood level, and if approaching them from the state level often seem too diffuse to me.

Integrated planning means dealing with air sheds, watersheds, transportation-sheds, and economic areas of influence, and these geographies tend to line up at the metropolitan scale.

The Transportation/ Land Use Connection

Terry Moore and Paul Thorsnes, with Bruce Appleyard   New Edition

APA American Planning Association

Planning Advisory Service
Report Number 546/547

Terry Moore is author of *The Transportation/Land Use Connection,* published in 2007 by the American Planning Association. This publication, part of the Planners' Advisory Service series, provides planning professionals with a detailed but concise overview of the topic. © AMERICAN PLANNING ASSOCIATION.

The planning analysis focuses on what the metropolitan area or region could look like in the long run. Also, the market analysis that supports the planning tends to work best at the regional level, so there is a logic as to how it comes together.

Why did you decide to focus your work on land use and transportation? What is the connection?

❯ If you don't talk about land use, it's hard to do the transportation planning: We're building roads out here for . . . what exactly? If you put the transportation improvements first, you can plan land use around the access those improvements provide, but should transportation be the organizing principle for a long-run vision of place and livability?

There is a tension among people trained in transportation planning, transportation engineers, and land use planners. That was certainly more true 20 years ago when states were implementing transportation plans purely to combat congestion. Then the direction was to plan roads and bridges and get them built. Today there's more talk about planning, land use, and addressing issues of environmental quality by looking at all of these issues together.

None of the disciplines would disagree that if you are doing land use planning, you need to pay attention to transportation issues, and vice versa. That is not what the land use/transportation connection is all about. The idea is that we have to do more than talk about it—we have to adopt policies and change the way we invest public money.

Even though most transportation engineers would not say they can build our way out of congestion, the reality is that most states are working as if it were possible. It is hard institutionally and politically to get traction for a preferable policy: one of doing better pricing, and better project evaluation based on pricing and willingness to pay, that would probably change congestion, our perception of it, and the policies and investments we prescribe to cope with it. That's the next step, but we are not there yet.

Transportation agencies have the power because they have the money and they're centralized. MPOs are less well funded, and it's difficult for the local land use vision to drive the investments of powerful state agencies. Therefore, it can't be just a local vision. It has to become a regional vision, and to

get there, there has to be some common idea of what local governments are trying to achieve, what makes sense, how the locals are going to divide the pie and create infrastructure that serves the land use vision.

How has this work changed your views of planning?

❯ When I got out of school, I was a lot more confident that I could change the world. I thought, I'm smart, I have all of these analytical tools, if I do the analysis, I'll get the right answer, and it will be so clear to everybody that we'll all do it and get it done.

Now, when I look into the world that I work in, with metropolitan areas of millions of people and tens of millions of transportation trips, and at how to integrate land use, transportation, and environmental quality, in a world of constant change and political considerations, it seems impossible to me that a model is going to tell us how to proceed.

What planners can do is to bring together the best information they can and package it in a way that people can understand and make factual decisions based on it. We need to get more information when people say they need more information, and facilitate discussion that can lead to some type of decision. That decision may be temporary, but at least it can be adjusted as we move forward. The incrementalist in me says we're never going to get it just right.

It's not so much about the ultimate outcome but about moving in a direction that has some of the right answers in it. There are a lot of possible futures. The important thing is to get agreement as to the direction that we should be going in and move that way. It may be the best we can do.

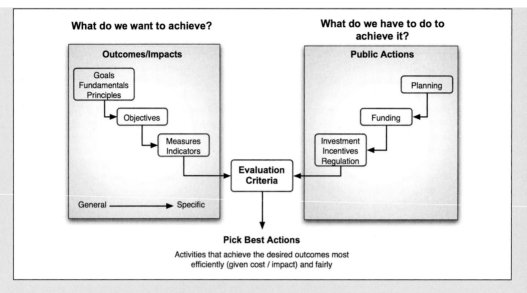

What do we want to achieve?

What do we have to do to achieve it?

Good planning analysis requires information, but it also requires an understanding of what a community or region is trying to achieve. Helping communities to be clear about their goals is a key service that planners provide. ECONORTHWEST.

PLANNING FOR SUSTAINABILITY

Sustainability planning has become the most prominent and important new emphasis in the planning profession. "Sustainable development" has many definitions, the most common being the one adopted by the Brundtland Commission in 1987

> *Development that meets the needs of the present without compromising the ability of future generations to meet their own needs.*

Over the past two centuries various scientists and economists have observed the exponential growth of human population and resource use and have concluded that such growth and consumption are not sustainable. Though dismissed by the majority for many decades, these views gained prominence in the late twentieth century because of well-documented and dramatic examples of environmental degradation attributable to human activity. In the first decade of the twenty-first century a majority of Americans have accepted as valid the scientific data on global warming and many have concluded that we must somehow change how we live in order to halt and reverse our collective impact on the planet.

Planners have come to recognize that resource use is greatly affected by community design, especially by how and how far we must travel each day to meet our daily needs for employment, goods and services, and recreation. The American Planning Association adopted a *Policy Guide on Planning for Sustainability* in April of 2000 (American Planning Association 2000). This document identifies four core ideas that should motivate and guide planners in their work:

1   We want to sustain communities as good places to live, and that offer economic and other opportunities to their inhabitants.

2   We want to sustain the values of our society—things like individual liberty and democracy.

3   We want to sustain the biodiversity of the natural environment, both for the contribution that it makes to the quality of human life and for its own inherent value.

4   We want to sustain the ability of natural systems to provide the life-supporting "services" that are rarely counted by economists, but that have recently been estimated to be worth nearly as much as total gross human economic product.

Since that policy was adopted, sustainability has been embraced by a broad spectrum of American society, most notably the business community.

Those four ideas have been boiled down to become the "triple bottom line" of sustainability, sometimes referring to the "Three E's" (Environment, Economy, and social Equity), and sometimes the "Three P's" (People, Planet, and Profit). The "triple bottom line" approach requires the evaluation of alternative solutions to a problem ("Should we expand the highways, build a light rail system, or do nothing?") according to the impact that each alternative will have on the local and global environment, on the local economy, and on quality of life for residents. Though widely used and generally understood among planners, the triple bottom line approach is not yet supported by common standards. Planners young and old will be challenged over the coming decades to help communities and organizations figure out how to translate the idea of sustainability into decisions and actions that change how we live.

Some existing specialization areas in planning are especially relevant to planning for sustainability. These include urban design, including New Urbanism and Transit-Oriented Development (TOD), bike and pedestrian planning, and hazard mitigation planning. Planning community systems of energy conservation and renewable energy implementation is beginning to emerge as a growing area of specialization.

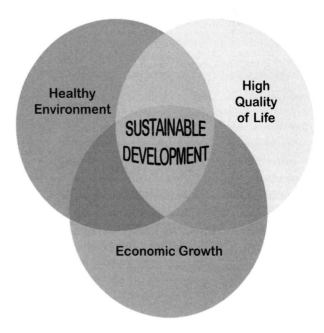

Sustainable Development is about more than just protecting the environment, or keeping the local economy going, or improving people's lives. It is about finding the intersection of all three of these considerations. Planners interested in sustainable development seek programs and community design solutions that promote environmental quality, economic prosperity, and social equity—all at the same time. JASON VALERIUS.

Urban designers seek to balance competing demands for space through smart design. Here, a busy four-lane street in Appleton, Wisconsin, could be an uncomfortable place for people traveling by foot. But by providing a wide sidewalk, and by establishing a buffer zone through the placement of street trees and benches, the designer has made this street hospitable to both cars and pedestrians. JASON VALERIUS.

New Urbanism

Today, as the planning profession gears up to meet the challenges of peak oil and climate change, and as experts warn that we cannot meet carbon reduction goals without changing the way we move about in cities, urban design is experiencing a rebound, like a species coming back from near extinction. The New Urbanism is a major element of this resurgence.

Density is essential if people are to be encouraged to leave their cars behind and use transit, bikes, and their own two feet to reach their destinations. But density brings its own challenges. Urban designers are trained to use space efficiently but elegantly. They design dense urban districts that feel good rather than feeling harsh and stressful. New Urbanism is a set of principles and design techniques that aim to achieve density that people will love to be in.

Applying the Principles of New Urbanism

STUART SIROTA, AICP

Principal, TND Planning Group

Baltimore, Maryland

How did you become interested in New Urbanism?

❭ During the first 10 years of my career, I became increasingly disillusioned with the planning profession. As I became more aware of the realities and consequences of sprawl and automobile-dependence, the more I came to the realization that current planning policies and practices were merely perpetuating the problem.

Around 1996, I began to become aware of and very interested in the emerging principles of transit-oriented development, livability, placemaking, smart growth, New Urbanism, and sustainability. This completely changed my attitude, and filled me with a renewed sense of hope that, as a planner, I could become part of the solution.

From that point forward, I dedicated myself to advancing these principles by infusing them into my work and by educating other colleagues about them.

I feel so passionate about New Urbanism that I launched my own practice.

What types of projects do you do?

❭ I work for the public and private sectors, primarily on downtown and revitalization projects where we try to create more walkable, vibrant destinations. I also work on projects to retrofit existing suburban areas into walkable and pedestrian-friendly areas to create a true center or heart of a community where one doesn't exist. I also provide master planning for developers who are interested in traditional neighborhood design (TND) or transit-oriented development. That's my bread and butter.

I also work for nonprofits, doing master planning for inner city neighborhoods or for community groups that want a better sense of place in their communities and to become more pedestrian friendly.

What else does the job involve?

❭ As the principal of a consulting practice, I am responsible for all aspects of running the business. This includes performing technical work, project management, client coordination, business development and marketing, administrative tasks, and report writing and production, to name a few.

How do you market your work?

❭ My consulting practice is built on a highly collaborative model, in which I am part of a network of consultants across North America that focuses exclusively on planning, designing, and implementing "walkable urbanism" and the transportation infrastructure that supports it. I typically form or am part of multidisciplinary teams that work on a wide array of projects, which are often done through a charrette process.

A lot of your work is done in charrettes.

❭ About three quarters of my work is charrette-based. It's a format that's almost always open to the public, as a public forum.

Stu Sirota and his firm, TND Planning Group, use "before and after" illustrations like this to show how a place can be transformed by smart urban design. The "before" photo shows an existing parking garage fronted by an underutilized public plaza, as well as a single-use institutional building with limited street orientation in the foreground. The infill concept retains the parking garage but creates a series of mixed use "liner" buildings and a more functional, intimate public plaza that masks the garage while activating the street. The concept also includes introduction of ground-level commercial and façade improvements to the institutional building. These give the building a stronger street orientation and contribute to a more pedestrian-friendly, mixed-use streetscape. The addition of balconies creates visual interest for pedestrians and an attractive amenity for upper-floor building tenants. TND PLANNING GROUP.

In the past year or so, I led or participated in about a dozen charrettes, each lasting upwards of a week. Some were located in my own region and some were in different parts of the country. All of this can be quite demanding, yet is also intensely rewarding. The periods leading up to and following charrettes are just as demanding with preparation, analysis, and production activities.

I'm cognizant that it's a different kind of effort and goes beyond the regular public process. At the other end of the process are the NIMBYs who are extremely hostile to what we're trying to do, people who fear density and traffic and are really fearful of trying something different. That's a real challenge, to work with those folks to educate them on the benefits of density.

What other challenges do you face?

❯ Despite my continued enthusiasm and passion, the last decade or so has been extremely challenging, and at times, frustrating. There has been much resistance among planning organizations and personnel to embracing planning practices and policies that result in sustainable, walkable urbanism.

Recently, however, there has been a growing interest within the planning profession to embrace just such a paradigm shift. A new sense of urgency within the profession, brought about by the mounting evidence of automobile emissions as a major contributor of global warming being caused by automobiles, rising energy prices, and housing affordability, are all acting to accelerate the shift away from the status quo.

Despite these encouraging signs within the profession, the uphill battles that are still encountered when trying to convince planning commissioners, neighbors, traffic engineers, fire marshals, and others outside the profession of the benefits of creating de-

ACP designed and implemented a three-part intensive charrette process, named Blueprint Plus for the City of Fort Wayne to help develop a vision to guide public policy and private investments in downtown, design the public places and the buildings that frame the vision, and identify site-specific catalytic projects. ACP VISIONING+PLANNING

velopment at walkable densities, mixing of uses, and pedestrian-friendly streets, continually reminds me that we still have a long way to go as a society.

Even though I'm not always able to sway everybody, it's great when you are able to engage someone who comes in not understanding the process and are able to turn them around into an ally. It's happened a lot on my projects.

I enjoy the process of winning people over to what we're doing, to get them to view things in a new way. Education is a big part of it. You have to have an incredible amount of patience, and empathy, too. It's a process that builds over a long period of time.

NIMBY—it strikes terror in the heart of every planner. NIMBY stands for Not In My Backyard. Communities need places to generate power, but people want neither power plants nor wind turbines in their own backyards. "Put them someplace else, anyplace else!" Communities need places to dispose of solid waste, whether they are burying the waste in landfills, incinerating it in a state-of-the-art Combined Heat and Power (CHP) plant, or recycling it. Neighbors, however, typically want none of it. Processing waste, no matter how sustainable the process is, generates heavy truck traffic and causes neighbors to worry about bad smells and fumes of all sorts. While energy production and waste management are commonly cited NIMBYs, even seemingly benign land uses can generate objections. Add to the NIMBY list any land use that generates traffic or that might conceivably lower property values.

Working through NIMBY concerns—both the founded and the unfounded—is a large part of every planner's work.

Fostering Transit-Oriented Development

GB ARRINGTON

Vice President and Principal Practice Leader, PB PlaceMaking

Portland, Oregon

How did you become a planner?

❯ I think we all went to planning school to change the world. My whole career has been about aligning political science with planning. Political science is the art of the possible, and planning is the art of what should be.

I came out of college with a liberal arts degree. I wanted to go to law school but decided not to become a lawyer, so decided to go to Europe and take photographs or to go to graduate school and

ended up doing both by going to planning school in Edinburgh. Europe has been doing planning for a very long time, and I wanted to bring that experience back to the United States.

You are known for your work in Portland integrating transportation and land use planning. How did it happen?

❯ I fell into the transportation side of it. I wrote my thesis on the politics of planning. On my first day out of planning school, I was able to start working in the Planning Bureau with the City of Portland.

When the funding for that position ran out, I became the first person hired at TriMet (the Tri-County Metropolitan Transportation District of Oregon) to work on the Banfield Busway Project. The state had recently withdrawn plans for a freeway through the City of Portland and was moving toward supporting bus and transit service by creating a pot of funding to develop and implement alternative transit projects.

I worked on the Banfield project, leading the analysis looking at the land use implications. The project spanned the decade and became a leading project to develop transit in Portland and to link transit to land use. Ultimately, it became the first light rail project in Portland and the start of what you would now call transit-oriented development in Portland.

Linking transportation infrastructure with land use as an integrated approach is now a very strong and powerful concept in planning, but when I started in the 1970s, that was not the case. It has been gratifying to see that happen, and it has provided great career opportunities for me.

Was there something particular about Portland that helped make it happen there?

❯ Working at an agency that wrote transportation plans, influenced land use plans, and developed transit, I assumed that it was the normal way to do things. In this region, planners have long shared common values, and there are interpersonal relationships among planners at different agencies that enables them to build integrated and interconnected strategies across agencies. That was a very important ingredient because no one agency had the tools on its own to be effective.

How have you integrated transportation and land use?

❯ What my career has been all about is using infrastructure as a means to an end. It starts by developing the transportation infrastructure to support land use. You put transit stations in different places than you would if you were planning for transportation

alone. You arrange parking in other ways. You fund local land use plans that support transit by providing funding to local governments through the transportation project. When we started, no one told us to do that. It was never a federal requirement, to complete a local land use plan and get it adopted as part of a regional land use framework.

To do that, we used the funding from the rail project. Later, as the debate started to heat up nationally about how to integrate transportation and land use, we were asked about how to do that as a federal policy, and we worked with FTA to develop federal rules in support of it.

What skills are needed to do this kind of work?

❯ Integrating transit and land use is institutionally messy, so you need good political skills to navigate through the institutional barriers. At the same time you need a fundamental understanding of what local governments expect from land use and the tools to help achieve that, what developers are looking for to make a project feasible, and how a transit agency thinks about the flow of modes and people to make transit work. Those are the ingredients; the skill is knowing how to mix them together to get something that is greater than the sum of the parts.

Why did you decide to enter the private sector?

❯ I left Tri-Met in 1999 after the second rail line opened, a year before the third rail line opened, and a couple of years before the fourth line opened. At the time, it seemed like I had made as big of an impact as I could in Portland, and I wanted to see if there was a bigger barn to play in.

I joined Parsons Brinckerhoff with a vision for creating a national practice for transit-oriented development, to see if I could do at the national level what we were doing in Portland, which was reshaping communities through transit.

My niche is linking transportation and land use in a multidisciplinary way. To do that, you need to be careful about listening to the community. Today we are working in 42 different communities, in seven or eight countries around the world, and I never went into any of those projects thinking I know what the answer is. The answer comes out of listening to what the community is saying, what their hopes, needs, and desires are. Then we give some examples and try to move in a direction that is feasible.

We don't have any transportation projects that don't have a land use nexus where transportation and land use touch each other. We look at the core of each community, then work at the regional scale.

Three-dimensional models, whether physical models made of cardboard and wood or digital models made of pixels on a screen, are essential tools for visualizing how an area will change in the future. PB PLACEMAKING.

We may approach each project with the same fundamental idea, where the values are the same, but the ideals will play themselves out differently. You can't translate Portland into Dubai.

Every place has a different starting point, with different degrees of civic infrastructure. We look at how the different levels of government get along with each other, their funding tools, and the organizational structure.

As a consultant, one quickly figures out that my job is like being a grandparent. When I was in local government, I felt like a parent. My job never stopped. You are always nurturing your child 24 hours a day, and there is no vacation from that.

As a consultant, no one can afford your services 24 hours a day. So we come in like a grandparent. It's the parent's job to raise the child and implement the plan. It's the grandparent's job to be a steward to help make that happen. It's a very different skill set.

What I do is give them the tools, reinforce good behavior, and try to stop them from making mistakes.

What are the keys to becoming a successful planner?

❯ It's important to find something you're passionate about, something that you wake up and feel excited about. It's also important to have a long-term vision and realize that you can make a difference.

I found that being a generalist backed by having a lot of knowledge of specific details is really, really helpful. In my job, I have to know a lot about a lot of things but try not to get lost in the details. And you can get lost quickly when you're working on complex projects with large teams and a lot of different people.

There can only be so many people in the room with a big vision or you'll end up with chaos. My job isn't always to have the big vision. Sometimes it's about synthesis, bringing ideas together and making the project more cohesive. I think my biggest strength is listening to everyone and synthesizing the ideas of the group.

I'm always looking for opportunities to grow my skills. I would be completely bored in my job if I had to do the same thing over and over again. I want to take what I do further down the road. So I am always looking to find people who can take things further, looking for great clients to make great things happen.

What's really interesting to me is that I'm working in China, in Dubai, in Australia, and on both coasts of the United States, and what I hear are common dreams to develop alternatives for the automobile. No matter where we work, people want to make their communities more walkable, with more mixed use, and great places to live. That's common across all demographics and political policies. So I think it's a great time to be working in this field. There is no finish line.

Creating Change and Livable Communities

DAN BURDEN

Principal and Senior Urban Designer

Glatting Jackson Kercher Anglin

High Springs, Florida

Walking is the key to success of a town, a neighborhood, a town center. The chemistry of a good city is based around human interaction and connections. When I came back to Florida, I decided to change my title to Bicycle/Pedestrian Coordinator to address the need for both modes.

I filled that role for 16 years in Florida. By 1996, I got so many requests to work outside of the state that I chose to retire early. I formed a nonprofit organization known as Walkable Communities, Inc., and I've been on the road ever since.

In 2004, I decided I no longer wanted to go it alone. I thought I needed more support, so I folded my practice into Glatting Jackson, a firm known for building sustainable and livable communities.

How do you envision your role as a planner?

❯ One of the important jobs of any planner is not just to address the current conditions of a city or community, but to think to the future. If we know that current practices and policies are not sustainable, then it's the duty of the planner to be a change agent.

Throughout my life, I've been a change agent, and the best planners get that. It's not our job just to tread water. It's to come up with innovative ways to make ourselves less dependent on the car, to create more balance in our lives, to address public needs and social integration, to promote inclusiveness, and to get rid of practices that isolate us.

What sprawl has done in this country is induce more depression and feelings of loneliness and isolation. It's the role of the planner to be a visionary and be willing to make change, because so much needs to be changed.

Do you experience a lot of resistance?

❯ Oh, a tremendous amount. People who are put on planning commissions often are good at supporting conventional development. They make sure they do things the old way.

In other towns, a planner may put his career on the line, doing what he knows he should do. Sometimes people just don't get it. Some people think that anything that increases traffic is bad.

Over time, I think attitudes will change. I haven't sensed how quickly it will happen just yet across the country, but you see with the latest changes in the economy (especially when gas prices were rising) that a lot of people are packing into transit, and agencies are ordering buses as fast as they can. You can't put enough fleet out there. With bicycling, we're seeing the same kind of phenomenon. We don't have enough bike racks out there. But we still get pushback.

What are the details of your planning approach?

❯ A high percentage of my work is to orchestrate one-day events, two-day events, to engage with the public and media and staff, and bring agencies together around the ideas of sustainability.

My message is that change is okay, change is important. I talk about the importance of change.

What's so fascinating about measuring the street? Residents are taking part in a walking tour of their neighborhood. Through this process, people communicate to transportation planners the places where walking feels uncomfortable, or downright dangerous. Listening to the people who live in a place is critical to understanding the issues and possible solutions.
COURTESY OF DAN BURDEN, GLADDING JACKSON.

Planning for Bicyclists and Pedestrians

JENNIFER TOOLE, AICP

Principal, Toole Design Group

Hyattsville, Maryland

Why are so many more people working on bicycle and pedestrian planning today?

❯ I think it's two major things. First, the federal government started funding this kind of work through the first ISTEA (the Intermodal Surface Transportation Efficiency Act of 1991), and every subsequent transportation bill has increased support for these kinds of programs.

Also, bicycle and pedestrian planning has become legitimized. Cities are under such pressure to optimize their transportation systems and make them more efficient. There is a lot of interest on the part of major cities to make their systems more bike friendly and pedestrian friendly. And they are making progress. We have some cities where 10 percent of trips are being made on a bicycle.

There's a lot of public support for it as well. Advocacy has been growing, from the local level, to the state level, to the national level. Strong advocates are pushing for this. And the bicycle industry has become a lot more active in funding bicycle advocacy programs.

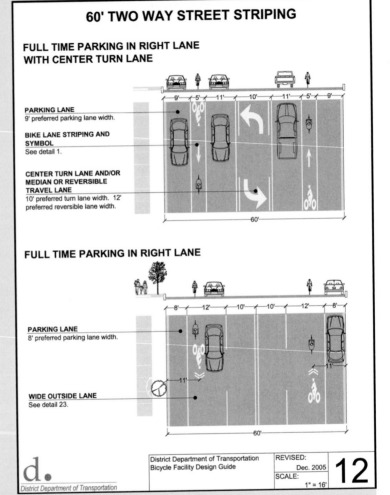

These street cross-sections show different options for placing a new bike lane relative to the auto lanes. Good street design is the key to drivers and bikers getting along together on heavily trafficked streets. TOOLE DESIGN GROUP.

Do you find more people are interested in this type of work?

❭ Eight or ten years ago, when we put out job ads to focus on bike and ped planning, we'd get back three resumes. Now I'm getting a lot of interest from students in college who tell me that they want to focus their career on bicycle and pedestrian issues. So I would say there is a lot more rec-ognition about this area within the transportation profession.

What's interesting about this type of career is that you can come at it from a lot of different angles. We have engineers, transportation planners, and landscape architects, and we try to draw on their skills in a diverse professional environment. That's one of the reasons I think it's an up-and-coming area.

EMERGING SPECIALIZATIONS IN THE ERA OF SUSTAINABILITY

The increasing interest in and urgency for sustainability planning has spawned several new specialization areas that are still emerging. These include hazard mitigation planning, planning for green communities, and sustainable energy planning.

Hazard mitigation planning is not a new specialization, but it is taking on renewed importance as communities begin to cope with the mounting impacts of global climate change. Scientists warn of many climatic changes that will produce flooding, increased risk of landslides, increased risk of wind damage, higher tide surges, and other effects. Planners work with local communities to anticipate these risks and plan land use and infrastructure in ways that will reduce the risk of injury and property damage, as well as protecting the natural environment.

Planning for green communities integrates the green building movement with the New Urbanism movement, combining the tools of each in order to create new kinds of communities to reduce negative impacts on the environment. New Urbanism argues that building communities at higher densities is essential for sustainability, but high density development can have devastating effects on the local environment unless systems are designed to manage the impacts of concentrating many people in a small area. Planning for green communities looks at all of the systems and processes in cities and finds ways of putting these systems together in ways that reduce both regional and local impacts from development.

Finally, the future of planning will require specialists in planning for sustainable energy for communities. Chapter 5 looks at the future of planning and sustainability in greater detail. Here, planners on the leading edge of these trends in the profession share their stories.

Planning for Hazards and Emergencies

DEEPA SRINIVASAN, AICP, CFM

President, Vision Planning and Consulting

Columbia, Maryland

Between 80 and 90 percent of my business is related to hazard mitigation. It's a big percentage because I am working in a niche market, and there aren't too many hazard mitigation planners in the country.

Hazard mitigation has come more into focus recently. There was some hazard mitigation planning going on in the 1980s and '90s, but in 2000, a federal law came into effect, the Disaster Management Act, that required that every community have a hazard mitigation plan in place to qualify for pre- and post-disaster-related funding. In simple terms: if a community does not have a plan in place, they are not eligible for pre- and post-disaster funds.

It's a valuable exercise, because the research shows that for every dollar you spend planning pre-disaster, you can save three dollars after a disaster happens.

What's the difference between hazard mitigation and emergency management planning?

❯ Mitigation plans are developed prior to a disaster in order to reduce the impacts of a disaster while emergency management plans tell you how to respond to an emergency situation.

What are some examples of the recommendations you develop?

❯ Mitigation actions span a variety of topics. We may recommend retrofitting or buying out repeatedly flooded properties, making buildings wind resistant, enhance code enforcement through zoning and subdivision regulations, improved public awareness and training, bridge modifications, and so on. We will put mitigation-related projects in the CIP (Capital Improvement Program).

What are your greatest challenges?

❯ Working with engineers and getting them to understand the importance of planning.

Trying to educate comprehensive planners on the importance of integrating hazards into their plans.

Trying to get the various agencies within local government (public works, emergency management, engineering, and planning) to communicate with one another.

Is it rewarding?

❯ I love what I do and find it very rewarding. The plans that I create help make communities safer and eventually save lives and properties during a hazard event. It's my way of giving back to the community.

I have never regretted doing what I do. I think it's very fulfilling because you feel like you're making an impact on society. Even if only a few mitigation projects are realized, you are saving millions of dollars in potential losses and have improved community awareness in the process.

City of Salisbury
Flood Mitigation Plan

Prepared for the Department of Public Works of the City of Salisbury, Maryland - January 2008

Prepared by:

The "100-year flood" is a misnomer that has become entrenched in the way people talk about flooding. It does *not* mean that the area within the 100-year floodplain will flood only once every 100 years. It means that *every year* that area faces a 1 percent chance of flooding. Planners use zoning to limit the kinds of structures that can be located in floodplains. But floodplains move, usually getting bigger and encompassing more existing buildings. Specialists like Deepa Srinivasan help communities to prepare for hazards like this and to make physical changes on the ground to avoid having floods and other hazards occur. CITY OF SALISBURY, MARYLAND, 2008.

Developing Green Communities

DANA BOURLAND, AICP

Vice President, Green Initiatives at Enterprise Community Partners

Columbia, Maryland

What does your job involve?

❯ I direct all aspects of our Green Communities program, including strategic planning and program development, grants, technical assistance and training support, research and evaluation, and public policy advocacy.

I work with the Enterprise Foundation's financial affiliates to deliver project financing to Green Communities developments. I also co-lead environmental strategy for Enterprise and serve as managing director of the Green Communities Offset Fund.

Why did you choose to work on issues related to green communities?

❯ I think there is tremendous opportunity by rethinking the way we develop to bring significant health, economic, and environmental benefits to low-income people who stand to benefit the most from green communities. Working on issues related to green communities brings together my interests in placemaking, social equity, environmental justice, and smart growth.

You worked as a state planner before moving into this role. How difficult was it for you to make the transition to working on planning issues related to sustainability?

❯ It was not a difficult transition for me because of my background in environmental resource economics and smart growth. I have learned a great deal, however, about how buildings work and how they could work much better.

When I started the transition towards sustainability, I began reading everything I could on the topic—*Green to Gold*, *Ecology of Commerce*, *Natural Capitalism*, *Cradle to Cradle*, *EcoCities*, and plenty of other documents, as well as scanning the web for green planning efforts in other countries.

I also enrolled in a one-week course at MIT on sustainable real estate and became a LEED accredited professional. I continue to read and try and learn what else is going on. It is an incredible time of innovation and difficult to keep up.

Sustainability and green building technologies have received a lot of attention from planners and the public in recent years. What do planners who may work with sustainability issues, generally, need to know and/or do to educate themselves about these issues and make sustainability real in their work?

❯ Planners who have been focused on smart growth issues will probably be at an advantage when it comes to sustainability issues, although I would hope all planners are tuned into the issues of future generations, our impact on the environment, and durability.

Fundamentally, though, I think we need to educate ourselves on matters related to performance, particularly around benchmarks for reducing greenhouse gas emissions and using nonrenewable resources. It will be incredibly important to learn about best possibilities on how to rethink the way we are planning. Focusing on performance, climate change, and sustainability open up great new opportunities to reimagine the way we do business.

What is your greatest challenge?

❯ Perhaps the greatest challenge in being a planner is that I'm not a developer.

Ensuring that plans are executed properly and that buildings and places perform the way they were designed is often a challenge but a critical part of the equation.

What are the most satisfying parts of your job?

❭ Providing green housing for persons that have formerly been homeless and also seeing the quick improvement in children's health by living in a green home are among the more satisfying parts of my job.

The least?

❭ Knowing that we have not found a solution to providing the opportunity for all Americans to have fit and affordable housing is the least satisfying part of my job. Knowing that seniors, children, and people of all ages are homeless and that others are living in substandard housing making decisions between food, housing, and medical care every day is equally unsatisfying.

Money that people spend on heating their homes cannot be saved for college—or for a beach vacation. Green buildings have lower energy bills, which is like taking money to the bank. Planners specializing in green building do cost/benefit analysis to demonstrate the feasibility of green building on a more widespread basis. ENTERPRISE COMMUNITY PARTNERS.

PART I   The Marriage of 'Affordable' and 'Green'

'RESIDENTS SAID THEY WERE WARMER AND MORE COMFORTABLE THAN THEY HAD EVER BEEN, AND AT THE SAME TIME OUR BILLS WENT DOWN. IT DOESN'T GET MUCH BETTER THAN THAT.'

— Lucille McEwen,
Harlem Congregations for Community Improvement

The U.S. Green Building Council, a national nonprofit group, created a system of sustainability ratings for buildings, and now for neighborhoods, known as LEED. LEED stands for Leadership in Energy and Environmental Design. Green buildings, buildings that reduce their energy and environmental impacts, may apply for LEED certification. Like voluntary certifications of "organically grown" and "fair trade," LEED certification tells consumers that a building or development project has achieved certain minimal standards of energy reduction and environmental performance.

In addition to certifications for development projects, individuals may receive LEED accreditation by passing an exam that verifies that the person knows the correct methods for assigning points in the LEED rating system.

For more information on the LEED program and rating system, see www.usgbc.org.

Planning for Sustainable Energy

INGRID KELLEY, LEED-AP

Project Manager, Energy Center of Wisconsin

Madison, Wisconsin

❯ I went back to planning school to earn my master's degree relatively late in my career. I was hoping to integrate my experience as an HVAC designer and an energy program manager for the State of New Mexico with my passionate and growing interest in sustainable community design, by acquiring the skills of an urban planner. I had learned a lot about energy efficiency and renewable energy and had done hands-on workshops in straw bale construction and other alternative building methods. I had attended Permaculture basic and advanced courses, and read everything I could find about sustainable agriculture and community design. I figured combining my energy and sustainability experience with the excellent community-based planning program at the University of New Mexico would make me a desirable candidate for what was obviously the next big career opportunity for planners.

That was 2001 and I was about five years too early. While there were progressive planning firms designing walkable neighborhoods and mixed-use developments, the planning profession in general was not yet concerned about carbon footprints or particularly aware of the relationship between fossil fuels and global warming. I found a job back in the energy sector managing programs for the state of Wisconsin through a private nonprofit, hoping eventually to find a way to work with communities on sustainable energy planning.

This is where I discovered I had one foot in each of two worlds that had never much thought about the other. My energy colleagues were immersed in research, consultation, and training about energy efficiency in individual homes and buildings or residential-scale renewable energy systems. They hadn't given any thought to looking at how a whole community could plan to make itself more energy efficient or energy self-reliant, and, in the process, exceed the combined results of individual efforts. They had no experience with how the idea of sustainable energy planning for communities could be woven into other municipal priorities such as economic development or environmental quality.

Luckily (and most likely due to Al Gore), the last couple of years have seen the concept of sustainability redefined around meeting the challenges of climate change, with our energy use in the foreground. I still work for the Energy Center of Wisconsin, and we are very busy responding to the rapidly growing demand for knowledge about community energy planning. I am pleased that the two separate professional worlds of energy and planning are beginning to learn about each other. My own interests have moved away from sustainable community design toward helping planners and energy professionals understand each other's priorities and expertise. I help planners understand that energy issues are only partly about engineering and a lot about communities making decisions, and I talk to energy consultants and engineers about how meeting those carefully calculated energy reduction goals means empowering the whole community.

As we move forward, I see planners being asked to provide more and more leadership on energy and sustainability in their communities, and to serve as coordinators and information conduits as we

The times they are a-changing. Planners today face a steep learning curve to gain a strong grounding in the problems and possibilities of sustainable energy. Smart communities are getting ahead of the curve. WARWICK GREED.

sort out the massive and complex challenges of reducing our use of fossil fuels and adapting to the effects of climate change. Planning schools need to promote energy literacy as part of course requirements, and planners already in practice would do well to participate in workshops and read about energy technologies on their own. It's not necessary to be an engineer—indeed, much of what needs to be done to reach energy sustainability has little to do with engineering.

In addition to writing my recent book, I am now developing curricula on energy technologies and

issues for planning and community design professionals, both for continuing education credit and for student course requirements. I foresee demand for a variety of brand new professions such as community energy program manager or sustainable energy planner—both new directions for planning students. This is exciting work although it's still a challenge to convince both energy professionals and planners that in order to reach our ambitious carbon reduction goals we will need a strong combination of technological savvy and a knack for old-fashioned community engagement.

Ingrid Kelley recently published a primer on energy entitled *Energy in America: A Tour of Our Fossil Fuel Culture and Beyond.* In it, she shows explicitly how planners can and should incorporate thinking about energy and carbon emissions in their comprehensive plans. Land use, transportation, community facilities, waste management, utilities, housing, and economic development elements of the comprehensive planning process all link back to energy. This roadmap shows where planners need to look for opportunities to do integrated resource management.

Teaching Others to Become Planners

Planning schools cannot train professional planners without the participation of practicing planners in the education of students and without the participation of full-time faculty in the practice of planning. Because planning schools focus on the preparation of students to become professionals, bringing real-world experience into the classroom is essential.

Planning schools accomplish this in two ways. First, full-time planning faculty are encouraged to participate in planning activities at the local, state, national, and international levels. Their participation may be in the form of paid consulting on grants or contracts.

Often, planning faculty engage in practice through pro bono activities (service free of charge), providing advice and services to communities that are unable to afford planning services on their own. These activities keep planning faculty engaged in real-world problems and the issues that practicing planners face every day.

But full-time faculty, no matter how engaged they are in applied research and community service, are insulated from the politics and day-to-day management issues of planning practice. Because planning students need to be prepared for those aspects of planning, schools ask experienced and talented planners to do guest lectures and to teach courses so that planning students benefit from their perspectives.

Below, three planning faculty describe how they became full-time teachers of planning and the special challenges and rewards that planning faculty experience. Their pathways represent three distinct routes, each fairly representative of a segment of the planning academy.

Teaching the next generation of planners. UNIVERSITY OF WISCONSIN–MILWAUKEE, SCHOOL OF ARCHITECTURE AND URBAN PLANNING, MEDIA CENTER, 2009.

Professor Bartholomew, seeking a career of activism, stumbled into a career teaching planning—and is new to it.

Professor Bradbury started out in her career as a practicing planner and drifted into an academic career as she pursued increased understanding of the problems and solutions familiar to practicing planners.

Professor Clark was motivated by an intense curiosity and intellectualism, first channeled in the direction of an education in physics but then found himself drawn by personal history and historical events to seek a career that might blend his interest in being engaged in social improvement with an intense life of the mind.

Becoming a Planning Professor

KEITH BARTHOLOMEW

Assistant Professor of City & Metropolitan Planning

College of Architecture and Urban Planning, University of Utah

Salt Lake City, Utah

Why did you decide to become a planner?

❯ I became a planner by accident. I went to graduate school (law school, actually) to become an environmental lawyer. My aim was to work on public lands issues such as roadless area protection, endangered species habitat, and so on.

When I finished school and a judicial clerkship, a job opened up at 1000 Friends of Oregon, arguably the nation's preeminent planning advocacy organization. I jumped at the chance, but I really had no clue what planning was or what the issues were. Somewhere during the first or second month on the job, I realized that I had found,

maybe stumbled across, the perfect profession for me. I became a planner on the job.

My training is in law, but I'm a planner by experience.

Today you are an academic. How did you make the change?

❯ I am an assistant professor in the Department of City & Metropolitan Planning at the University of Utah. I teach five courses per academic year and I am expected to do research and publish scholarly writings.

I moved here when my ex-wife got a medical residency in Utah. Our son was six at the time. So I quit my job and moved to Salt Lake City. I got a job as an administrator for the law school and began teaching in the urban planning program. Now I have a full-time position. I'm on the tenure track, but I'm not yet tenured.

I am also expected to provide service to the community and the profession. In my case, most of my service is the result of my position on the Utah Transit Authority's board of trustees.

Was it a difficult transition?

❭ I can't imagine it's ever easy, going from a nonprofit organization to being an academic. The teaching part is easy. When you're in an advocacy organization, teaching is a part of the trade. It wasn't a problem. I have some background in research but no academic training. It's a hard transition. I don't think I've made it over the hump yet.

When I was in law school, I swore to myself that I would never do it. In law school, I saw the political backbiting that is not uncommon in an academic environment, and I swore off that life. So it's the height of irony that I am here.

Planning is often about deciding when, where, and how to grow communities. Keith Bartholomew explains the significance of wine in one such planning process in Portland, Oregon: "The LUTRAQ project was all about defeating a proposed new suburban beltway on Portland's west side called the Western Bypass. Most of the Bypass would have been located outside of the region's urban growth boundary, on some of the most productive farmland in America. When we first got started in fighting the Bypass, way before we began the LUTRAQ research, there were a number of local families that became active in opposing the freeway. One of these families was the Ponzi family. The Ponzis have been growing wine grapes in western Oregon for decades, and they produce some of the region's best wines, in my humble opinion. Well, the Bypass corridor included a significant amount of the family's estate vineyard, and what the freeway wouldn't have destroyed, the air pollution from the cars on the freeway would have. A picture of their estate vineyard is right there on the label. It's now been more than ten years since the Bypass was defeated and the Ponzis are still growing grapes and making excellent wines. Every year, on the anniversary of the Bypass' defeat (and sometimes other occasions, too!), I enjoy a bottle of Ponzi wine, look at the label, and remind myself why it is that I'm a planner." PONZI VINEYARDS.

Did your training in law and experience as a planner prepare you for this job?

❯ In part. I think people coming into academic careers are better equipped if they have the background, experience, and training in a graduate program. Because that's what a Ph.D. program trains you to do.

What are the most and least satisfying parts of your job?

❯ The most satisfying parts relate to teaching—delivering a good lecture, advising students on class projects, etc. The least satisfying is always feeling behind (and panicked).

Prior to joining the faculty at the University of Utah, Professor Bartholomew worked for 1000 Friends of Oregon on the LUTRAQ project. LUTRAQ, short for "Making the Land Use, Transportation, Air Quality Connection," tried to find alternatives to building a new freeway that would meet Portland's transportation needs without spurring additional suburban sprawl and without generating more air pollution from increased traffic. Professor Bartholomew views his experiences on that project, especially the combination of searching for politically feasible solutions to problems and then selling that solution, at the heart of planners' work and what he works to teach his students.

For most full-time university teaching positions, the doctoral degree, usually a Ph.D., is the required credential. To complete a Ph.D., students need to complete substantial coursework beyond the master's degree and then design and complete a dissertation, which is a major piece of independent scholarship of the sort that full-time faculty are expected to complete in order to receive tenure and promotion.

For some tenure-track planning faculty positions, an educational background other than a Ph.D. may be desirable. Every planning program needs to teach planning law, and at least one planning faculty position may be reserved for someone who has earned a J.D. in law. Planning schools with a strong emphasis on design and physical planning may also reserve some positions for someone with a master's degree in one of the design professions—architecture, urban design, or landscape architecture. In these fields, the master's degree is referred to as a "terminal master's," meaning that the master's degree is considered the university teaching credential.

Most planning school faculties are composed of two types of faculty: full-time, tenure-track faculty and adjunct faculty, who are usually part-time employees.

When a planning school hires a practicing planner to teach a course, the planner becomes an adjunct professor. Typically, the planner is hired just one semester at a time and has no responsibilities except to teach the course and teach it well.

Most of the faculty in planning school are full-time, tenured or tenure-track faculty. These faculty teach multiple courses each year and have other job duties, principally doing research as well as participating in the management of the academic department and university and doing public service.

A new assistant professor is on the tenure track, that is, on the way to tenure, but not yet tenured. Associate and full professors have already been awarded tenure and are in charge of deciding whether assistant professors will be granted this benefit before the end of their seven-year probationary period. Once tenured, a faculty member generally cannot be dismissed except in cases of serious misconduct or an extreme financial emergency at the university. Given this, universities want to assure that the people they tenure are the sorts of people who will continue to work hard and contribute to the mission of the university even after they receive tenure.

Throughout the university, the main way that assistant professors are expected to demonstrate their long-term commitment to hard work is through conducting research and publishing the results in academic journals—hence the saying "Publish or perish." Increasingly, faculty are also expected to obtain outside research funds to support the time they spend on research. Consequently, the life of an assistant professor is intense—writing grant proposals, designing and completing research projects, all while teaching courses, often for the first time.

The research that planning faculty do today become the new tools of planning practice tomorrow. Planning faculty explore new ways of collecting data, new ways of analyzing and presenting information, and new tools for influencing the millions of individual choices that shape cities. Planning research, for example, studies the effectiveness of government action in changing the behavior of developers or consumers. For example, do subsidies to developers really increase the ability of a community to attract new investment? Do subsidies to transit riders, through subsidized fares, significantly increase transit ridership?

While some planning research focuses on cities and the people in cities, other planning research focuses on planning and the practice of planning. Planning research attempts to identify the best practices in planning. Planning research led the way during the 1960s to the strong emphasis today on participation in planning.

Moving from Planner to Professor

SUSAN L. BRADBURY, Ph.D.

Associate Professor

Iowa State University

Did you work as a professional planner before becoming a planning educator? If so, can you describe your practice briefly?

❯ Yes, I worked as a professional planner between my master's work and before starting my doctoral program. I worked for a relatively small town with a population of approximately 28,000 people. It was located near my hometown (basically it was a neighboring town), which was great because I was very familiar with the local issues that the community was facing.

I really enjoyed my work as a planner. My master's education was more academic in focus than practical, so I really enjoyed learning the practical side of things, including handling the front counter, making presentations at city council or at planning commission meetings, learning how to write a planning report and how to review site plans, for example. I learned a great deal about basic office management and about the actual process of planning. I was extremely fortunate in where I worked in that it was a relatively small office with a small staff who were very generous with their time and who mentored me.

There was a planning director, a senior planner, and I served as the assistant planner. We talked planning a lot during the week; I was able to ask lots of questions, and they would answer them. They were also very generous with the projects that came in and how they were distributed among the staff. As new

projects came into the office, I was asked if I had done that type of project before, and if not, then I had first choice at the project. As a result, I was able to work on a variety of different projects from site plan review, site inspections, subdivision reviews, playground design, tree planting, and so on.

Although a small office and relatively small town, there was a considerable amount of activity and never a dull moment in the office. I was constantly learning new things about the practice of planning. When I left to pursue my doctoral studies I was rather sad to leave, mainly because my work situation provided me with such a rich learning environment among colleagues who I not only enjoyed interacting with but who I highly respected as professionals.

What made you decide to change course and become a planning educator?

❯ I must confess that I was extremely naïve and really didn't consciously make the decision to become a planning educator. I was dedicated to becoming a professional planner and upon the completion of my master's degree I felt that many of the questions I had about the field of planning and my understanding of cities and city development remained unanswered. The only way I knew to be able to learn more and seek the answers I wanted was to continue my education. I really thought that I would go and study for another year and then I would have my answers or at least increase my knowledge, and then I would return home and enter the planning field.

Instead, of course, the more I learned the more I realized I didn't know, and thus my thirst for knowledge grew instead of diminished, and before I knew it I had completed my course work towards my Ph.D. At that point I figured I might as well keep going and finish the degree given all my efforts. Even as I approached the completion of my doctorate, I still thought that I would work as a practicing planner. It wasn't until I was given the opportunity to teach a class toward the end of my doctoral program that I started to think about becoming a professor.

Where did you go to school? What was doctoral study like? What did you enjoy about it? What did you not enjoy about it?

❯ I attended the University of Florida for my doctorate degree and selected that program simply because there was a professor there whose research I was very familiar with and interested in, and I simply wanted to learn more about this particular aspect of economic development. As a result, my doctoral program resembled an apprenticeship.

I enjoyed my doctoral studies mainly because I had previously attended somewhat smaller schools, and the University of Florida offered a much wider range of classes and programs from which I could select. I was very fortunate in that I had received an excellent foundation during my bachelor's and master's programs and thus there were a lot of classes within the doctoral program I didn't have to take. As a result, I was able to replace some classes within the department with those from outside the department, and I loaded up on methods classes and statistics.

This turned out to be particularly helpful to me since the university at that time required doctoral students to either satisfy a foreign language requirement or else be proficient in computers and statistics in order to satisfy that requirement. The ability to be able to focus on computers and statistics in place of a foreign language enabled me to satisfy

that degree requirement. That was the only aspect of my doctoral studies that I found particularly "challenging." The other aspect about my doctoral studies that I enjoyed was, of course, being able to pursue my own research. I entered my Ph.D. program with a clear idea of where my interests lay, so I think that was very beneficial. Having a clear research focus helped me to matriculate through my course work quickly and complete my doctoral program in three years.

What is most rewarding about being a planning educator?

❯ This is my 20th year as a planning educator and I have started to reflect back on my experiences. I would have to say without a doubt what I enjoy the most and find the most rewarding is working with students. Watching students grow and develop into competent professional planners is really a treat. Some students really surprise you—they blossom when you least expect it. One of my greatest pleasures is to receive a phone call or an email from a former student. It is usually a brief message but they bring me up to date on their professional careers and often they will tell me how they utilize some of the knowledge or skills that they learned in my classes. I find this very satisfying.

What skills or temperament are important for being a successful planning educator?

❯ The answer to this question partly depends upon one's definition of success. One of the tendencies that I have noticed during my career is that those educators who are considered the most successful by the academy are often those who have excelled at research. Despite the increasing focus on teaching within universities, being a good teacher is not particularly rewarded or recognized within the academy. Writing articles or books, and getting grants, are what counts.

Related to this is another aspect typically not acknowledged, which concerns a person's collegiality. As educators our training and our work experience takes place within an independent and yet highly competitive environment. However, for departments and programs to be successful they require educators to work as a team. One of the dichotomies within the academy is that individualism and independent thinking is rewarded, while being a team player within your department is not. To build strong programs and departments you need individuals who work well with others, so attitude and collegiality do matter. Lastly, to succeed in this line of work you need to have good organizational skills. You cannot be successful in teaching or research if you are not organized.

How do you balance teaching, research, and staying in touch with practice in your work?

❯ I think that this is one of the greatest challenges that any (planning) educator faces, but I do believe that this is particularly more difficult for women than it is for men. I also think this is one of the great benefits associated with being a planning educator, but it can also be a curse.

What I mean by this is that as a planning educator our professional lives are very rich, our work is very diverse, and thus, at least for me as someone who gets bored easily, I like the multifaceted nature of our work. On the other hand, getting pulled in many directions can be difficult and stressful. For women, I think this is even more challenging because we are typically held to a different standard within the academy. Women are more often expected to be an excellent teacher, a competent and productive researcher, and professionally engaged all at the same time and continuously over long periods of time during their career.

Women, in other words, need to demonstrate that they have the capability and the stamina to do the job. Men, on the other hand, don't seem to have to so much prove that they can do the job as they have to demonstrate the potential to do the job. Thus, they seem to be able to be successful in one area and merely competent in the others in order to be successful. As a result, finding the "balance" between teaching, research, and practice is much easier for men than women. However, I do think the differences in expectations have narrowed as more women have entered and succeeded within the academy.

I must confess that I still struggle with finding a balance but have over time learned how to better achieve balance. The best way to achieve balance is by streamlining one's teaching with one's research and outreach or service activities. In other words, align your teaching interests with your research interests and professional activities so that you teach what you do. This will help you to be more efficient, enabling you to achieve a better "balance" among the various activities.

While all university departments recognize public service as an element of their mission, departments of urban and regional planning place much greater emphasis on this aspect of the university mission than their colleagues in other academic departments (Frank, 2008). Planning schools actively encourage their faculty members to do engaged research and to participate in other public service activities related to planning. Few planning faculty fit the "ivory tower" stereotype. Planning faculty regularly interact with professionals, working alongside them in finding solutions to problems.

In some cases, this may take the form of funded research addressing new ways of planning for transportation, environmental improvement, or economic development. In other cases, it may involve the faculty member in directing a studio course, teaching students how to carry out a planning process by assisting a local (or distant) planning agency or community organization. Studios may take place in the university's "own back yard," or students may travel to other countries to work on a planning problem facing a community in Sri Lanka, Germany, or Costa Rica.

Faculty members also participate in practice through their involvement in organizations related to planning. Planning faculty sit on the boards of planning-related organizations. The most obvious of these is when a faculty member serves on a local planning commission. But many other opportunities exist. Planning faculty often work with organizations promoting Smart Growth, transportation options, or policies promoting jobs for people in distressed areas in the community. Planning faculty also serve as advisors to local, state, and federal government agencies, as well as to the United Nations, World Bank, and other international development agencies. Planning faculty are often called upon to serve on blue ribbon commissions and other advisory panels, investigating the causes of problems and searching for public policy solutions to them.

Being Called to a University Career—With a Practical Slant

THOMAS CLARK, Ph.D.

Professor and Chairperson

Department of Planning and Design

College of Architecture and Planning

Denver, Colorado

How did you come to your career as a university faculty member teaching planning?

❯ I was born in 1944, under the reign of FDR. Pearl Harbor got our attention in 1941 much as did 9/11 years later. Hiroshima and Nagasaki had been bombed just months before I came into the world. World War II was still underway. Prospects for my parents, living in a small apartment in Cleveland, were doubtful. War had affected all.

There was at least a tacit acceptance that government was probably doing its job. If the war would only end, then recovery would require similar effort. The end of war, of course, also marked the onset of massive suburbanization driven by accelerating household and capital formation rates. I myself couldn't have appreciated the meaning of this historical context in my early years, but it profoundly affected all that was to follow.

In my teens, dinner-table conversation tended to the political. In my high school years, I was chosen class president three times over, a progression cut short in my senior year when my best friend voted against me, and for good reason. Term limits then have their place!

Presidencies then and now are time's essential metric. Truman, then Eisenhower followed FDR. The election of 1960 brought Kennedy to the White House, an apparent break with the past. His death, and ascent of Johnson, carried forward a more aggressive national policy agenda even as Vietnam sapped resolve. Nixon and all the rest were to follow.

At Brown I studied math and physics at the start. While in a physics lab in my freshman year we got the news: Kennedy had been assassinated. Sometime in the months that followed my direction began to shift away from the arcane complexities of the inanimate to a life of public engagement. Those past conversations over dinner, leadership roles in high school, and the fervor over the youthful exuberance of Kennedy and then the regret of his passing drew me away from physics and towards political science.

On graduation, choices had to be made. I was on my own and the money had run out. Interviews with New York City banks and Hartford insurance companies failed to inspire at the time. Law school and the Peace Corps seemed like possibilities so I dabbled in both, but when my family relocated from Connecticut to Iowa, I embarked on the study of planning at the University of Iowa, in a new program that, even then, could attract some very committed professors and some wonderful students who shared my enthusiasms. So began my earnest pursuit of "planning."

Where did you go to school? What was doctoral study like? What did you enjoy about it? What did you not enjoy about it?

❯ Undergraduate study at Brown University gave way to graduate work in planning at the University of Iowa, and while in that program I began to find in geography—at least in Iowa geography which was a global pioneer in quantitative and theoretic aspects of spatial matters—a second home. The invitation there to pursue the doctorate, coupled with the offer of a full ride on a National Defense Education Act Fellowship, was all it took to draw me upon graduation into further study in that ancillary discipline.

The study of planning was captivating, and purposeful. In geography I found a somewhat firmer paradigm. I was determined there to develop mathematical models of metropolitan form that might allow us to "test out" the future before it would actually occur, and to weigh the efficacy of possible urban public interventions meant to yield more favorable spatial outcomes.

The pursuit was full of intrigue and the possible prize quite compelling. Researching my dissertation was the single most important experience in my intellectual life. Those insights, well outside the domains of conventional wisdom, ground my thinking even today, almost 40 years later. Doctoral study was for me a joyful opportunity to explore widely, to joust passionately.

Despite these fine times, by 1972 I was ready to leave Iowa. The dissertation would take three more years. Seeking positions worldwide, on three continents and in five nations, I landed at McGill, in geography. A one-year visiting appointment led to three years, again in geography, at Middlebury College in Vermont, followed by a stint at Rutgers, New Brunswick, this time in planning with secondary involvements in geography. I had returned to my central passion, which was and is planning. Geography is a fine discipline, but in planning one finds a marriage of thought and action that geography lacks. Planners are the masters of purposeful action and of the modes of intervention by which the course of change can be redirected in cities and regions. We understand moreover that the client for our services is expansive. Sustainability requires no less.

A PASSION FOR RESEARCH BY PROFESSOR THOMAS CLARK

I learned then that research is like spelunking. It is an opportunity to see things, comprehend things, never before witnessed, much as would those entering underground chambers for the first time, filled with mystery. I loath the notion that the doctorate is nothing more than the dissertation. The doctoral student's aspirations should be renaissance in reach. How else to contextualize knowledge. Today, too many fail to live or acknowledge this necessity, which is all the more critical if we are to inspire the following generations of scholars.

Challenges and Rewards

In researching this book and talking to planners, we asked them to talk about their greatest challenges and the least and most satisfying aspects of their work. Here is what they told us.

GREATEST CHALLENGES

Keeping the Big Picture in the Forefront

❯ The biggest challenges are keeping focus on the "big picture" while addressing specific project issues and unforeseen events, maintaining public understanding of the planning process and rationale for our recommendations, and trying to work expeditiously within a bureaucracy.

William Anderson, FAICP, City of San Diego

❯ If I had to put a label such as this on it, my greatest challenge would be getting local people to look at the big picture and the long term. For most communities it's all about short-term, tax base and growth/expansion.

James Segedy, FAICP, AIA, Pennsylvania Environmental Council

❯ To overcome "we've always done it that way."

Lisa Hollingsworth-Segedy, American Rivers

Working in Multidisciplinary Teams

❯   My consulting experience has afforded me the opportunity to work on a wide range of project types, with a wide range of scientific experts, engineers, specialists, and planners. My project teams are all multidisciplined, and every project teaches me new lessons on the strengths and weaknesses a team brings to a project. Scientists,

▼ Putting together a planning charrette, like this one, requires a whole palette of experts: public participation specialists, urban designers, civil engineers, and many others. Planners need to be able to work with these diverse disciplines, and the best planners serve as a bridge between different experts. CHESTER COUNTY PLANNING COMMISSION.

Challenges and Rewards (Continued)

Night meetings are very common in planning. A city planner in the public sector can expect at least two night meetings a month—one with the planning commission and one with a committee of the city council. Add to that public meetings as part of a participatory planning process as well as meetings with neighborhood organizations to offer them advice and to hear their concerns. And for planning consultants, the schedule can be even worse, especially with travel added on to an already hectic meeting schedule. COURTESY OF DAN BURDEN, GLADDING JACKSON.

engineers, and planners do not process information in the same manner. The greatest challenge is often finding the common denominator, and getting a project team working as a team when you have so many professional approaches that are part of the mix.

Alyse Getty, Parsons Infrastructure and Technology

Implementation

❯ Planners generally have no ability to implement a plan. Implementation requires budget commitments that often have to be granted by various governing bodies and funders. Moreover, implementation requires a commitment to action. A good plan is one that does not remain on the shelf. In general, I think the greatest challenge for any planner is to create a plan that will actually be used.

Specifically, my challenge has been to limit sprawl by protecting resource lands, on the one hand, while developing vital communities on the other.

Ronald Bailey, AICP, Chester County, Pennsylvania Planning Commission

Balancing Life and Work

❭ It has been exceptionally difficult not to get consumed by the amount of work there is to be done. There is always one more study, one more meeting, one more perspective on various issues. It's tough to balance work with the personal time you need not to burn out because so much needs to be done to improve the condition of our cities.

Otis Rolley III, Central Maryland Transportation Alliance

❭ I really do enjoy coming to work and being able to be an adult who's not a mom and do what I'm used to doing, and working on something I have control over.

Evening meetings are tough now. As a single parent, I've learned to depend on friends. Any friends who have offered to help me, I take them up on that.

My daughter also comes to meetings with me sometimes. With our Bicycle Advisory Committee, that has worked out, as the people on the committee are really, really flexible and meet at the end of the day, instead of after dinner.

So far, it's daunting, but it's okay. And I think it depends on the work environment and your boss. If you have a good boss who's flexible and you're a good employee that they want to keep, they will enable you to work through it.

Kelley Segars, AICP, Knoxville Regional Transportation Planning Organization

❭ Working at home—with the dual full-time responsibilities of caring for a child and home, and completing my professional responsibilities—is quite a challenge.

Every day is a new balancing act between meeting deadlines, caring for my son, and completing daily household tasks. There are always conflicts and the right choice is never clear-cut.

A successful work-at-home parent requires a good deal of judgment and ability to understand priorities. It also requires a strong recognition of what your personal, professional, and parenting goals are and what must happen for you to achieve each of those goals.

Kathie Ebaugh, AICP, Bell David Planning Group

LEAST SATISFYING PARTS OF THE WORK

Waiting to Make a Difference

❭ The least satisfying part of my job is how hard it is to see progress. There are no quarterly reports with profit and loss; practically the best one can hope for is a vague sense of "more" or "less" progress, "more" or "less" commitment, "more" or "less" drama.

One of the gut checks of being a planner is whether you can live with the constant difference between what you want and what actually is. If you're a planner, things are never the way you want them to be. You have to get comfortable with that fact, as well as the fact that things happen over time.

Nat Bottigheimer, Washington Metropolitan Area Transit Authority

Wrong Decisions Made for the Wrong Reasons

❭ The big one is a common complaint among planners—that we have this vision of how things should work and then political reality knocks it down, and we end up with a project that isn't what it could have been.

Sometimes it is hard to keep trying to do your best when you keep seeing the failures. It's also hard to convey to the public that we really are working on accomplishing things, but that it takes time (and money and political will).

Challenges and Rewards (Continued)

The least satisfying is what I talked about as one of the greatest challenges—that planners often get ignored, like when one developer complains or a neighbor argues against a greenway next to his property.

Kelley Segars, AICP, Knoxville Regional Transportation Planning Organization

❭ The least satisfying are the projects that get killed off by politicians pandering to NIMBYs and other squeaky wheels, being unable to persuade communities to prioritize because politically they are obliged to treat all possibilities as equally promising and all concerns as equally valid, and projects where no one cares about the outcome and the purpose is simply to fulfill a statutory requirement.

Elaine Van S. Carmichael, AICP, Economic Stewardship, Inc.

❭ Least satisfying is working on a "bad" project—defined as one with poor local support in the planning department, weak political leaders with no vision, and too little funding.

Lee Einsweiler, AICP, Code Studio

❭ The least satisfying part is when people make decisions solely on what will give them the greatest financial gain and have no regard for the precious water resources that we all must protect and share in order to survive.

Lisa Hollingsworth-Segedy, American Rivers

Working with the Public—Sometimes

❭ The fact that it's an occupational hazard of this work to be belittled by citizens, elected officials, columnists, etc. is also not particularly rewarding, but it's the kind of thing that you have to be calm about because it just is—there's no sense getting upset about the force of gravity—it just is.

Nat Bottigheimer, Washington Metropolitan Area Transit Authority

❭ I am dissatisfied with the inability of planners to deal with those who game the civic engagement process and the failure of most public sector planners to offer leadership and use their authority as professionals to influence changes to the built and natural environments. Too many planners assume that citizens know what's best for a community simply by virtue of living within it.

Elaine Van S. Carmichael, AICP, Economic Stewardship, Inc.

❭ The profession has embraced citizen participation, hearing endlessly statements from citizens who can express fears, but simply do not know. This empowers the NIMBY at the expense of professional. We have not reached the level of status with elected officials, lay boards, or citizens equal to that which lawyers and engineers often exert. Overcoming this is a daily battle that is wearing. Too many of the profession are unwilling to stand up in front of their citizens and say that their fears are groundless.

Lane Kendig, Kendig/Keast Collaborative

Paperwork and Administrative Tasks

❭ That's simple. Paperwork and administrivia.

James Segedy, FAICP, AIA, Pennsylvania Environmental Council

❭ The mundane but necessary responsibilities of keeping a consulting practice running, which includes invoicing, administrative tasks, marketing, and so forth.

Stuart Sirota, AICP, TND Planning Group

❭ The least satisfying part is the bureaucratic portions. Rules, regulations, and paperwork that are often inefficient and counterproductive.

Otis Rolley III, Central Maryland Transportation Alliance

❭ Least satisfying—dealing with entrenched power centers, particularly with planning and engineering firms who will do what is necessary to satisfy a client, or public officials that act in their self-interest or succumb to political pressure rather than the public interest.

J. Richard Kuzmyak, Transportation Consultant, LLC

REWARDS

Diversity of the Work

❭ I enjoy the diversity of projects I work on and the diverse groups of people I work with. As the project manager of a statewide visioning project known as *Reality Check Plus*, I worked with people across Maryland to develop a vision for future growth. To be able to work with and hear the concerns and hopes of farmers, environmentalists, homebuilders, elected officials, community activists, housing advocates, and many others was quite enlightening to me.

Jason Sartori, Integrated Planning Consultants

❭ My job changes gears every few months. Right now I am working on public involvement techniques, but next month I will begin work collecting survey data. By December I will be writing a national report and interviewing MPO directors. This field requires mental flexibility and helps stave off workplace boredom, which I am prone to.

Alexander Bond, AICP, University of South Florida Center for Urban Transportation Research

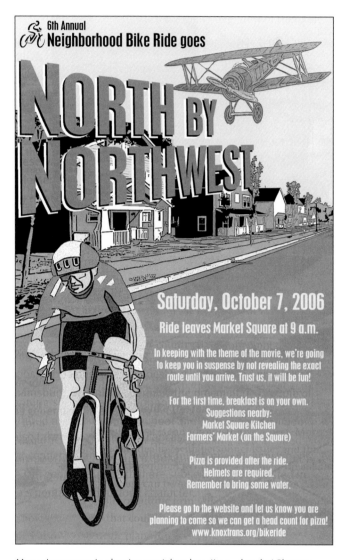

Measuring success in planning can take a long time—decades! Planners learn to take satisfaction in small victories and see those successes accumulate over time. SARAH POWELL, KNOXVILLE REGIONAL TPO.

Challenges and Rewards (Continued)

Working with Great People

❭ I feel really rewarded when mentoring younger planners and working with other Econ Stew folks. I enjoy my colleagues, working and traveling with other members of the consulting team.

Elaine Van S. Carmichael, AICP, Economic Stewardship, Inc.

Seeing Success

❭ It's usually the small successes that end up being the most satisfying. For instance, one person says that Bike to Work Day last year convinced them to stop driving to work, or that Smart Trips resulted in their family getting rid of a car. I try not to look at the big picture because it seems impossible that we can make a significant difference.

Kelley Segars, AICP, Knoxville Regional Transportation Planning Organization

❭ The most satisfying parts of my job are watching things fall into place. Especially gratifying is seeing a community embrace an idea and make it happen as their own.

James Segedy, FAICP, AIA, Pennsylvania Environmental Council

❭ The most satisfying part of the job involves connecting with the people involved in a project and finding ways to address everyone's issues to develop a successful project that restores the river and improves the environment.

Lisa Hollingsworth-Segedy, American Rivers

❭ The most satisfying is the support of prior clients when we reach out to do either additional work for them or new work for other communities. Our reputation means everything in the personal services business, and a good rep is very satisfying.

Lee Einsweiler, AICP, Code Studio

❭ Coming up with new techniques that are a revelation to decision makers, and also the use of these techniques or underlying research to "make a difference" and come out to a different and unexpected outcome that defies conventional wisdom.

J. Richard Kuzmyak, Transportation Consultant, LLC

❭ The most satisfying part is seeing a plan get implemented and seeing people's lives improved from it.

Otis Rolley III, Central Maryland Transportation Alliance

❭ I sometimes have to pinch myself when I get up each morning and realize that I am able to do what I am passionate about. Knowing that I am part of the solution and helping create a more sustainable future is very gratifying. Being in the role of "change agent" and dealing with the conflict that often comes with challenging the status quo can sometimes be stressful.

However, I find nothing more satisfying than achieving an innovative "win-win" solution to a challenging situation, or turning a skeptical stakeholder or decision maker into an ally. In addition, I also enjoy the camaraderie and fellowship of the associates and clients with whom I collaborate. The relationships I have formed with people who share the same values and ideals transcend that of just a professional relationship, and many have become dear friends and confidants.

Stuart Sirota, AICP, TND Planning Group

❭ The greatest satisfaction comes from seeing great places and neighborhoods evolve out of the policies developed, the project review process, and proactive implementation. The least satisfying aspect is that it takes years for this to happen.

William Anderson, FAICP, City of San Diego

If you had to do it over again, would you choose planning as a career?

❯ I am not sure I ever "chose" planning; rather it chose me. It is who I am. Luckily, I had a professor in college who saw that and helped me steer down this career path.

Kathie Ebaugh, AICP, Bell David Planning Group

❯ I can't imagine doing anything else. My colleagues like to call me "the planner's planner," which I take as a sublime compliment. Every time I hear friends and acquaintances complain about their careers and pine for retirement, I think about how lucky I am. Not that I don't have bad days—I do—but that's usually because my workload is too intense, or I've had a bad meeting.

That said, I do struggle with career issues of a different kind: Should I stay self-employed or go to work for a consulting firm? Should I stay in the private sector or go to work for a city? How can I deal with the isolation of working by myself? How can I continue to find interesting work and avoid committing myself to the wrong projects? What's the next professional frontier? And so on.

I would absolutely do it again if I had to do it over. But here's a confession—I have daydreams about leveraging my planning skills into a career in travel writing or television. I'd love to host a weekly show about how cities work, or about great cities of the world. But until talent scouts from the Discovery Channel show up at my door, I think I'll stick to planning.

Barry Miller, AICP, Planning Consultant, Berkeley, California

❯ No. If I had my time over again, I would not have embraced the words of John F. Kennedy, nor misread the false signs of hope implicit in the moon landing.

▼ Great places don't just happen. They're planned. CITY OF SAN DIEGO.

Challenges and Rewards (Continued)

Planning has the potential to bridge the gap between what is and what could be, but people in general, and the planning profession in particular, sabotage and undermine this potential at every turn.

If I was starting over I'd study law with the objective of becoming the chief judge of the Planning and Environment Court or the head of one of world's great development companies or real estate investment houses.

Geoffrey Booth, Youngblood Endowed Professor of Land Development, Texas A&M University

❯ It absolutely was the right choice for me. After wandering around several other careers and jobs, there is no doubt that this is what I was placed on this earth to do. Yes, I would do it again—perhaps not following the same path, but I would definitely do it again.

James Segedy, FAICP, AIA, Pennsylvania Environmental Council

❯ I've often reflected upon this and have told prospective planners that I would not have changed a thing. The planning profession is interesting, dynamic, and personally rewarding. You will not be bored and you will make a difference.

Brad Steinke, City of Apache Junction, Arizona

❯ Absolutely! Landscape architecture has so many facets, and provides one with the tools to venture into a wide array of choices.

Elizabeth "Boo" Thomas, ASLA, Center for Planning Excellence

❯ Looking back, I think I did the right thing, though like anyone, I think of what "else" could I have done or could still do. I believe few people ever have the "dream" job, but I think my overall level of satisfaction has been very good.

As with any career you have your ups and downs and wonder what else I could have done. I believe having a passion in life, whether a job, family, or a hobby, is important. I think being a planner is as close as I have gotten to having a passion.

This career has allowed me to mature in many ways. I never dreamed I would speak in front of large crowds about contentious projects or become a negotiator between different views.

Dirk Geratz, AICP, City of Alexandria, Virginia

❯ Although I did not set out to be an urban planner, and to a large degree still consider myself an urban geographer, I believe I went in the right direction.

Planning, both in my years as a government staff member and as a consultant, has allowed me to enjoy a wide range of experiences and produce products that I believe have contributed to making the communities I worked with better places. I think of the variety of projects in which I participated and find it difficult to see how any other profession would have given me the opportunity to go to the office each day knowing that it will not be routine. It has given me an exposure to all aspects of government at all levels and has allowed me to travel extensively throughout the United States. The travel itself becomes tiring quickly but the opportunity to see so many communities and work with a broad range of government professionals makes that seem trivial.

Yes! I would do it again. Would I take the consultant route or remain a government staff member? That is a difficult question. As a consultant I have enjoyed tremendous variety and personal growth but I also enjoyed variety as a staff member and had the satisfaction of continuity with the community.

Howard Geisler, President, Geisler/Smith Associates

❭ Yes, I believe it was a good career choice. I would do it again, and as an undergraduate I would certainly want an architecture or landscape architecture background. I think the profession has too few practitioners today who have the technical training. A lot of the issues we face require technical expertise, not a liberal arts training that is suited for talking about policy without the ability to shape it to the real physical world, either the environment or built environment.

Lane Kendig, Kendig/Keast Collaborative

❭ I am doing exactly what I want to be doing, and hope to keep doing it for some time to come. How I got here was rather circuitous but reflects my different interests and passions. I don't know where my career will take me in the next 30–40 years or more—that's a lot of time to make an impact, and I look forward to continuing to figure out how I can be most effective as I go. I would not bother to pursue a Ph.D. again—but if I hadn't done that, I probably wouldn't have come to Baltimore, and then a lot of other things wouldn't have happened either. . . .

Amy Menzer, Executive Director, Dundalk Renaissance Corporation

❭ Planning was a vocation that found me and it was an excellent career choice. It is a career where one can interface with both concepts and people. Often, in planning, we called ourselves the "Department of Damage Control" and were disappointed that our plans were always being ruined by community realities. But, in retrospect, I think that this is the point of planning: working from an ideal to a best scenario based on reality, and doing that well, takes far more skill than just dreaming up the textbook "perfect" solution.

Joan Kennedy, City of Hampton, Virginia

❭ My career is continually evolving, and encompasses more than work in public participation

and civic engagement. It is rooted in key themes of place, community, inclusiveness, and culture. For me it has been the perfect choice, because I have always sought to stay true to my calling, my deepest interests and values, and my unique talents and gifts. Several books in particular have helped me along my career path: *Wishcraft: How to Get What You Really Want, Finding Your Own North Star, The Pathfinder,* and *Feel the Fear and Do It Anyway.*

I wouldn't change any part of my career path. When you love what you do, and stay true to your sense of calling, you are likely to hone your favorite gifts and talents in ways that will continue to open doors for you. I have taken plenty of risks, but it has all been worth it. I love what I do: what more could I ask for?

Corinna Moebius, Bordercross Consulting Group

❭ I love my work and it's been a good fit for me. I joke that I'm a consultant because I have a short attention span and like to be the center of attention, but really it's for the intellectual and personal freedom and the opportunity to see how things are done all over the place. The consultants tend to be the savviest, too; the academics and government folks are all very earnest, but they move really slowly and they tend to lack courage. I'm writing a book now that I hope will make a lasting contribution, which would be very difficult to accomplish in other fields or while working for a jurisdiction.

Elaine Van Carmichael, AICP, Economic Stewardship Inc.

❭ Yes it was a good choice. My inclinations towards design, creative intervention, analysis, performance, and self-expression are fairly well satisfied within the profession's tent. My frustrations have to do with the profession's inherent tendency to limit cause and effect—the ability to see and ascribe the impacts of one's actions. The glacial pace of change

Challenges and Rewards (Continued)

in the U.S. planning process makes this a reality. Architecture, my original training, does not suffer from this limitation anywhere near as much. Alternative career choices I would likely make today include movie directing, teaching, or performance arts.

Uri Avin, FAICP, PB PlaceMaking

❯ Absolutely. It was not the career I had intended. I got into the planning field because it was the best environmental law job I could find at the time. After I started, I realized that it was where I belonged all the time—I just didn't know it before. So, too, with teaching. I never planned to have an academic life. It just followed from what I was doing before. That sense of natural progression is very satisfying, if somewhat unpredictable.

Keith Bartholomew, University of Utah

❯ For me, work is a calling, not a career. It is a values-driven, values-based exercise. My only regret is that I didn't speculate on stocks when I could have done so profitably—I could then have stopped worrying about getting paid for what I do, and I could be speculating (taking riskier positions) in life.

Sam Seskin, Transportation Planning Director, CH2MHill, Portland, Oregon

❯ Yes, I probably would do it over again, but ideally with the insight to know how to work around the many political and institutional impediments to "doing the right thing" the first time.

J. Richard Kuzmyak, Transportation Consultant, LLC

❯ I'm so happy in my career choice it's unreasonable. I would absolutely do it over again, and I only wish I could have known about the field I'm in now when I was in college—or before.

Nat Bottigheimer, Washington Metropolitan Area Transit Authority

❯ I have been very happy with my career. My work is fast-paced and diverse. I fear that many planning jobs become frustrating because they do not result in tangible products, but my career as a transportation planner has been very positive from that perspective.

Henry Kay, Deputy Administrator for Planning and Engineering, Maryland Transit Administration

❯ While it can be frustrating at times, when you look back at what we are trying to do, it is critical that we figure out how to grow smarter in Maryland, in the U.S., and for the planet. You get to do many different things, work with interesting people, and all for a good cause.

Richard Eberhardt Hall, AICP, Maryland Secretary of Planning

❯ I believe that I have been very fortunate and that I did make a great career choice. I have worked on some very exciting projects with some extremely talented individuals. I think it would have been interesting to have had the opportunity to work directly for an agency rather than in the private sector, so perhaps if I were to reconstruct my past, I might have tried that course as well.

Alyse Getty, Parsons Infrastructure and Technology, Inc.

❯ My original motivation to leave "geology" and enter "planning" was to have more at the end of the day to give to family. My motivation to stay was that I applied my training in geology and water resources in practical ways. I expanded my skill sets and interests, and I believe I became a much more rounded professional than if I had stayed in a more traditional career track for geology. I would only agree to do it over again if I could know then what I know now!

Lisa Hollingsworth-Segedy, American Rivers

❭ Very much so. It's very rewarding. Every job isn't going to be satisfying 100 percent of the time, but the people who work for the Park Service are dedicated to the mission of the Park Service and want to shape the role of parks in the future.

I see our role as being very, very important, from general management plans to determining whether a park should be a park in the first place. Particularly for the folks who work in the Planning and Compliance Division, I think it's really rewarding, despite the frustration you might have about the length of time that projects may take.

I know we're making a difference. We're working in wonderful places. We're meeting with senators and congressmen. It's tough to beat.

I'll never be a millionaire, but I don't have any regrets.

Richard Sussman, National Park Service

❭ I have no regrets regarding my career choice, especially given how it has worked out with transition to consulting early on. However, to be honest, I'm not sure how I'd answer that question if 18 years into my career I was still working in the public sector! Although I enjoy the subject matter, I'm not sure I would be entirely happy in the local government environment.

L. Carson Bise II, AICP, TishlerBise

❭ There's nothing I'd rather be doing than what I'm doing now, and my enthusiasm has never been greater. I believe that the disillusionment and setbacks that I experienced in the first part of my career was part of the impetus that set me on the path towards what I was destined to do.

Stuart Sirota, AICP, TND Planning Group

❭ From the time I was four years old, I wanted to be a pilot. Growing up under the approach to LaGuardia Airport in New York City, I have always been fascinated by aircraft.

As I begin to see a future end to my career and reflect on it, I have found it to be a rewarding one. During both my county planner and aviation planner jobs, I feel like I've made a difference and provided benefits to a great many people in both the communities that I helped "plan" and the airport facilities across the country that I have helped improve.

All things considered, it has been a rewarding and excellent career choice, and was based on a passion and love for being around aircraft. I believe I would do it again—in many self-assessments, I'm not certain that I was ever suited for other types of careers.

Wayne Schuster, AICP, CM, Maryland Aviation Administration

5 What Is the Future of Planning?

As part of their jobs, planners are always peering into the future, trying to see what the future holds and how communities can anticipate what is coming in order to be prepared to meet new challenges and to take advantage of new opportunities. So what do planners see for the future of our own profession? Planners see a number of important challenges ahead that will increase the importance of good planning and increase the need for planners with new skills to tackle new problems.

Economic Recession and Planning

IN 2008 AND EARLY 2009, planners were thinking a lot about the effect of the global economic crisis on communities and the role of planners in addressing this problem. Lisa Hollingsworth-Segedy, associate director for river restoration for American Rivers in Pittsburgh, noted that the planning job market tends to decline during hard economic times. "I believe that, in the short run, the current economic crisis will cause many planners to lose their jobs."

As the economy declines, especially the development sector, the amount of work for planners declines as well. When developers cannot get loans or attract investors, they put off starting new projects. When developers see the housing market collapsing, they postpone plans to build new subdivisions, apartments, and condos. As a result, they don't need the services of planners.

While municipal planners are unlikely to be laid off, cities typically reduce their hiring of planners during recessions. An economic recession typically results in lower tax revenues for cities, and that translates into city budget cuts. That means that students completing their preparation for a career in planning may find that it takes many months to land their first job if they happen to graduate during an economic downturn.

Once hired, however, planners are unlikely to be laid off. Layoffs in local government are less common than in private industry. In the private sector of planning, consulting firms look to their planning sections to produce work for their engineering sections. So while the planning job market is cyclical—ebbing and flowing with the larger economic cycle—the swings in the planning job market are usually less dramatic than in many other industrial sectors.

"While construction activity ebbs and flows, infrastructure, housing, and the location and type of economic activity that drives human interaction will always be important issues. I expect that planners will always be an important part of the dialogue on these issues," said S. Mark White, AICP, of White and Smith Planning and Law Group, Kansas City, Missouri.

Coping with Layoff

MARYA MORRIS, AICP

Independent Consultant

Chicago, Illinois

Your experience out of college has a parallel in the recent recession. Like many planners, you recently lost your job. What was that experience like?

❯ I worked at APA for 18 years; then I took a job and worked for my friend Kirk at a consulting firm. I never thought I would ever get another job. I did not see the purpose of having to look for another one. In retrospect, I could see what happened. We lost clients and they were my clients. I found myself pinch-hitting for Kirk. So when Kirk brought me into his office and gave me the news, I was horrified. How on earth did I ever get into this situation? So I went home and slept for two weeks. My husband would greet me in the morning and say, "Another day of moping, honey?"

While layoffs in planning are unusual, the economic recession of 2008–09 hit housing development especially hard—much harder than other recessions in recent times. That downturn in development activity hit the planning industry as well. A few planners who offered interviews for this book had been laid off between their first interview and a follow-up interview. Here is how one viewed that experience.

Geospatial Technology and Planning

The digital revolution of the past three decades has had a profound effect on planning and the way planners do their work. Planners expect future developments in digital technologies, such as CAD and GIS, to have continuing effects on what planners can do and how they do it.

"There are several changes that are having a significant impact on the planning profession," said David Kuehn, Program Manager, U.S. Department of Transportation.

"First is technology around geospatial systems and remote sensing that exponentially increases the amount of data about the physical environment and the ability to assess and display that information.

"Second is a new role as for an active public, again with supporting technology. Activist planning from the 1960s also included community-participatory planning. I had been involved in community mapping with paper maps or disposable cameras. But new technology has really increased the value of community participation in the collection and analysis of information. This breaks down the barrier between experts and nonexperts and provides a more balanced position when discussing options and alternatives."

Adapting Zoning to the Twenty-first Century

GEOFFREY BOOTH

Youngblood Endowed Professor of Land Development

Texas A&M University

College Station, TX

Prior to your current position, you worked on sustainable development in the private sector. What did that job involve?

❯ I was the Senior Fellow, Sustainable Development at Environmental Resources Management. My role was to develop and deliver consulting services and products that drew on environmental science and solutions to create real estate value.

I advised a local government on its green building policy; prepared a strategy plan for a large power generating company's 32,000 acre real estate portfolio;

advised, along with my colleagues, the World Bank on its global city indicators program; and demonstrated to a major property developer how it could use environmental science to create a major (4,000 residents) mixed-use community on a contaminated site.

You critique zoning law rather severely. Do you have an alternative?

❯ Zoning law is deliberately written in the most sterile and unevocative language—uninviting and unintelligible to all but a few urban planners and zoning lawyers—the rest of the community is effectively locked out of the placemaking process.

A new "sensory law" must draw instead on the complete palette of human expression—evocative language, the combination of interactive digital motion "pictures and sound" to evoke the companion senses of taste, touch, and smell—so as to properly express what we want from the future development of our cities.

Under sensory law, the city plan and regulatory instruments must take an interactive digital, visual, and auditory form, because it is simply impossible to adequately express the places we love, in black letter legal terminology.

The new sensory law will be intelligible to all, not just lawyers and planners because it draws on all the senses we use every day to assess place. It will thereby empower all who live in the community to contribute to the regulatory standards for the places we wish to create.

Developers will be required to present their proposals in an interactive digital and auditory form to demonstrate compliance, and secure development entitlement. Unless the completed development is true to, or better than, the digital development approval that allowed it to be built. It will be unlawful to commence the use.

In regard to your views on sensory law, what should planners do to get us closer to your vision? Is it a matter of developing and using better tools, or do we need to make better planners?

❯ Think about how you assess place using all five of your senses. Think about how we currently communicate and enforce our planning visions, laws and policies and then map the disconnect. Go to http://www.urbancircus.com.au/ and ask yourself why urban planners aren't utilizing this technology to improve the quality of their plans, the public support needed to implement them, and avoid the costs of the great planning disasters and misalignment of investment caused by their clinging with their cold dead hands to "black letter" zoning law. Use the technology to both your and the city's advantage. Use your comfort level and proficiency with new technology to undermine and sweep away the older generation of urban planners who have a vested interest in clinging to the old ways merely because it protects their position, income, and influence. Combine your knowledge and understanding of the substance of sustainable development with the power of the new "sensory law" to virtually design, create, and experience with all your senses, better cities as the platform to secure broad political support. Only then will public and private sector investment be allocated to convert your virtual design into actual places that we enjoy and that deliver an enduring sustainability dividend. The planning profession can, in this way, turn its young talent to the future.

Rediscovering Public Health

When the planning profession first emerged in the late nineteenth century, protecting public health was a major part of planning's role in cities. By separating uses that were incompatible, people believed that planning could prevent illness. Efforts to segregate housing away from noxious smells and fumes, for example, were believed to protect health as well as protect property values and quality of life.

Planning Healthy Communities

JESSICA OSBORNE

Physical Activity/Active Community Environment Coordinator

Colorado Department of Public Health and Environment

Denver, Colorado

You recently took a job in public health. How do you tie that to your previous work?

❭ I'm very excited because I think the focus in planning is shifting away from issues of growth and sprawl to more talk about public health.

When you frame land use issues in the context of public health, I think people "get it" in a way they don't when you talk about public works or infrastructure.

Public health is a novelty for a lot of planners. They're not comfortable in talking about it. But I find health to be a more legitimate argument in support of the need to change land use. People can see and understand that we have neighborhoods that don't support pedestrian activity. So public health is a way to talk about transit and walkability with people who may be intimidated or confused when the topic is infrastructure or public works.

It's my next frontier. I still want to accomplish the same goals but in a different way.

Today, public health is reemerging as a driver of planning approaches, after lying dormant for many decades. "Several recent studies have linked planning to issues of obesity and public health," said Jason Sartori of Integrated Planning Consultants. "When we design cities in ways that require people to drive rather than walk, and when we design streets that make biking dangerous, we discourage people from engaging in physical activity."

"If planners, engineers, designers, and public health agencies don't already realize it, we have to be on the same page in terms of how communities function, we just don't speak the same language," said Jessica Osborne of the Colorado Department of Public Health and Environment. "The old mechanism for planning and roadway design is broken, and if we hope to have healthy, sustainable, vibrant communities, we have to come together and create a common dialogue to create places people want to live, work, and walk in. We have to break the dysfunctional silos of thought and practice down and learn from each other in order to come up with solutions for our towns and cities."

Fortunately, planners are working with public health professionals to create city environments that protect people from disease and traumatic injury. Once, public health professionals and planners worked together to protect people from typhoid and dysentery. Today, they are working together to protect people from heart disease, stroke, diabetes, and traffic accidents.

Demonstration Project 3:
Alice's Garden

Milwaukee County Supervisor Elizabeth Coggs-Jones, who helped establish Johnsons Park, designated a section of the park as Alice's Garden. "Alice" was Alice Meade-Taylor, former director of the Milwaukee County Office of UW-Extension. The garden is named for her in recognition of her dedication and commitment to children in Milwaukee's inner city.

In the center of Alice's Garden would be an open-air shelter for teaching various small groups about a variety of garden and landscape subjects, and for the posting of notices (see Map 1.2). The design and construction of the structure provides a valuable learning opportunity for architecture students at UW-Milwaukee's School of Architecture and Urban Planning.

Physical improvements to the garden would include restructuring of the garden layout, improved paths, removal of old asphalt and unsightly compost piles, and replacing the cyclone fence with shorter, more attractive fencing. Well-designed paths will lead through a renovated garden. Interpretive signage of the style and quality found elsewhere in Johnsons Park would inform visitors and gardeners about urban agriculture and edible landscaping. Signs near an enhanced orchard may suggest fruit trees for homeowners to consider in their yards. A sign near a prairie garden may list native species appropriate for perennial gardening at home. Harvest festivals, jam and jelly workshops, and other events will bring people from throughout the community to the site.

The perimeter of the garden would be fenced with a nearly invisible 4-foot black cyclone fence. Two dimensional art elements expressing garden themes would be placed on the fence facing the adjacent streets. All three streetscapes surrounding the garden would be planted with new storm water trees as part of the overall Legacy community streetscape plan described in the next demonstration project.

Demonstration Project 4:
The Legacy—A Green Community
for a New Generation

This recently approved $20 million redevelopment project is expected to create over 50 market-rate single-family homes and at least 48 condominium townhouses, and up to 15,000 square feet of developed retail space. Homes are expected to cost from $180,000 to $250,000. Legacy Development Partners is a limited liability corporation comprising Legacy Redevelopment Corp., Irgens Development Partners, and Williams Development Corp. Recommended green infrastructure goals for the redevelopment plan include urban reforestation, reductions in home heating costs through canopy tree plantings, storm water retention and infiltration, safe pedestrian

Fond du Lac and North Avenue Green Infrastructure Initiative / Center for Resilient Cities

Transporting food over long distances wastes energy and increases carbon emissions. Growing food locally builds community ties and encourages self-sufficiency. In March of 2009, First Lady Michelle Obama set an example by digging up a patch of the White House lawn to plant a vegetable garden. She was not alone, as sales of seed skyrocketed during the economic crisis. Planners will be looking for ways to integrate community gardens into neighborhoods, like this plan from the Center for Resilient Cities. Good food, moderate exercise. Good for us. CENTER FOR RESILIENT CITIES, 2007.

In the future, planners will work harder to make communities walkable and bike-able so that children grow up healthy and fit, and so adults stay that way. COURTESY OF DAN BURDEN, GLATTING JACKSON.

The Centers for Disease Control (CDC) now has an Active Community Environments Initiative that studies walking, biking, and the creation of accessible recreation spaces. As just one part of this effort engaging planners, the CDC has developed an "Active Community Environments guidebook for public health practitioners to use to partner with transportation and city planning organizations to promote walking, bicycling, and close to home recreation facilities" (Centers for Disease Control, no date). As research findings and understanding of the importance of active community design grows, planners will work increasingly on educating the public about the public health costs of sprawling, auto-dominant city forms and how to make cities more walkable, bike-able, and livable.

"In the coming years, I think we're going to see more links between planning and these types of social ills and there will be a growing recognition that good planning can help improve communities and society as a whole in ways we had previously never considered. Of course, comprehensive models must be developed to more fully understand these relationships for planners to do their job effectively," Jason Sartori said.

As a result, planning is creating new tools and new specializations.

"Planning is expanding its attention to design issues, and trends like form-based codes that follow that desire for improved place making will be hot in the near future," said Lee Einsweiler, AICP, of Code Studio.

Carbon, Climate Change, Peak Oil, and Planning for Sustainable Energy

Good city planning will be an essential part of the global response to global climate change and the depletion of petroleum reserves. Scientists have predicted for over 50 years that sometime in the first half of the twenty-first century, the world will have used half the oil that has ever existed (U.S. Government Accountability Office, 2007, 12). The point at which half of the world's oil supply has already been used up is called "peak oil." After that point, as oil becomes more and more scarce, prices begin to rise.

The approach of peak oil has been eclipsed in recent years by a second major trend scientists have been warning about. Since the first Intergovernmental Panel on Climate Change (IPCC) issued its report in 1990 and on through the issuance of the fourth IPCC report in 2007, scientists have been warning—first quietly and then more insistently—that the earth's climate is getting warmer and that human activity is likely the cause. In 2008, the scientists who prepared the Fourth IPCC Report in 2007 shared the Nobel Prize with former Vice President Al Gore, author of *An Inconvenient Truth*, a film explaining the causes and predicted consequences of global climate change.

As communities make the transition away from high carbon sources of energy, like this coal-fired power plant, planners will need to be fully engaged in making cities more energy efficient and finding space for the full range of renewable energy production facilities. Already, planners are looking at zoning codes to understand how solar, wind, and other renewables may be "zoned out" in ways that are counterproductive in the new energy environment. NANCY FRANK, 2009.

Increasingly, planners are facing new issues related to the integration of renewable energy into existing urban areas. For example, planners will be balancing the benefits of on-site generation of electricity from solar collectors and wind turbines against potential hazards and disturbance to neighbors. Here, Discovery World Museum in Milwaukee, Wisconsin, has installed a demonstration of solar and wind to show people the immediate effect of noise and other concerns and to show the energy-generating potential. NANCY FRANK, 2009.

Following the 2007 IPCC report, skepticism about the realities of climate change withered dramatically and increasing numbers of people began to support immediate action to curb carbon emissions (the chief cause of climate change) and to begin to prepare for inevitable changes. Planners have been gearing up to meet this challenge.

Good city and regional planning is central to efforts to reduce carbon emissions. In addition, because some continuing change in climate is now inevitable, planners are on the front lines in adapting to the changes that communities can anticipate.

PLANNING FOR CLIMATE ADAPTATION

Because of the quantity of carbon that has already built up in the atmosphere, scientists tell us that even an immediate and dramatic reduction in carbon emissions would not eliminate some of the predicted climate change. Adapting to the changing climate will engage many professions, but planners will be in the thick of it.

While global climate is getting warmer, scientists tell us that specific geographic areas will experience widely varying effects. Some places will become wetter and others drier. Some places will get hotter, and others cooler. In some places storms will become more frequent. In other areas, storms will become more intense, resulting in heavier downpours and increased flooding. In many places, the climate will become more variable, hitting extremes of hot and then cold, wetter and then drier, from one season to the next.

Whatever the resulting changes, cities need to be prepared to adapt to those changes. Drier conditions, leading to drought, can deplete water resources for drinking water. Increased irrigation of lawns and gardens can make matters even worse in drought conditions. More intense rainfalls can result in increased flushing of pollutants from city streets and parking lots. Swollen rivers and streams erode their banks, and severe flooding becomes more common. Heat waves become more frequent and extreme. The heat in cities, magnified by acres of roofs, streets, and parking lots, creates a heat island that can become as deadly as disease. In France, an August 2005 heat wave resulted in the death of 15,000 people.

Planners are working with climate scientists, engineers, and public health professionals to anticipate the likely changes and to plan urban infrastructure to cope with these changes. Stormwater pipes may need to be sized larger in the future to cope with more frequent torrential rains; so cities need to plan how and when to replace existing pipes. Planners are working with other professionals to expand the area along rivers where development needs to be restricted in order to prevent damage and danger in case of flooding.

If reservoirs and groundwater supplies will be stressed by droughts and long periods of below normal rainfall, planners need to develop strategies for reducing cities' demand for water.

In addition to adapting the built infrastructure of cities to cope with climate change, planners are also looking at the benefits of green infrastructure. Green infrastructure mimics the natural processes of nature to deal with wastes and to prevent the concentration of pollutants, heat, and stormwater. Working with landscape architects and engineers, planners can design living green ribbons of plants and trees to be strategically placed throughout neighborhoods to retain and absorb water, to provide cooling shade, and to prevent rainwater from carrying pollutants to streams and lakes.

Tree-lined streets, tree-covered bike and jogging trails, and trees along the banks of urban rivers can reduce the overall heat build-up in cities and, importantly, create cooler spaces where residents can enjoy the outdoors without risking adverse health effects, such as heat stroke. Trees shading houses can also reduce the heat island effect while reducing demand on air conditioners.

In the face of anticipated climate change, an increasing number of planners are pursuing specialized training in hazard management. Planners trained in hazard management look at ways of modifying urban land use to reduce the risks associated with forest and grass fires, earthquakes, tornadoes, hurricanes, floods, and other natural disasters. Planners explore policies that can reduce

At one time, planners and engineers dealt with the public health hazards caused by urban flooding by encasing river channels in concrete so that rainwater would flow quickly and unimpeded away from populated areas. Unfortunately, this increases drowning hazards when people get caught in the channel of rushing water. NANCY FRANK, 2009.

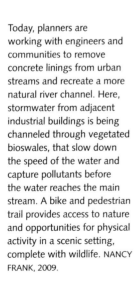

Today, planners are working with engineers and communities to remove concrete linings from urban streams and recreate a more natural river channel. Here, stormwater from adjacent industrial buildings is being channeled through vegetated bioswales, that slow down the speed of the water and capture pollutants before the water reaches the main stream. A bike and pedestrian trail provides access to nature and opportunities for physical activity in a scenic setting, complete with wildlife. NANCY FRANK, 2009.

the likelihood of property damage, injury, and death when such disasters occur. In addition, planners look for ways to reduce the frequency of disasters that are influenced by human activity. For example, land use regulations can reduce the likelihood of wildfires invading subdivisions and wiping out whole neighborhoods; floodplain regulations can restrict building in areas that are more likely to flood under conditions of climate change.

PLANNING FOR CLIMATE MITIGATION

Planning is also on the frontlines of efforts to mitigate climate change by reducing the output of greenhouse gases.

"Smart planning is critical to the future of our country. Rising energy prices, coupled with a very unstable market, require that we protect and leverage our resources to preserve the quality of life in America. Planners have been trying to promote quality-of-life issues for decades (growth management, smart growth policies, sustainability, global warming, new urbanism, traditional neighborhood developments, green building etc.), said Elizabeth "Boo" Thomas of the Center for Planning Excellence. "I think America is listening now!"

Cities account for 80 percent of greenhouse gas emissions. This means that any meaningful effort to reduce carbon emissions will need to happen in cities. In addition, "studies show that higher-density development results in lower greenhouse gas emissions" (Newman, Beatley, and Boyer, 2009, 18).

Climate mitigation opportunities in planning cover a broad range of options and activities for planners. "Climate change profoundly influences the profession. It is the new organizing principle and adds a compelling rationale for all we do," said Luther Propst, Executive Director of the Sonoran Institute in Tucson, Arizona. Here are just a few ideas that practicing planners are thinking about today.

Alternative energy options—from solar and wind to biofuels and nuclear energy—will require careful attention to siting issues to avoid undesirable conflicts with neighborhoods and property rights. The surge in solar collectors installed during the energy crisis of the 1970s foretells the conflicts between landowners that occurs when people compete in cities for access to the sun's rays. Already, planners in dense urban areas are struggling to make the right decisions about the siting of wind turbines, with neighbors concerned about noise, visual impact, effects on wildlife, and dangers from towers and turbine blades. In addition, preserving agricultural land to meet an expanding demand for both food and fuel will become increasingly urgent.

Even with careful planning of a diverse energy mix, many energy experts predict that the U.S. will be unable to achieve carbon emission targets without dramatically reducing energy demands. Alternative fuels suffer from a number of drawbacks, including lower energy density, intermittent availability, and competition for space with other important human goals (e.g., land competing between food and fuel production, shade trees in cities competing with solar collectors).

"The issue of climate change relates directly to transportation planning in that we've built an auto-dependent society that relies heavily on fossil fuels and carbon emissions," said Marya Morris, AICP, a planning consultant in Chicago. "Planners can be part of the climate change solution if we raise awareness about the contribution low-density development patterns have on the problem"

Transportation accounts for 27 percent of all energy consumption in the U.S. (Architecture 2030, 2009). How we plan our cities influences whether people need to drive or can get where they need to by bike or walking. Designing cities to encourage mass transit will be critical to achieving energy and carbon reductions.

"As the fuse of global climate change keeps burning . . . I think planning will increasingly be viewed through the lens of energy consumption both associated with buildings and relative to transportation," said Ted Knowlton, AICP, of the Planning Center in Draper, Utah.

Buildings in the U.S. account for 48 percent of all energy consumed in the U.S. (Architecture 2030, 2009). Architects have been at the forefront in raising awareness of the energy and carbon savings that can be achieved through green building practices through organizations like the U.S. Green Building Council and Architecture 2030. While planners do not design or construct buildings, planners influence what kinds of buildings are built by influencing local policies on building codes. Across the country, cities are adopting new "green codes" that encourage or require new buildings to achieve a minimum standard of energy efficiency. All the green buildings in the world won't solve the carbon problem, however, if people travel in unsustainable ways to reach those buildings. For green buildings, energy used in commuting can exceed building operating energy by over 130 percent (Environmental Building News, 2007).

"To increase their effectiveness, planners need to address more issues at their appropriate geographic scale," said Kelley Segars, AICP, of the Knoxville Regional Transportation Planning Organization. "For many planning issues, the geographic boundary that encompasses the problem is the region, not the municipality. Regional visioning and planning is a growing trend but it will remain to be seen how much this trend penetrates into typical metropolitan areas."

Connections between cities and their surrounding regions will be critical in meeting carbon reduction targets. For example, planners are learning about the energy and carbon impacts of transporting food and are creating regional plans to preserve local farmland and creating new partnerships to promote food grown for local consumption. For example, in Wisconsin, planners in Dane County (the location of Madison, the capital of Wisconsin) are "connecting Wisconsin producers with Wisconsin consumers . . . through an innovative project called Institutional Food Market Coalition" (Peterangelo 2008, 1). Regional transportation networks, linking denser neighborhoods of homes, shops, offices, and manufacturing facilities will be an essential feature of the carbon neutral city of the future. A host of environmental problems—from water quality and water resource conservation to air quality—need to be addressed at a regional scale. Our new energy crisis may help planners to forge stronger regional institutions to achieve all of these goals.

A Bright Future for Planning

Most planners we talked to see planning as growing in importance in the coming decades:

> I hope that planners can continue to improve how we communicate with elected officials and the public. With that should come better understanding, and ideally, better decisions.
>
> KELLEY SEGARS, AICP, Knoxville Regional Transportation Planning Organization, Knoxville, Tennessee

> Planning's importance will only increase as the demands of resource limitations (especially with peak oil) and the challenges of climate change become ever more present.
>
> KEITH BARTHOLOMEW, University of Utah

> The future of planning is very bright as we struggle with equity, poverty, sprawl, and climate change. Planners have the tools and the perspective to address these issues.
>
> HENRY KAY, Deputy Administrator for Planning and Engineering, Maryland Transit Administration, Baltimore, Maryland

The challenges ahead will require planners to draw upon all of their traditional skills—analyzing problems and creatively solving them, communicating effectively with public officials and the general public, and then forging a vision and a path forward. Be a planner.

RESOURCES

INFORMATION ABOUT PLANNING CAREERS AND EDUCATIONAL PROGRAMS

American Planning Association, www.planning.org

- Planning Education, http://planning.org/ education/resources/index.htm
- Information for Youth and Teachers, http:// planning.org/education/youth/
- APA/AICP Salary Survey, http://www .planning.org/salary/

The summary can be viewed for free. Membership is required to access the full report. Students memberships are available for $60.

Association of Collegiate Schools of Planning, www.acsp.org

The Association of Collegiate Schools of Planning (ACSP) is a consortium of university-based programs offering credentials in urban and regional planning. Acting together, the ACSP member school faculty are able to express their shared commitments to understanding the dynamics of urban and regional development, enhancing planning practices, and improving the education of both novice and experienced planners.

ACSP Guide to Undergraduate and Graduate Education in Urban and Regional Planning

Updated annually or biannually, the ACSP Guide includes detailed descriptions of planning educational programs at over 90 colleg-

es and universities. The Guide also includes information about careers in planning. Download is available free of charge. Print and CD copies may be available for a charge.

Croby, Olivia. *Geography Jobs*

Downloadable from Bureau of Labor Statistics at http://www.bls.gov/opub/ooq/2005/spring/ art01.pdf

Guide to Graduate Programs in Urban Planning, **Planetizen, http://www.planetizen.com/guide**

Planetizen's Guide provides some of the same information about graduate programs as the guide put together by the Association of Collegiate Schools of Planning. Planetizen's guide provides basic program information as well as rankings of programs.

Occupational Outlook Handbook

Updated annually by the U.S. Bureau of Labor Statistics, the Occupational Outlook Handbook provides information about: the training and education needed, earnings, expected job prospects, what workers do on the job, and working conditions. Search for:

- Urban and regional planners

The Handbook also provides information on the following related occupations:

- Architects
- Civil engineers
- Environmental engineers

- Landscape architects
- Geographers
- Property, real estate, and community association managers
- Surveyors, cartographers, photogrammetrists, and surveying technicians
- Market and survey researchers

ORGANIZATIONS YOU CAN JOIN

American Planning Association (APA), www.planning.org

APA is a nonprofit education and membership organization. Members include practicing planners, planning students, elected and appointed officials, planning commissioners, and interested citizens. Student memberships are available for $60, http://www.planning.org/join/students/index.htm.

APA-affiliated Planning Student Organizations (PSOs), http://www.planning.org/students/pso/list.htm

PSOs are university-based student organizations that formally designate themselves as Planning Student Organizations with APA. If your university has a planning program but is not listed, contact the department chair of the planning degree program. Many student organizations neglect to formally connect to APA.

Congress for the New Urbanism (CNU), www.cnu.org

The Congress for the New Urbanism (CNU) is the leading organization promoting walkable, neighborhood-based development as an alternative to sprawl. Student memberships are available.

International Society of City and Regional Planners (ISOCARP), www.isocarp.org

ISOCARP is a global association of experienced, professional planners. Founded in 1965 with a vision of bringing together recognized and highly qualified planners in an international network. ISOCARP has members from over 70 countries. ISOCARP is a nongovernmental organization, recognized by the United Nations and the Council of Europe and with a consultative status with UNESCO.

Planners Network, www.plannersnetwork.org

Planners Network is an association of progressive planning. Its members are professionals, activists, academics, and students involved in physical, social, economic, and environmental planning in urban and rural areas. Planners Network serves as a voice for social, economic, and environmental justice through planning.

Urban and Regional Information Systems Association (URISA), www.urisa.org

The Urban and Regional Information Systems Association (URISA) is a nonprofit association of professionals using Geographic Information Systems (GIS) and other information technologies to solve challenges in state/provincial, regional, and local government agencies and departments.

PORTALS ABOUT PLANNING

About Planning, www.aboutplanning.org

About Planning is an Internet clearing house for information about websites, publications, essays, and news related to land use planning, growth management, comprehensive planning, smart growth, new urbanism, and much more.

Cyburbia, www.cyburbia.org

Cyburbia, established in 1994, is the Internet's oldest portal and social networking site for urban planners and others interested in cities and the built environment. Cyburbia includes a very active message board (almost 300,000 messages to date), an image hosting gallery, syndicated feeds of hundreds of planning-related weblogs, and a selective directory of Internet resources relevant to planning and urbanism.

Planetizen, www.planetizen.com

Planetizen is a public-interest information exchange provided by Urban Insight for the urban planning, design, and development community. It is a one-stop source for urban planning news, commentary, interviews, event coverage, book reviews, announcements, jobs, consultant listings, training, and more.

PlannersWeb, www.plannersweb.com

Home of the Planning Commissioners Journal, oriented to the needs to citizen planners. Fees apply to use many of the resources on the site.

Planum, www.planum.net

Webpage of the *European Journal of Planning,* offers more resources than just access to the journal.

Smart Growth America, www.smartgrowthamerica.org

Smart Growth America is a coalition of national, state, and local organizations working to improve the ways we plan and build the towns, cities, and metro areas we call home. The coalition includes many of the best-known national organizations advocating on behalf of historic preservation, the environment, farmland and open space preservation, neighborhood revitalization, and more.

Urbanicity, www.urbanicity.org

Urbanicity is a global resource aimed at local government and urban development. It is a broad-based, international portal. The Education page includes a comprehensive and extensive series of links to courses and training including undergraduate degrees, master's programs and professional development courses, including online and distance learning education, in Europe and North America, with links to programs in countries in South America, Asia, and Africa in development.

Urban Land Institute, www.uli.org

The mission of the Urban Land Institute is to provide leadership in the responsible use of land and in creating and sustaining thriving communities worldwide. ULI has more than 40,000 members worldwide representing the entire spectrum of land use and real estate development disciplines, working in private enterprise and public service.

Urban Planning Research blog, http://planning-research.com/

Administered by UCLA faculty members Randall Crane, this blog is directed at urban planning researchers (i.e., faculty in planning programs).

ACTIVITIES AND EVENTS

Box City, Center for Understanding the Built Environment (CUBE), www.cubekc.org

The Center for Understanding the Built Environment (CUBE) brings together educators with community partners to effect change that will lead to a quality built and natural environment, one and interdependent.

CUBE is a resource center where schools and event sponsors can purchase curriculum kits for conducting a Box City event. State and local chapters of the American Institute of Architects (AIA) and the American Planning Association (APA) are common sponsors of Box City events across the country. Find a chapter in your area through the national organizations of APA and AIA.

National Engineers' Week Future Cities Competition, http://www.futurecity.org/

National Engineers Week Future City Competition is a program developed to help seventh- and eighth-grade students to discover and foster interests in math, science, and engineering. As you'll soon discover, it's a program that's both challenging and stimulating for everyone involved.

Smart City Radio, www.smartcityradio.com

Smart City™ is a weekly, hour-long public radio talk show that takes an in-depth look at urban life, the people, places, ideas, and trends shaping cities. Host Carol Coletta talks with national and international public policy experts, elected officials, economists, business leaders, artists, developers, planners, and others for a penetrating discussion of urban issues. (Podcast available.)

REFERENCES

American Institute of Certified Planners. "Ethics," http://www.planning.org/ethics/index.htm (accessed March 28, 2009).

American Planning Association. APA/AICP 2008 Planners Salary Survey.

http://www.planning.org/salary/index.htm (accessed March 22, 2009).

Architecture 2030. 2009. The Building Sector: A Hidden Culprit. http://www.architecture2030 .org/current_situation/building_sector.html (accessed March 7, 2009).

Association of Collegiate Schools of Planning (ACSP). 2008. *Guide to Undergraduate and Graduate Education in Urban and Regional Planning, 14th edition*. Association of Collegiate Schools of Planning.

Bureau of Labor Statistics. Occupational Outlook Handbook 2008–09 Edition. "Urban and Regional Planning," http://www.bls.gov/oco/ ocos057.htm#emply (accessed January 19, 2009 and March 21, 2009).

Bureau of Labor Statistics. OES. *Occupational Employment and Wages, May 2007*. "19-3051 Urban and Regional Planners." http://www.bls .gov/oes/current/oes193051.htm (accessed March 22, 2009).

Centers for Disease Control. No date. Physical Activity Resources for Health Professionals, http://www.cdc.gov/nccdphp/dnpa/physical/ health_professionals/active_environments/ aces.htm (accessed July 13, 2009).

Environmental Building News. 2007. "Driving to Green Buildings: The Transportation Energy Intensity of Buildings," September 1, 2007. http://www.buildinggreen.com/auth/article .cfm/2007/8/30/Driving-to-Green-Buildings- The-Transportation-Energy-Intensity-of- Buildings/ (accessed March 7, 2009).

Frank, Nancy. 2008. "Measuring Public Service: Assessment and Accountability—To Ourselves and Others." *Journal of Planning Education and Research* 27: 499–506.

Hoch, Charles, Linda C. Dalton, and Frank S. So. 2000. *The Practice of Local Government Planning*. International City County Management Association. Washington, DC.

Kelley, Ingrid. 2008. *Energy in America: A Tour of Our Fossil Fuel Culture and Beyond*. Burlington, VT: University of Vermont Press.

Koncz, Andrea. No date. "Work Experience Key for New College Grads Seeking Employment." National Association of Colleges and Employers (NACE), http://www.naceweb.org/press/ display.asp?year=&prid=294 (accessed February 21, 2009).

National Congress for Community Economic Development. 2009. http://www.ncced.org/ (accessed January 19, 2009).

National Commission on Coop Education. No date. "The Cooperative Education Model," http:// www.co-op.edu/aboutcoop.htm (accessed February 22, 2009).

NCI Charrette System. No date. "The NCI Charrette System," http://www.charretteinstitute.org/charrette.html (accessed February 14, 2009).

Nemko, Marty. 2009. "Best Careers 2009: Urban Regional Planner: A multi-faceted job for a multi-talented person." U.S. News and World Report, online. December 11, 2008, https://pantherlink.uwm.edu/service/home/~/Best%20Careers%202009%20Urban%20Regional%20Planner%20-%20US%20News%20and%20World%20Report.mht?auth=co&loc=en_US&id=405771&part=2 (accessed April 2, 2009).

Newman, Peter, Timothy Beatley, and Heather Boyer. 2009. Resilient Cities: Responding to Peak Oil and Climate Change. Washington, DC: Island Press.

Ozawa, Connie P., and Ethan P. Seltzer. 1999. "Taking Our Bearings: Mapping a Relationship Among Planning Practice, Theory, and Education." Journal of Planning Education and Research 18(3): 257–266.

Peace Corps. No date. "Environment," http://www.peacecorps.gov/index.cfm?shell=learn.whatvol.env (accessed December 15, 2008).

Peace Corps. No date. "Urban and Regional Development" http://www.peacecorps.gov/index.cfm?shell=learn.whatvol.busdev_01.urban (accessed December 15, 2008).

Peterangelo, Joseph. 2008. "IMF and Local Food: Expanding on Success." WAPA Newsletter, Fall 2008: 1, 3–4. http://www.wisconsinplanners.org/wapanews/WAPA_Fall_2008.pdf (accessed September 7, 2009).

Peterson, Jon A. 2003. The Birth of City Planning in the United States: 1840–1917. Baltimore: Johns Hopkins University Press.

Peirce, Neal. 2008. "As the Nation's Top Metro Regions Show, It's Time to Reinvent Our Energy Future," Seattle Times, June 10, 2008.

QuintCareers.com. "Informational Interviewing Tutorial" http://www.quintcareers.com/informational_interviewing.html (accessed July 13, 2009).

University of Cincinnati. "Urban Planning," http://www.uc.edu/degreeprograms/program.aspx?program=23BUP-URPL (accessed February 22, 2009).

U.S. Government Accountability Office. 2007. "Uncertainty about Future Oil Supply Makes It Important to Develop a Strategy for Addressing a Peak and Decline in Oil Production." GAO Highlights, GAO-07-283. February 2007.

Woolhouse, Megan. 2007. "Urban Planning Sparks Pupils' Creativity." Boston Globe, December 14, 2007. http://www.boston.com/news/local/articles/2007/12/14/urban_planning_sparks_pupils_creativity/ (accessed February 22, 2009).

INDEX